SHAPING
LANGUAGE
POLICY IN
THE U.S.

SHAPING LANGUAGE POLICY IN THE U.S.

THE ROLE OF COMPOSITION STUDIES

SCOTT WIBLE

SOUTHERN ILLINOIS UNIVERSITY PRESS
CARBONDALE AND EDWARDSVILLE

Copyright © 2013 by the Board of Trustees,
Southern Illinois University
All rights reserved
Printed in the United States of America

16 15 14 13   4 3 2 1

Chapter 1 was adapted, with permission, from "Pedagogies of the 'Students' Right' Era: The Language Curriculum Research Group's Project for Linguistic Diversity," *College Composition and Communication* 57.3 (2006), 442–78. Chapter 3 was adapted, with permission, from "Composing Alternatives to a National Security Language Policy," *College English* 71.5 (2009), 460–85. Both articles were published and copyrighted by the National Council of Teachers of English (NCTE), Urbana, Illinois. Permission to quote from archival materials regarding the CCCC Language Policy was granted by the NCTE. Permission to quote from Ford Foundation records in chapter 1 was granted by the Ford Foundation. Permission to quote from interviews with Carol Reed and with Geneva Smitherman was granted by the interview subjects.

Publication was partially supported by a grant from the Department of English at the University of Maryland.

Library of Congress Cataloging-in-Publication Data
Wible, Scott, 1978–
Shaping language policy in the U.S. : the role of composition studies / Scott Wible.
    p. cm.
Includes bibliographical references and index.
ISBN 978-0-8093-3134-5 (pbk. : alk. paper) — ISBN 0-8093-3134-9 (pbk. : alk. paper) — ISBN 978-0-8093-3135-2 (ebook) — ISBN 0-8093-3135-7 (ebook)
1. Language policy—United States. 2. English language—Rhetoric—Study and teaching—United States. 3. English language—Political aspects—United States. 4. National security—United States. I. Title.
P119.32.U6W53 2012
306.44'973—dc23   2012024414

Printed on recycled paper. ♻
The paper used in this publication meets the minimum requirements of American National Standard for Information Sciences—Permanence of Paper for Printed Library Materials, ANSI Z39.48-1992. ∞

CONTENTS

Acknowledgments   vii

Introduction:
   Situating Language Policy within Composition's
   Past, Present, and Future   1

1. The Language Curriculum Research Group:
   Translating the Students' Right to Their Own
   Language Resolution into Pedagogical Practice   30

2. The CCCC National Language Policy:
   Reframing the Rhetoric of an English-Only United States   70

3. The Defense Department's National Security Language Policy:
   Composing Local Responses to the United States'
   Critical Language Needs   117

Conclusion:
   Redefining Language Policy's Role in Composition Studies   167

Notes   183
Works Cited and Consulted   199
Index   221

ACKNOWLEDGMENTS

I OWE THANKS TO MY ADVISERS AND TEACHERS WHO GUIDED ME through the earliest stages of writing this book, especially Cheryl Glenn, Elaine Richardson, Keith Gilyard, Jack Selzer, Patrick Shannon, Stuart Selber, and Jon Olson. I also want to thank several colleagues at both my former and present institutions, West Virginia University and the University of Maryland, for their intellectual and collegial support, especially Brian Ballentine, Laura Brady, Jonathan Burton, Ryan Claycomb, Jo Ann Dadisman, Jay Dolmage, Catherine Gouge, and Nathalie Singh-Corcoran. This project also benefitted from spirited exchanges with fellow participants in the "Rhetoric and Transnationalism" and "Toward a Rhetoric of Multilingualism" workshops at the 2007 and 2009 Rhetoric Society of America Summer Institutes.

At two key moments in drafting this book, I profited greatly from a Riggle Fellowship in the Humanities from West Virginia University as well as a fourth-year research leave arranged by Donald Hall, former English Department chair at WVU. Jonathan Green, formerly a research associate at the Ford Foundation, and Margaret Chambers, staff member at the National Council of Teachers of English, made it possible for me to navigate the archives at their respective organizations. Deborah Holdstein, former editor of *College Composition and Communication*, Jonathan Schilb, former editor of *College English*, and two anonymous reviewers from each of these journals helped me to sharpen my analyses in previous article-length versions of chapters 1 and 3. The two reviewers for Southern Illinois University Press similarly provided many excellent revision suggestions that helped me to clarify and contextualize my argument. I also thank Karl Kageff, editor-in-chief at Southern Illinois University Press, for his enthusiastic support of this project and the Press's editorial staff for bringing it into published form.

I want to express my appreciation to my families and friends for their encouragement, especially Bob and Barb Enoch, Rob and Carleen

Enoch, and Lucy Enoch. My grandmother Anna Holesa, my brothers Brad and Andrew Wible, and my parents Bernie and Elizabeth Wible have been enthusiastic supporters throughout my entire time working on this project. Jack and Nancy Wible have inspired me through their joy in living and their love of learning during their first few years of life. And finally, I give loving thanks to Jessica Enoch for sharing her wisdom, patience, humor, and unwavering support.

INTRODUCTION
SITUATING LANGUAGE POLICY WITHIN COMPOSITION'S PAST, PRESENT, AND FUTURE

IN HER CHAIR'S ADDRESS AT THE 2003 MEETING OF THE CONFERENCE on College Composition and Communication (CCCC), Shirley Wilson Logan asserted the importance of the organization's language policies. She called on rhetoric and composition scholars to reread texts such as the 1974 Students' Right to Their Own Language resolution and 1988 National Language Policy in order to better understand "the important principles they uphold" as well as "their salience in this moment in history" ("Changing" 333). Logan claimed that these language policies could usefully guide CCCC members in their efforts to improve language instruction and to advocate for literacy education in a moment when the student population is becoming ever more linguistically diverse. She declared, "As language arts educators, we ought to be at the center of all policy decisions that affect the teaching and learning of communication skills," and she charged scholars "to have ready answers" when questions about linguistic diversity in education arise (335). Analyzing the CCCC language policies, Logan argued, can help rhetoric and composition scholars to discover "ready answers" and compose effective arguments in public debates about language diversity in schools and society.

While Logan sees value in returning to these documents, at the time of their creation the CCCC language policies created confusion and sparked criticism about their efficacy for rhetoric and composition studies. Many scholars have been confused by the 1974 Students' Right resolution, for example, because they expected it to offer more strategies for bringing its ideal to life inside the writing classroom. *English Journal* editor Stephen Judy used his December 1978 column to express such a view about the Students' Right resolution: "One great weakness in the

CCCC statement is that it talks about respecting and not interfering, but it doesn't say anything about what the schools should do in a *positive* vein. It doesn't attempt to describe what teachers can and should be doing to help kids learn language" (7). In 1976 Allen Smith similarly lamented that the "Students' Right" policy seems to "spin in . . . circles" and leave us with the questions "what should we be teaching and for what purpose" (155–56), but he also challenged the policy's theoretical soundness, describing it as "a contradiction," "muddled," and "mythical" (155). More strident were those compositionists in the early 1980s who believed that the Students' Right resolution and any subsequent CCCC language policies were simply the result of scholars becoming "wrapped up in ideological wars which [are] of little concern to them" (Parks 212). Contemporary responses to this language policy reveal similar disagreement and confusion about the specific contribution it makes to rhetoric and composition studies. Jerrie Cobb Scott, Dolores Y. Straker, and Laurie Katz talk about the "business" of the Students' Right resolution solely in terms of specific teaching strategies (Preface xviii), while Patrick Bruch and Richard Marback believe that the policy is meant not to generate pedagogical talk about "practical problems and concrete solutions" but instead to foster public and professional dialogue about "visionary ideals and abstract ideas" such as dignity, justice, and rights (*Hope* 51).

The 1988 National Language Policy, meanwhile, has recently been criticized by Bruce Horner for "attract[ing] little attention" ("Students' Right" 741), but it has in fact generated confusion about its usefulness for the field's efforts to improve conditions for language learning. Some scholars said they didn't see how one could adopt a language policy that promotes multilingualism without ignoring the real-world demands for English language competency placed on students in their other classes and future jobs. In 1988, for example, Trudy J. Sundberg complained that the National Language Policy and the National Council of Teachers of English (NCTE) Resolution on English as the "Official Language" did nothing but encourage teachers to let immigrants "avoid learning English, thus confining many of these students to self-perpetuating linguistic ghettos" ("Case" 17). Others were simply puzzled as to whether or not these language policies were even relevant. Harvey Daniels explained that many NCTE members were confused as to why the organization would oppose the English-only movement of the 1980s, for they believed that declaring English as the United States' official language would seem to bring with it "the apparent uplifting of their own professional specialty" (Preface, viii). Writing more recently, Geneva Smitherman suggested that we should see the National Language Policy not as attracting little attention but rather as prompting "minimal" negative reaction, a response due at least in part to the field's "developing sociolinguistic sophistication and political maturity about language rights issues" ("CCCC's Role" 369).

Just as significant as the confusion, criticism, and disagreement about these language policies is the ignorance of them among language arts educators. The CCCC Language Policy Committee reported in its 2000 *Language Knowledge and Awareness Survey* that two-thirds of CCCC and NCTE members have no knowledge of the CCCC's Students' Right resolution or National Language Policy (14–15). Indeed, confusion about these language policies' pedagogical value and political relevance has resulted in the fact that they have rarely been included in the professional training of either the present or future generations of composition scholars.

Shaping Language Policy in the U.S. takes up Logan's call and addresses this confusion about both the past and present importance of language policies for rhetoric and composition studies. It first revisits two of the CCCC's key language policy statements, the 1974 Students' Right resolution and the 1988 National Language Policy, in order to identify "the important principles" that each one holds. The book then articulates each policy's "salience at this moment in history" as it turns toward a contemporary policy debate, the post–September 11 emergence of a national security language policy. More specifically, the approach in *Shaping Language Policy in the U.S.* is to conduct a historical analysis of the Students' Right resolution and the National Language Policy in order to better understand the theoretical richness of these policies and the activities that scholars have used to create, promote, circulate, and respond to them. While understanding each of these CCCC policies is a crucial disciplinary endeavor in its own right, the two historical analyses frame the subsequent examination of the federal government's national security language policy, as the Students' Right resolution and National Language Policy prompt invention of several different strategies that rhetoric and composition scholars can pursue to engage this still-evolving debate. Contrary to various critiques about and confusion over these two CCCC language polices, *Shaping Language Policy in the U.S.* demonstrates ways that the CCCC language policies have usefully informed educators' professional practices and public service. It also explores how these policies can guide scholars and teachers as they pursue interventions both now and in the future, for the national security language policy debate is just one among many contemporary language policy debates that are of vital concern to students, the profession, and the nation's communities.

Each of the policies discussed in this study makes a specific argument for preserving linguistic diversity in education and in society. The CCCC's 1974 Students' Right to Their Own Language resolution countered the widespread attitude among educators that most ethnic minority students then matriculating to college in increasing numbers were "verbally disadvantaged" and, consequently, uneducable. The CCCC's language policy challenged this assumption by calling on teachers to affirm the linguistic skills and abilities that speakers of nonstandardized language varieties brought with them to college. Many scholars questioned the usefulness of the Students' Right policy, arguing that it was long on theory but short on practice. Chapter 1 reconsiders the policy's efficacy by investigating how one group of compositionists, the Language Curriculum Research Group, made use of the theory at the heart of the Students' Right policy as it developed a progressive pedagogy for first-year composition in the City University of New York system.

Fourteen years later, in 1988, the CCCC published its National Language Policy in order to neutralize a constitutional amendment sponsored by the English-only movement that would declare English the official language of the United States. Assessments of the National Language Policy were negative: some scholars saw the policy as encouraging teachers to shirk their duties to help all students learn English, while others believed that it undermined their status at a moment when English-only laws seemed to be "uplifting" the profession. Chapter 2 reenvisions the work of the National Language Policy. It examines rhetorical strategies the CCCC Language Policy Committee used to respond to the English-only movement and explores activities the committee performed alongside the National Language Policy to strengthen it and promote language education as a means of ensuring linguistic pluralism in the country. The National Language Policy and all of the Language Policy Committee's work can be read as arguments for compositionists to see their professional responsibilities extending beyond the classroom walls and into surrounding communities. Together, chapters 1 and 2 resolve confusion about these language policies' pedagogical, professional, and political implications and explore their salience for rhetoric and composition scholars who engage contemporary debates about the politics of linguistic diversity and language arts education in the United States.

Chapter 3 explores the possibilities for such interventions. It focuses on a debate that emerged following the September 11, 2001, terrorist attacks on New York City and Washington, D.C., as several federal agencies have come to see language policy as not only an educational but also a national security concern. Many government leaders believe that warning signs of the terrorist plot were "lost in translation" (Holt). U.S. military and intelligence officials have since talked about foreign language skills as valuable war-fighting tools, ones that can be used to infiltrate and defeat the nation's enemies. The U.S. Department of Defense hosted the National Language Conference in June 2004 to bring together government officials, corporate executives, linguists, and language educators in a collective effort to comprehend the military, intelligence, and diplomatic communities' pressing language needs and outline a plan to meet them by developing a comprehensive foreign language program throughout the entire U.S. educational system, kindergarten through graduate school. These conference deliberations informed the Defense Department's February 2005 white paper, *A Call to Action for National Foreign Language Capabilities*. Chapter 3 describes how this document, along with the Defense Department's January 2005 *Defense Language Transformation Roadmap* and then-president George W. Bush's 2006 National Security Language Initiative, laid the foundation for a national security language policy, and it analyzes the theories about language, education, and national identity that inform such a policy.

This reading of the national security language policy in chapter 3 suggests that in some ways this policy echoes the CCCC's earlier language policies. Indeed, it too seeks to persuade U.S. citizens and their elected officials that the nation's linguistic diversity can be leveraged as a valuable resource. In other ways, however, the national security language policy presents a narrow view of the uses toward which the nation should put its language resources. Foreign language scholars in the Modern Language Association (MLA), led by Mary Louise Pratt, Rosemary Feal, and Heidi Byrnes, have begun to develop a multifaceted response to the Defense Department's language policy, but chapter 3 demonstrates why this debate should concern rhetoric and composition scholars as well. This chapter applies the lessons gleaned from the earlier historical analyses to develop action-oriented possibilities for response. It demonstrates how compositionists can use the Students' Right resolution and National Language Policy as guides to invent pedagogical and political strategies for working in their classrooms, academic institutions, and communities in ways that build a broader public commitment not only to addressing the nation's security needs but also to supporting the nation's diverse language communities in their efforts to participate in mainstream political life.

Shaping Language Policy in the U.S., then, follows Logan's lead in bringing language policy back to the center of rhetoric and composition's disciplinary concerns. It clarifies the theoretical grounding and rhetorical purpose of language policies in relation to public and professional debates about language diversity and literacy education. Groups such as the CCCC, the English-only movement, and the Defense Department compose language policies in order to synthesize their theories about language into a plan for shaping the classroom and the larger society in specific ways. Given this emphasis on articulating broad arguments, language policies do not always present compositionists with concrete strategies for classroom, institutional, or political practice. Nevertheless, *Shaping Language Policy in the U.S.* gives compositionists direction on how scholars have in the past and can in the future adopt an active stance toward language policies, reading them as a means to guide their own interventions in contemporary debates and revising their pedagogy, research, and service in ways that work toward the goals these policies represent.

Defining *Language Policy*

Articulating the salience of language policies for present-day work in composition studies first requires defining the concept of *language policy*. Applied linguists, political scientists, scholars of education, law, and modern languages, and, in ever-increasing numbers, rhetoricians and compositionists have all studied language policy. From this scholarship, two approaches to defining it are most relevant to this book's argument.

First, some scholars have expanded their view of language policy from government-related documents to consider texts that emerge from a wide variety of public and private spheres of activity. For too long, argues linguist Thom Huebner, language policy scholars have only attended to what he calls "overt language policy," that is, those legal documents and administrative codes concerning language "which are explicit, formalized, and/or codified," such as English-only laws in private workplaces or San Francisco's Proposition O, which banned bilingual ballots in 1983. While Heubner acknowledges that documents created by the government and the courts are important, he also contends, "language policy formation and enforcement is more ubiquitous than that." He explains: "Private enterprises from small businesses and multinational corporations, the media, publishing houses, professional and religious organizations, foundations, and supranational alliances and confederations have language policies." These organizations and institutions each enact a "covert language policy" that makes no reference to specific laws or government regulations but still affects uses of or attitudes toward language (4). The Federal Communications Commission, for example, produces a covert language policy through its tendency to award broadcasting licenses in ways that suggest the "desirability" of delivering at least some programs that serve linguistic-minority communities (Piatt 15). This attention to the "ubiquitous" nature of language policy is particularly important in countries such as the United States, where no single government document explicitly states a language policy. For this reason, scholars seeking to better understand language policy in the United States are beginning to focus not only on court decisions and amendments to state constitutions but also the management practices of private and public employers, programming or publishing decisions by media outlets, and school standards and curricula.

The second approach to defining *language policy* that is relevant to the present study is applied linguists' broadening of this concept to encompass more than just texts. Bernard Spolsky maintains that scholars need to think about language policy in this expanded way because "even where there is a formal, written language policy, its effect on language practices is neither guaranteed nor consistent" (8). For these reasons, Spolsky proposes a definition that encompasses three specific yet interrelated parts that constitute a nation's or a community's language policy:

1. language practices: community members' habitual pattern of selecting among the varieties that make up its linguistic repertoire;
2. language beliefs or ideology: community members' beliefs about language and language use; and
3. language intervention, planning, or management: any specific efforts by someone with or claiming authority to modify the practices or beliefs of someone else within that community. (5)

In Spolsky's broader definition, then, the "language policy as written document" definition used by many legal and policy studies scholars falls under the category "language intervention, planning, or management." For applied linguists such as Spolsky, the language policy of any community instead emerges from the interanimation of these three dimensions, rather than being prescribed in a specific text alone.

Shaping Language Policy in the U.S. focuses on language policy documents that have emerged within professional, civic, and governmental contexts as a means of "language management." Specifically, throughout this book, the term *language policy* refers to written texts that outline plans for directing particular language practices toward specific political, economic, or cultural ends. The groups authoring these language policy texts aim to set priorities and propose strategies for developing languages that meet certain national or communal needs and to clarify the reasons that they believe should guide people's decisions about language use. The CCCC Students' Right policy advocates for the rights of all students to produce "precise, effective, and appropriate communication" in a wide range of language varieties (Committee on CCCC Language Statement 2). The CCCC National Language Policy supports efforts to create a multilingual public sphere in the United States. And the Defense Department's national security language policy proposes a specific understanding of the nation's language needs and outlines strategies for developing and managing the language resources to meet these needs.

To be clear, though, the three language policies at the heart of this book do not carry legal force or serve an official function. All of these policies are "overt" in the sense that they explicitly focus on language, although only one of these policies, the English Language Amendment proposed by the English-only movement, has been "codified"—and then only where it has been adopted by an individual state's legislature or voters. Neither the CCCC Students' Right resolution and National Language Policy nor the Defense Department's *Call to Action* white paper and *Defense Language Transformation Roadmap* impose rules that regulate any person's behavior, as an English-only amendment to the U.S. Constitution necessarily would. Instead, these language policy statements have been published and circulated as a means to clarify and communicate a particular group's vision for language learning and language use in the United States. Collectively, the policies examined in this book speak to the ubiquitous nature of language policy in the United States, as these texts emerge from different organizations and attempt to direct language practices toward various ends within a range of contexts, from the classroom and schools' surrounding communities to the military institutions and offices of federal, state, and local agencies.

Even as this study focuses on language policy texts that attempt language management, it also attends to the other two aspects of language policy that Spolsky outlines. One, this book examines how each language policy statement reflects particular beliefs and attitudes about language. Two, this discussion also repeatedly emphasizes the fact that language policy texts do not control people's language practices but instead serve only to guide pedagogical practices, research projects, and management decisions as well as the deliberations of education, corporate, and legislative leaders.

SITUATING LANGUAGE POLICY ANALYSIS INSIDE RHETORIC AND COMPOSITION STUDIES

The focus on language policy texts aligns this study with those of rhetoric and composition scholars such as Arnetha Ball, Suresh Canagarajah, Keith Gilyard, Bruce Horner, Valerie Felita Kinloch, Ted Lardner, Richard Marback, Paul Kei Matsuda, Stephen Parks, Elaine Richardson, Geneva Smitherman, Christine Tardy, John Trimbur, and Victor Villanueva. As with their work, this book contributes both to the larger multidisciplinary effort to study language politics and policies in the United States as well as to conversations inside rhetoric and composition studies regarding pedagogical approaches to language diversity in the writing classroom. This study of two historical language policies from the CCCC and one present-day policy from the Defense Department also speaks to the concerns of scholars investigating how political, social, and economic contexts affect literacy education, and it adds texture to rhetoric and composition's disciplinary histories.

Identifying Language Policy Work within Rhetoric and Composition Studies

Shaping Language Policy in the U.S. intervenes most explicitly in composition's sixty-year effort to understand and shape language policies affecting literacy education and political participation. As Smitherman explains in "CCCC's Role in the Struggle for Language Rights," compositionists engaged in language policy work as early as 1951, just two years after the founding of the CCCC. In that year's February issue of *College Composition and Communication* (*CCC*), Donald Lloyd launched an attack against writing instructors who trivialized the language of students who did not speak "correct" English. Lloyd declared, "In our day, to make statements about English and about language which do not square with linguistics is professionally reprehensible" (qtd. in Smitherman, "CCCC's Role" 350). Lloyd called for students to retain their Mother Tongue while learning Standardized English as a set of "alternative language habits" (354).[1] Smitherman suggests that in so doing, Lloyd anticipated the ideas and attitudes that would lead the CCCC to adopt the Students' Right policy two decades later (354).

The CCCC's 1974 publication of the Students' Right resolution marked the organization's entry into broader public conversations about educational politics and language policy, and rhetoric and composition scholars have engaged in similar debates that emerged since that time. Smitherman served on the CCCC committee that drafted the Students' Right resolution. Later that decade she reasserted the language policy's theoretical foundations and pedagogical applications when she testified as an expert witness in the 1979 *Martin Luther King Junior Elementary School Children v. Ann Arbor School District* court case, in which Judge Charles W. Joiner ruled that the district and its teachers had failed to take African American students' language backgrounds into account when developing strategies for teaching them to read and write. In May 1998 the CCCC made a similar assertion for linguistically and culturally relevant pedagogies with its Statement on Ebonics, which provided theoretical grounding to support the Oakland (California) Unified School District's decision to create a literacy education program conducted in Ebonics in order to help them both develop greater competencies in Standardized English and appreciate more deeply "the legitimacy and richness" of African American students' primary languages (Oakland Unified). Meanwhile, the English-only movement emerged in the mid-1980s as an attempt to restrict bilingual education and government provision of bilingual services; as chapter 2 explains, the CCCC created its 1988 National Language Policy to articulate an alternative vision of how the United States could build on the presence of languages other than English within the public sphere. Since that time, the CCCC has responded to the presence of speakers of languages other than English within the composition classroom, as well. The CCCC Statement on Second Language Writing and Writers, published in January 2001 and revised in November 2009, calls for rhetoric and composition scholars to account for second language writers when planning research studies, writing textbooks, designing curricula, drafting syllabi, and training new teachers. And most recently, when in April 2010 the Arizona Department of Education began removing instructors of Limited English Proficiency students from their positions if their spoken English was "heavily accented or ungrammatical" (Jordan), the NCTE responded with a public statement: "Teachers who have deep roots in the culture and linguistic experiences of their students are well equipped for success in teaching English, regardless of their spoken dialect or accent" ("NCTE Speaks Out"). All of these examples illustrate rhetoric and composition scholars' continual engagement with public debates about language. At each turn, they have used policies or position statements to articulate a theoretically informed stance on how public laws, educational policies, and teaching practices can better promote linguistic and cultural diversity in the United States.

While these policy statements have spoken to audiences both inside the profession and across the wider public, rhetoric and composition scholars have also contributed to academic conversations about U.S. language policy. One strand of this scholarship has been studies that examine the material and symbolic effects of language policies as well as the ideological foundations on which they are constructed. For example, as the CCCC Language Policy Committee drafted and circulated its 1988 National Language Policy, Geneva Smitherman, Victor Villanueva, Dennis Baron, Vivian I. Davis, Roseann Dueñas González, and James Sledd contributed to *Not Only English: Affirming America's Multilingual Heritage*, an essay collection that explained the CCCC and NCTE's grounds for objecting to English-only legislation. Davis and Sledd in particular examined how one key part of the English-only movement's rhetorical strategy involves masking xenophobia, racism, and nativism behind arguments for preserving national unity. Victor Villanueva, meanwhile, engaged Richard Rodriguez in debates over English-only legislation and bilingual education policies in the pages of monographs and journals during the 1980s ("Whose Voices"; "Voice of Voices"; *Bootstraps* 34–50), and since that time Villanueva has written extensively about how the English-only movement reinforces amnesia about the history of linguistic and cultural diversity in the United States ("On English Only").

Scholars have similarly examined the Students' Right policy, the Ebonics resolution, and the Statement on Second Language Writing and Writers. Horner, for example, argues that the Students' Right resolution reinforced a traditional conception of language that fails to adequately attend to how material, social, and political dynamics affect how meaning gets made, while Richard Marback and Patrick Bruch read the Students' Right resolution within the discursive context of the civil rights movement, arguing that the language policy encourages teachers to define "competence" not only in terms of attaining identifiable writing skills but also learning how to dignify human beings across lines of racial, ethnic, and linguistic difference ("Race Identity"). Marback critiques the CCCC Statement on Ebonics for the way it seemingly downplays negative reaction to Oakland's Ebonics policy as "ill-informed" and, in so doing, ignores legitimate concerns about education and literacy underlying these complaints ("Ebonics" 13). Paul Matsuda analyzes the CCCC Statement on Second Language Writing and Writers in relation to histories of the fields of composition studies and second-language writing, suggesting that this policy reflects composition scholars' commitment to correcting the disciplinary division of labor whereby concerns for English as a Second Language (ESL) students fall solely to scholars in applied linguistics or Teachers of English as a Second Language programs ("Second-Language"). More recently, Christina Ortmeier-Hooper analyzed the revision process leading to the 2009 version of this CCCC statement, and she explored how several writing program administrators have been working to implement this document's recommendations within their local institutions. Collectively, then, these scholars have deepened the field's understanding of the political, linguistic, and cultural values that inform different language policy texts.

A second strand of scholarship has examined how composition studies contributes more to the shape of a U.S. language policy than just overt policy texts such as the Students' Right resolution and the National Language Policy. In their 2002 *CCC* article "English Only and U.S. College Composition," Horner and Trimbur contend that despite its public protests to the contrary, composition studies actually reinforces the goals of the English-only movement. Through their historical analysis of writing instruction in U.S. colleges, they find that "the first-year writing course actually *embodies* a language policy that privileges English in relation to other languages" (595). More recently, Horner, Lu, and Matsuda's 2010 edited collection *Cross-Language Relations in Composition* attends to different ways that compositionists reproduce or challenge a dominant U.S. language policy through composition program policies and objectives, textbook publishing, teaching practices, teacher-education curricula, and research priorities. Among the contributors to this collection, Suresh Canagarajah, John Trimbur, Elaine Richardson, Scott Richard Lyons, Kate Mangelsdorf, and Shondel Nero explore how these various activities and texts effectively manage the language practices and influence the language beliefs of students. This strand of scholarship prompts rhetoric and composition scholars to recognize that all writing pedagogies "embody" a language policy, no matter whether they reproduce or challenge the dominant social imperative to acquire facility in Standardized English only.

Recently, a third strand of scholarship has worked to situate analysis of U.S. college composition's language policies within a broader international context. More specifically, scholars have examined both explicit and implicit policies that affect the languages used for research, publication, and classroom teaching in academic institutions outside of the United States. Mary Jane Curry and Theresa Lillis, for example, have traced the economic and social pressures that are leading many multilingual scholars in Europe to publish their work in the English language and in U.S. and British academic journals. One consequence of this (sometimes implicit, more often explicit) language policy, Curry and Lillis argue, is that scholars are often being forced to turn their attention away from more locally pressing research questions, more locally relevant research sites, and more locally accessible non-English-language publications. Catherine Prendergast's ethnographic research in Slovakia similarly traces how and why English has become important for language professionals such as journalists and textbook authors in former Soviet bloc countries. She too challenges the myth that a country's investment in English-language education guarantees it a stronger position within the global economy. Matsuda, meanwhile, has examined how some academic interest groups in Taiwan are pressing for new criteria to measure faculty productivity and institutional quality in ways that give faculty more feasible options to conduct research studies and publish their results in languages other than English ("Politics"). Collectively, these scholars draw U.S.-based compositionists' attention to how language management policies, attitudes toward linguistic diversity, and literacy education practices are shaped by and helping to shape the larger international context. Their studies demonstrate that economic, political, and cultural pressures affecting language choices move across national boundaries and have consequences for knowledge production and cross-cultural understanding.

Shaping Language Policy in the U.S. joins this scholarly conversation about the discursive work that language policy statements do within the field. The three specific analyses at the center of this book examine how political and social agendas influence ideologies concerning language and in turn propel language policies in specific directions. Moreover, these examinations reveal ways that scholars and teachers can use the CCCC's language policies in particular to design research projects and pedagogies that respond to the linguistic realities of their students' lives and develop strategies for engaging pressing public debates about the nation's language needs in a globalizing, post–September 11 world.

Examining U.S. Language Policy through a Multidisciplinary Lens

Given the ubiquitous nature of language policy within the United States, this book's study of language policies related to composition studies specifically and language arts education more broadly should be seen as just one piece of a larger multidisciplinary effort to identify the various texts, values, and practices that give shape to the nation's language policy. Scholars in education, law, political science, and applied linguistics have conducted a variety of studies exploring different groups' beliefs about language diversity, linguistic majority and minority communities' language practices, and various organizational and governmental texts that attempt language management. Collectively, these studies advance the project of identifying a U.S. language policy (or policies) and explaining its effects and consequences for public and private life.

Legal scholars have made the most concerted effort to understand attempts at language management through overt language policy statements issued by legislators and the courts. They have focused in particular on legal challenges to policies that affect linguistic minorities' access to education, employment, political participation, and social services. Legal scholars have sought to understand the extent to which courts have interpreted a "language right" to exist within the framework of human and civil rights in the United States. Bill Piatt, for example, observes that the development of laws relating to language use has been inconsistent within the country, leading him to conclude, "It is as though the threads of language rights have not been woven into the fabric of the law, but rather surface as bothersome loose ends to be plucked off when inconvenient" (xi). As one example of this inconsistency, Piatt notes that the U.S. Constitution guarantees the right of undocumented persons to have access to an interpreter during their deportation proceedings but does not guarantee the same right to U.S. citizens "faced with administrative proceedings with potentially severe consequences such as the termination of public assistance" (149). Critical race theorist Juan F. Perea, on the other hand, has argued that the U.S. courts and legislatures in fact *have* been consistent—consistent, that is, in their refusal to recognize discrimination on the basis of a person's use of a non-English language as a form of racial or national origin discrimination. Drawing on Derrick Bell's theory of "interest convergence," Perea contends that linguistic minorities will gain rights to use non-English languages and language varieties "only when it is in the interest of the dominant majority to concede" such rights (136). Legal scholars, then, have reached different conclusions about the implications of court rulings on government laws and business policies relating to language use. Nevertheless, their work makes a significant contribution to the study of language policy in the United States because it attends not only to what overt and covert language policy texts say but also to how these texts get interpreted or enforced in legal settings.[2]

While legal scholars have focused on language management in the form of federal, state, and local laws, scholars from fields such as political science, history, and applied linguistics have attempted to trace how beliefs about and attitudes toward language have shaped U.S. language policy. Much of this research has focused on identifying the sources of people's support for or opposition to restrictive language policies. The most common type of study is analysis that identifies the racist, nativist, and xenophobic underpinnings of English-only laws (Crawford, "What's Behind"; Espinosa-Aguilar; Hill). More nuanced studies, though, show that support for English-only laws often represents, in linguist Joshua Fishman's words, "the displacement of middle-class Anglo fears and anxieties from the more difficult, if not intractable, *real* [economic, social, and political] causes of their fears and anxieties, to mythical and simplistic and stereotyped scapegoats" ("Displaced" 169). Linguist Geoffrey Nunberg concurs, noting that "language has always done the work of symbolizing cultural categories that are in themselves too deep and inchoate to be directly expressed" (494). Political scientist Deborah Schildkraut has since confirmed such arguments with empirical evidence. Through focus-group studies, Schildkraut demonstrates that one's particular conception of American identity influences, in predictable ways, one's support for, opposition to, or ambivalence about English-only laws. For example, some participants in Schildkraut's study conceived of America as a democracy that functions best when all citizens participate in the political process and make informed decisions, no matter the language they use to do so; these people tend to favor language policies such as bilingual ballots that enable linguistic minorities to participate in the political process. Other participants, meanwhile, imagined America as a democracy that requires a single medium of communication for all citizens to dialogue and arrive at the best decisions for the community; these people, not surprisingly, favor language policies that require political information and political debate to be in one language, namely, English. These types of studies, no matter whether they deliver extreme or more tempered conclusions, illuminate how beliefs and attitudes toward language influence public demand for or resistance to various language policy texts.

Education scholars and applied linguists have drawn on these two lines of research to analyze how language beliefs and language management have or have not affected the language practices of teachers, students, and their families. Sociolinguists such as Joshua Fishman, William Labov, and Lesley Milroy have shown, in fact, that larger political, social, and economic forces exert greater influences on the acquisition and use of different language varieties in minority communities than do overt language policies or language management activities. Robert S. Williams and Kathleen C. Riley's recent research serves to illuminate these conclusions. They studied generational language shift in one Franco-American family in Vermont and found that a shift toward English monolingualism intensified as political, social, and economic pressures manifested themselves in the dominant society's hostility toward multiculturalism and multilingualism. These pressures, Williams and Riley explain, made it difficult for "bilingual/bicultural-'friendly' institutions," such as the Francophone farming community, one-room schoolhouse, and church, to function (87).

Education scholar Stephen Krashen has analyzed public debates about language policies in order to better understand the sources of this hostility toward multicultural and multilingual education. He finds the U.S. public generally to be misinformed about what bilingual education programs entail; how the success of such programs can be measured; and what their potential benefits might be for students, for schools, and for communities. These misconceptions serve to erode public support for these programs and, in turn, undermine the aims not only of bilingual education but also of those very people who would favor English-language assimilation. Indeed, English-only policies such as California's Proposition 227, which in 1998 ended bilingual education programs and replaced them with an English-language immersion model, have been lauded as the most efficient means of helping non-English speakers to learn the language. As applied linguist Elliott L. Judd has found, however, such restrictive language policies force many Limited-English Proficiency students into mainstream classrooms before they are linguistically competent enough to master the academic material in English ("English Only").

To combat the pressures from public support for English-only policies, applied linguists, educators, and ethnic studies scholars have pursued another line of research that has taken them into linguistic minority communities. Here they have begun to develop programs aimed at revitalizing indigenous communities' use of heritage languages, such as various Native American and Hawaiian languages.[3] These scholars work alongside community leaders to develop curricula and other language management practices that help students to gain greater facility in the languages that reflect their communities' cultures and worldviews (K. Davis 84). For example, Mahealani Pai has developed a summer camp program in which children learn about indigenous perspectives on their culture's relationship to the ocean through the process of learning traditional Hawaiian chants, hula, and songs. Language policies that promote maintenance of heritage languages serve as overt attempts by scholars, teachers, and community leaders to manage the language practices of a community in ways that resist dominant social and economic forces.[4] In so doing, these language revitalization policies and programs counter the hegemony of English in both public and private life.

As this book situates composition's language policies in relation to the broader national scene of language practices, attitudes, and planning, one must also keep in mind that language policy work promoting multilingualism or monolingualism is being undertaken in other national contexts, as well. For example, Singapore's official bilingual education policy makes English the medium of instruction for all students in all content areas but also requires every student to learn his or her "mother tongue," which must be one of the nation's other three official languages: Mandarin Chinese, Malay, and Tamil. Education scholar L. Quentin Dixon observes that this government language policy has created a working multilingualism among the populace but nevertheless threatens language diversity in the sense of promoting the public and private use of standardized varieties of all four official languages, rather than local dialects. In Europe, meanwhile, the Council of Europe in 1996 issued the Common European Framework of Reference for Languages as part of its larger "Language Learning for European Citizenship" project. The Common Framework provides a detailed description of competencies at six different stages of learning a second language, and it now widely serves as a standard guiding the teaching of second languages within European schools (Council). While the Council of Europe does not make binding laws in the manner of the European Union, the Common Framework has come to serve as one piece of a language management plan within Europe to promote multilingualism as a means of fostering cross-national democracy (Little). Just across the northeast border of the United States, meanwhile, the National Assembly of Quebec in 1977 enacted the Charter of the French Language as a means to preserve the French language from perceived threats of English monolingualism. This legislation gives the provincial government power to promote French as the common language linking all Quebec citizens (Éditeur), and it has used this power to make French the mandatory language of government proceedings and primary and secondary schooling, among other requirements. Obviously, there are many more examples of national language policies that aim to cultivate either multilingualism or monolingualism as the normal linguistic practice within a respective country's public spheres. While *Shaping Language Policy in the U.S.* focuses on U.S. language policy in general and composition's language policies in particular, recognizing this broader international context underscores the interconnectedness of language policy work, as language practice, management, and attitudes in one country—say, for instance, the United States' implicit support of English monolingualism—affects language policy in other countries—as with governments that either promote or resist the incorporation of English into educational institutions and political and economic discourse.

Shaping Language Policy in the U.S., then, contributes to this larger intellectual project to trace the many material and discursive forces that form language policy within the United States. The analysis focuses on language policy documents that, while not written into law, were meant to frame the public conversation around issues of public uses of language in schools and in society. The trajectory throughout these chapters is one that shows language arts educators leading the way in calling for a policy that values public uses of languages other than Standardized English. The CCCC's policy texts show rhetoric and composition scholars taking the stance that their teaching and research, in the words of the Students' Right resolution, should not "reflect the prejudices held by the public" (Committee on CCCC Language Statement 1). Moreover, particularly in chapters 2 and 3 one sees language arts educators working in close relation to other civic groups, government agencies, and corporate institutions. Examining this dialogue, negotiation, and conflict contributes to the larger scholarly effort described here of telling a fuller story of how language policies in this country have been or continue to be formed in public life.

Fostering Linguistic Diversity in Composition Theory and Pedagogy

Although *Shaping Language Policy in the U.S.* foregrounds the significance of language policies for composition studies, the impetus for this study comes first and foremost from disciplinary conversations concerning the linguistic diversity of composition students. Each of the three language policies at the heart of this study argues for speakers and writers of marginalized languages and dialects to have greater opportunities to participate in public life. In making this argument, these language policies speak to concerns around linguistic diversity in the field of language arts education.

Early composition scholarship on language diversity drew on linguistics research. These studies documented specific syntactical, morphological, and semantic features of nonstandardized language varieties, particularly African American Language, that students learned in their communities or in their homes and that diverged from the assumed "correct" or "proper" language used and expected by these students' teachers (Labov). Compositionists used this linguistics research to build a case for the legitimacy of nonstandardized language varieties as tools for precise communication. Geneva Smitherman exerted the most consistent and forceful effort in bringing this research to audiences inside rhetoric and composition. In texts such as her 1977 *Talkin and Testifyin: The Language of Black America*, Smitherman did not stop at merely detailing the unique features of African American Language. She also painted a rich portrait of the cultural influences and worldviews that have molded the language's rhetorical features. A decade later, Keith Gilyard chose a slightly different route to dispel the notion that African Americans were linguistically deprived. He composed a personal literacy narrative, *Voices of the Self*, showing both his systematic and inventive uses of African American Language to negotiate the demands of home, community, and school.

More recently, Elaine Richardson in *African American Literacies* and Arnetha Ball and Ted Lardner in *African American Literacies Unleashed* have built on Smitherman's and Gilyard's efforts. These scholars articulate a fuller picture of the linguistic and rhetorical resources that African Americans use to communicate powerfully and intervene purposefully in their worlds. Ana Celia Zentella has made a similar contribution in describing the linguistic and rhetorical features used by Spanish/English/Spanglish-speaking students with her 1997 *Growing Up Bilingual: Puerto Rican Children in New York*. Compositionist Michelle Hall Kells and modern language scholars Guadalupe Valdés and Daniel Villa have continued to deepen our understanding of the influences of heritage language on Latino students' oral and written texts. And while rhetorical scholars LuMing Mao and Morris Young have articulated key principles that are coming to define Asian American rhetorics (Mao;

Mao and Young), Dorothy Aguilera and Margaret D. LeCompte, Galena Sells Dick, and Tarajean Yazzie-Mintz have critically analyzed indigenous students' language and cultural practices and begun tracing their effects on literacy education.

These studies of nonstandardized and nonprivileged language varieties prompt composition scholars to see that the languages of linguistic minority students are as robust as the Standardized English long valued in the writing classroom. Just as significantly, these findings reinforce the Students' Right resolution and National Language Policy with their calls for encouraging students to draw advantageously on their language backgrounds both inside and outside the classroom.

Another group of composition scholars have used these findings about the systematic nature and rhetorical sophistication of nonprestige language varieties to trouble long-held assumptions about the aims of education in general and literacy instruction in particular. Min-Zhan Lu, Victor Villanueva, Terry Dean, Margaret Marshall, Victoria Cliett, Charles F. Coleman, Peter Elbow, Rebecca Moore Howard, Kelvin Monroe, and Vershawn Ashanti Young have helped to elucidate how much of our pedagogy reinforces dominant societal conceptions of appropriate and effective language use. To quote Monroe, these scholars push us

> to recognize that as the daily lived experiences and the everyday languages of people diversify within this world, there are greater forces at work tellin us/students that cultural uniformity—employed by uniformed texts, readings, writin practices—is the only way to achieve anything worth acquiring. (110)

This strand of the conversation on language diversity prompts scholars to open their composition classrooms to reading, writing, and reflection on issues of language, identity, and power.

More recently, several scholars have aimed to refocus the composition classroom on fostering students' willingness and abilities to engage in cross-language and cross-cultural communication. Lu, Horner, Royster, and Trimbur argue for composition studies to move "toward a translingual approach" to writing instruction such that students come to see "differences in language not as a barrier to overcome or as a problem to manage, but as a resource for producing meaning in writing, speaking, reading, and listening" (303). This translingual approach to writing calls not just for identifying the different language practices that people use to engage in political, economic, and cultural activity in the globalizing world but also for revising both teachers' and students' attitudes and expectations about language practice.

Arnetha Ball, Ted Lardner, Terry Meier, Rashidah Jaami' Muhammad, and Gail Okawa have emphasized the need to bring language diversity issues into teacher-training courses, giving preservice teachers opportunities to reflect on these often-implicit attitudes toward language standards and linguistic difference as well as to identify the sources of these attitudes. More recently, composition scholars have begun in earnest to develop and share concrete pedagogical practices that teachers can use to foster respect for and allow students to draw on their diverse language backgrounds. Present-day members of the CCCC's Language Policy Committee have led the way in this regard with their 2005 collection *Language Diversity in the Classroom: From Intention to Practice* (Smitherman and Villanueva). As the title of this volume suggests, it addresses the intellectual and emotional barriers that have kept many teachers from doing more than just voicing their support of students' diverse languages and dialects. Compositionists such as Jaime Mejía and Louise Rodriguez Connal have also joined in this effort to articulate specific pedagogical practices that give students opportunities to develop skills in using a variety of linguistic forms and registers to achieve a wide range of rhetorical purposes.

Shaping Language Policy in the U.S. contributes to several strands of this disciplinary conversation about students' linguistic diversity. Chapter 1, for example, tells the story of the Language Curriculum Research Group, a collective of scholars who, like Smitherman, worked to translate linguistics research on African American Language for composition scholars and to create concrete pedagogical strategies for bringing the Students' Right ideal to life in the writing classroom. Chapters 2 and 3, meanwhile, investigate language policies that prompt English-language arts educators to see their work in relation to other languages and language communities both within the United States and around the world. Analyses of the debates surrounding English-only legislation, the CCCC National Language Policy, and the Defense Department's national security language policy call on compositionists to see students' language-learning needs within a political, economic, and cultural context that increasingly demands facility in multiple languages. All three main chapters, then, articulate the implications of the respective language policies for composition scholars' research, teaching, and service in colleges and in communities marked by increasing linguistic diversity.

Attending to the Contexts of Language and Literacy Education

As *Shaping Language Policy in the U.S.* explores the pedagogical implications of these three language policies, it also contributes to efforts by compositionists, education scholars, and literacy theorists to understand how social, political, and economic forces influence literacy education. This study connects most directly to Curt Dudley-Marling and Carole Edelsky's edited collection *The Fate of Progressive Language Policies and Practices*, a volume that underscores "the enduring truth that context matters" in how language arts educators can translate the field's language policies into pedagogical and civic action (xvii). Dudley-Marling and Edelsky explain in their introduction,

> As with any plan, the intentions behind progressive language practices [and policies] are not the entire story; nor is the practice as played out. The "players" are not only those directly involved in creating, revising, and participating in the innovative assessment project or the instructional program development or the policymaking activity. Parents, media, voters, local church groups, national movements, even disembodied current "commonsense" approaches participate in and affect the life histories of progressive educational language practices and policies. (ix)

In other words, the "success" of any particular language policy depends not just on the "quality" of the theories and ideas written into its pages. The interpretive frameworks of other scholars, school administrators, government officials, journalists, and citizens all affect how the policy circulates and gets used as well as how it does (or does not) get recorded and analyzed in our disciplinary history.

Of course, this understanding that dominant social forces influence language policy and literacy education is not new. Scholars such as James Paul Gee and Shirley Brice Heath have defined *literacy practices*, in the words of Brian Street, as both "behaviour" and "the social and cultural conceptualizations that give meaning to the uses of reading and/or writing" (2). In other words, compositionists do not simply teach students writing skills. They also convey a particular set of ideas about the purposes of writing and an accompanying set of values about appropriate or effective writing. These pedagogical practices reproduce or revise dominant ideas and values about writing and language difference.

More recent scholarship in literacy studies and rhetoric and composition has extended the work of Gee, Heath, and Street by focusing our attention on how the shift from a nation-based industrial economy to a global information economy has created new pressures on composition teachers. Min-Zhan Lu, Deborah Brandt, Romy Clark, Roz Ivanič, and scholars in the New London Group, including James Paul Gee, Joseph Lo Bianco, and Carmen Luke, have explored how the contexts for and demands placed on literacy education have changed dramatically as technological developments and changes in institutional structures are transforming peoples' working, civic, and personal lives. Lu, for example, has articulated how the global economy of "fast capitalism" has reinforced desires for language standards because they are seen as enabling efficient, clear transmission of information (43–44). These pressures, Lu argues, have reinforced many writing instructors' belief that their primary aim is teaching students to reproduce the standard conventions expected in workplaces as a means for communicating clearly and efficiently (43–45). In this way the economic context has influenced rhetoric and composition instruction in ways that encourage teachers and students to see nonstandardized dialects and languages other than English as barriers to clear and efficient communication rather than as important rhetorical resources for conveying information and making sense of the world.

Shaping Language Policy in the U.S. contributes in several ways to these ongoing conversations about how "context matters" for language policies and pedagogies that affirm linguistic diversity, as the three language policies in this study advocate for developing specific language practices as a means for creating particular social arrangements in the United States. Chapter 1, for example, examines how conservative political and economic pressures of the mid-1970s effectively sealed the fate of one progressive curricular project and, in turn, shaped how subsequent generations have perceived the CCCC's Students' Right language policy. Chapter 2, meanwhile, examines the English-only debates of the 1980s within the context of conservative political discourse of the Ronald Reagan era. This analytical framework highlights how debates about pedagogical aims and methods are also debates about the types of communities we want to live in and the role of schools in bringing about these social worlds. Finally, chapter 3 examines how the Department of Defense and several other government agencies view language education through a post–September 11 political and cultural lens that has in turn shaped debate about the priorities of the U.S. educational system and the nation's vision about what language arts education should prepare students to do. Throughout all three chapters, then, one sees language scholars such as Geneva Smitherman, Carol Reed of the Language Curriculum Research Group, and Mary Louise Pratt of the MLA both taking stock of how political, social, and cultural contexts shape language arts education and developing alternative language policies in order to bring about new visions for managing language practices toward progressive ends.

Writing Language Policy into Histories of Composition Studies

To emphasize the disciplinary significance of these three language policies, *Shaping Language Policy in the U.S.* is both grounded in and contributes to histories of U.S. composition studies. James Berlin, Robert Connors, Sharon Crowley, and Susan Miller have composed histories that explore the discipline's origins as well as the conditions that affect the field's position within colleges and universities. These histories view composition studies in broad strokes, dealing with pedagogical theories and professional issues. In their 1999 *CCC* essay "History in the Spaces Left," however, Jacqueline Jones Royster and Jean C. Williams complicate the historical narratives that too often dominate compositionists' thinking about the discipline's formation. They explain that many composition historians fail to acknowledge the cultural assumptions grounding their interpretive frameworks and, in so doing, produce histories that reinscribe the marginalization of African American scholars, teachers, students, and institutions within composition studies. Royster and Williams offer a new past for composition scholars to draw on, one that incorporates African American scholars' contributions to the field's theoretical and pedagogical development. Writing in the same 1999 issue of *CCC*, Keith Gilyard employed a similar analytical lens in "African American Contributions to Composition Studies," an essay in which he positions African American scholars' work on language diversity issues more centrally within composition studies' range of concerns.

Scholars such as Shirley Wilson Logan, Jessica Enoch, David Gold, Susan Kates, and Steven Schneider have since taken up this project of writing histories that complicate traditional disciplinary narratives portraying the composition classroom as the domain of white males. These historiographers instead account for the presence of marginalized students, teachers, and scholars in composition studies. They explore institutions, documents, and classrooms not often considered to be important sites of rhetorical education, and they examine places where dominant pedagogical approaches have been reworked to help marginalized students develop the rhetorical skills they need to fulfill their personal, professional, and political desires. Significantly, such historical analysis has often highlighted ways that compositionists have advocated for marginalized students' language rights.

Shaping Language Policy in the U.S. joins this effort to recover the work of marginalized scholars in composition studies and to situate language policy and linguistic diversity more centrally within disciplinary history. The narratives in chapters 1 and 2 describe compositionists in the 1970s and 1980s working within their classrooms, within their colleges and universities, and within their communities to generate a broader public commitment to literacy education that values students' diverse languages and dialects. Such historical analysis of the Students' Right resolution and the National Language Policy, two of the CCCC's key language policies, contributes to the discipline's efforts to create what Joseph Harris (channeling Van Wyck Brooks) calls "a usable past." For Harris, this concept means approaching the craft of writing history as a way "not simply of reconceiving our past as a field but of reshaping our actions as writers, teachers, intellectuals, activists, and administrators" ("Usable Past" 343). Toward these ends, this book presents a historical analysis of two key CCCC language policies and details scholars' efforts to implement these policies, and it proposes ways to draw on these histories in analyzing and responding to contemporary debates about a national security language policy. Through its attention to language policy and support for linguistic minorities, this history can inform composition scholars' efforts to negotiate the demands for pedagogical innovation and civic leadership presently facing them. Indeed, compositionists need to learn from and draw on this past as they attempt to make their voices heard in debates—such as the one sparked by the Defense Department's national security language policy—that affect their teaching and their students.

The Organization of This Book

Shaping Language Policy in the U.S. addresses the confusion of many rhetoric and composition scholars about the efficacy of language policies and articulates the significance of specific policies for the field. Each of this book's three main chapters first describes the context within which each language policy was written, paying particular attention to the political, cultural, economic, and educational situations to which it responded. This organizational strategy focuses the analysis on a specific aspect of the production and the use of each language policy.

Chapter 1 challenges claims that the Students' Right to Their Own Language resolution did not usefully inform compositionists' pedagogies during that era. The chapter begins with a brief analysis of the Students' Right language policy, highlighting how it responded to professional debates about the purpose of education sparked by open admissions policies at City University of New York (CUNY) in the early 1970s as well as sociolinguistics research exploring African American language practices. Attention centers on the Brooklyn College-based Language Curriculum Research Group, which, like the Committee on CCCC Language Statement that drafted the Students' Right policy, reimagined writing instruction in light of these educational initiatives, emerging research, and pressing concerns about how teachers could best work with linguistic minority students. Drawing on archival materials from the Ford Foundation, which sponsored the Language Curriculum Research Group's project, as well as two interviews with Carol Reed, the group's cofounder, this chapter describes the group's research, textbook writing, and teacher-training courses. This arrangement enables a reading of the Students' Right resolution through a historical analysis of how compositionists translated the language policy into pedagogical practice.

Chapter 2, meanwhile, analyzes the CCCC National Language Policy as a document intended to position the field as a civic-oriented body able to fill a "language leadership vacuum" (Smitherman, "Lessons" 30) in public debates about language politics and policies. This chapter situates the CCCC's 1988 language policy within the social, political, and cultural contexts from which it emerged, particularly rhetorical commonplaces about individual initiative, communal responsibility, and national identity that circulated widely during the Ronald Reagan era. While the English-only movement built on this conservative discourse to articulate a strong link between the English language and U.S. national identity, materials from the NCTE archives in Urbana, Illinois, suggest that the CCCC tried to redirect these rhetorical commonplaces in ways that could build greater support for multilingualism both inside the writing classroom and within the broader public sphere.

These two histories of CCCC language policies frame the analysis of and development of strategies for responding to the national security language policy in chapter 3. This study approaches the Defense Department's contemporary language policy as a text that can prompt rhetoric and composition scholars to dialogue with modern language scholars, government officials, corporate leaders, and language minority communities about what a linguistically competent U.S. society should be able to do. This analysis begins by highlighting how the Defense Department's *Language Transformation Roadmap* and *A Call to Action* white paper, former President George W. Bush's 2006 National Security Language Initiative, and several congressional legislative proposals present designs for a national education infrastructure grounded in definitions of foreign languages as military tools. It then draws on the work in chapters 1 and 2 as well as theories developed by Lu, Pratt, and Trimbur, among others, to critique this perspective on language and offer an alternative vision of how schools and communities can help bring about these ends. The chapter then moves from critique to action by proposing ways English scholars can use the CCCC's language policies as prompts to invent local strategies for implementing the emerging national security language policy so that it promotes multilingualism as a means of dialoguing to understand and resolve differences rather than translating to infiltrate and defeat enemies.

All three of the main chapters conclude by articulating how these language policies contribute to contemporary discussions inside composition studies. For example, chapter 1 highlights how scholars and teachers can link their arguments for progressive change in literacy education to analyses of the material conditions that enable or disable marginalized students from participating fully in academic life. Chapter 2 discusses what it means for the CCCC to operate as both a professional and a civic-minded organization. Chapter 3 highlights how public debate about the nation's foreign language resources underscores the need for composition scholars to expand the linguistic range of their research and teaching.

The conclusion of *Shaping Language Policy in the U.S.* steps back from these individual studies and examines the implications of language policies for the field of rhetoric and composition as a whole. The conclusion outlines how this book refines scholars' and teachers' understanding of the rhetorical purpose of language policies and their value inside the field; emphasizes the significance of language policies to discussions about how best to teach writing in ways that respect students' linguistic diversity; expands compositionists' conceptions of "academic work" and helps them to reenvision themselves not just as teachers and scholars but also as public intellectuals; and prompts them to develop strategies for working within local spaces to transform institutional practices in ways that build a greater public commitment to linguistic diversity.

An Exigent Moment

This book echoes the CCCC's call for composition scholars to value linguistic diversity and for all members of society to gain competency in multiple languages. While exploring the implications of composition's language policies, however, I continually reflected on my own language background. I am monolingual. My competency in non-English languages extends only to my reading ability in Latin, a "dead" language.

Examining the political, economic, and social contexts that shaped my own linguistic background has only strengthened my belief that the field of rhetoric and composition needs to change. Three decades after the CCCC affirmed the Students' Right to Their Own Language resolution, my own professional education—one conducted in English only—speaks to the field's need to see that composition scholars "have the experiences and training that will enable them to respect diversity and uphold the right of students to their own language" (Committee on CCCC Language Statement 3).

The language policies in this study should lead compositionists to reimagine their teaching and research in ways that attend more carefully to the writing that their students do in languages and dialects other than Standardized English. These language policies should lead rhetoric scholars to invent teaching practices that push students to expand their linguistic repertoires. And they should lead language arts teachers to give students opportunities to explore how and why they use different dialects and languages to compose their identities as they move between their classrooms, their homes, their neighborhoods, and their jobs.

Now is an important time to act on the principles at the heart of the discipline's language policies. Several congressional representatives have proposed legislation that would implement various aspects of the Defense Department's national security language policy. The ongoing deliberations about this language policy and its accompanying legislation hold significant implications for language arts educators, particularly in terms of funding priorities for teaching and research innovations. At the same time, however, states such as Arizona and Massachusetts are declaring Standardized English as their public schools' only language of instruction, policies that too often exacerbate the discrimination and difficult material conditions facing language-minority communities in the United States.

Rhetoric and composition scholars can provide valuable leadership in pedagogical, professional, and public debates about these types of language policy action. *Shaping Language Policy in the U.S.* aims to deepen our understanding of both the disciplinary and political significance of the CCCC Students' Right resolution and National Language Policy as texts that inform how composition scholars can respond to both national and local debates about linguistic diversity and literacy education. This historical analysis underscores the need to teach and serve alongside other professional and activist groups so that U.S. language policy reflects the field's democratic ideals—to teach language and literacy in ways that enable citizens to participate more fully in public life.

1 THE LANGUAGE CURRICULUM RESEARCH GROUP

TRANSLATING THE STUDENTS' RIGHT TO THEIR OWN LANGUAGE RESOLUTION INTO PEDAGOGICAL PRACTICE

> We affirm the students' right to their own patterns and varieties of language—the dialects of their nurture or whatever dialects in which they find their own identity and style.... The claim that any one dialect is unacceptable ... leads to false advice for speakers and writers, and immoral advice for humans. A nation proud of its diverse heritage and its cultural and racial variety will preserve its heritage of dialects. We affirm strongly that teachers must have the experiences and training that will enable them to respect diversity and uphold the right of students to their own language.
> —Committee on CCCC Language Statement, *Students' Right to Their Own Language*, 1974

> Although many compositionists and other language arts professionals greeted the Students' Right policy with high enthusiasm, still a great degree of lingering confusion existed: "Well, then, if I don't correct the grammatical errors, what do I do?" as one well-meaning instructor queried.
> —Geneva Smitherman, "CCCC's Role in the Struggle for Language Rights," 1999

WITH ITS 1972 STUDENTS' RIGHT TO THEIR OWN LANGUAGE RESOLUTION and accompanying 1974 background statement, the CCCC prompted the question, "What should the schools do about the language habits of students who come from a wide variety of social, economic, and cultural backgrounds?" (Committee on CCCC Language Statement 1).

As Smitherman recalls, however, many compositionists felt the Students' Right policy did not fully answer this question, leaving them with few specific strategies to take to the classroom.

This initial unsettled reception has influenced the field's current perceptions of the document, as composition scholars continue to debate the relevance of the Students' Right language policy to contemporary disciplinary concerns. For example, in the introduction to their 2005 collection *The Hope and the Legacy: The Past, Present, and Future of the "Students' Right to Their Own Language,"* Patrick Bruch and Richard Marback explain that compositionists past and present variously characterize the Students' Right policy "as a failed attempt at coalition, as an indirect influence, as a unique historical moment, and as an important inspiration" for literacy educators ("Critical" xii). Even with these disagreements, the most consistently reached conclusion among compositionists is that the theory informing Students' Right has rarely, if ever, materialized in the writing classroom. Michael Pennell, for example, suggests the Students' Right resolution and background statement, having not been "reinforced by actual pedagogical strategies," may be little more than "rhetorical ghosts with no substance below the ink and paper that [they] embody" (229). In fact, as the CCCC Language Policy Committee reported in a survey of CCCC and NCTE members in 2000, many compositionists have never even seen the ink and paper—let alone the substance—of the Students' Right policy, as two-thirds of survey respondents were unfamiliar with the resolution (14–15).

In most present-day work around issues of linguistic diversity and language policy, then, compositionists seem to agree that the conversations informing the Students' Right theory did not lead to pedagogical transformation inside the classroom. This chapter complicates this notion by recovering the work of the Language Curriculum Research Group (LCRG), a scholarly collective that in the late 1960s and early 1970s was building on the same sociolinguistic and cultural rhetorical theories that would eventually give shape to the Students' Right policy. Indeed, the LCRG created a textbook manuscript and trained writing instructors in ways that anticipated the policy's pressing question, "What should teachers do about students' varied languages?" The research group, based out of Brooklyn College and the Borough of Manhattan Community College, created a Standardized English as a Second Dialect course for African American and Puerto Rican students[1] whose writing displayed features of the Black English Vernacular (BEV) dialect.[2] Over a five-year period, the LCRG received financial support as well as professional legitimacy from prestigious Ford Foundation grants totaling over $250,000.[3] For reasons discussed later, however, few present-day scholars—and even fewer of the group's contemporaries—reference the LCRG's work, a fact that has only reinforced assumptions that the theory of the Students' Right policy did not usefully inform teachers' practices.[4]

While the LCRG created its curriculum and pedagogy alongside rather than in direct response to the Students' Right resolution, the group nevertheless intervened in the same public and professional debates about language diversity and literacy education that prompted the CCCC policy. For this reason, studying the history of the LCRG can contribute to the ongoing conversation among compositionists who are trying to understand more fully the educational and linguistic politics of the Students' Right era. Scholars can deepen their understanding of the Students' Right legacy by analyzing actual pedagogies, such as the LCRG's, that emerged from the scholarly discussions informing it. By drawing upon archival materials from the Ford Foundation, the LCRG's textbook manuscript and teachers' manual, and interviews with Carol Reed, a founding member of the LCRG, this chapter challenges perceptions of the Students' Right policy as a progressive theory divorced from the everyday practice of the composition classroom. Through this recovery of the LCRG's work, scholars can see the Students' Right ideal did in fact inspire teachers to invent pedagogies enabling students to leverage their linguistic diversity as a means for accessing academic literacies. Learning about the LCRG challenges common beliefs about the range of scholarly work that has gone on in the name of the Students' Right theory, for one sees not only the group's successes in helping students to use their own languages as resources for their academic writing and exploration but also how and why the LCRG's efforts to transform composition's pedagogical and political commitments have been nearly forgotten within disciplinary memory.

To make this argument, this chapter first considers the CCCC Students' Right policy and background document, examining their theoretical foundation and highlighting how these texts prompted compositionists to rethink their responsibilities to their students, to their discipline, to their colleagues in other fields, and to the communities outside school walls. Having thus examined the political and professional contexts within which the Students' Right policy documents emerged, the chapter's attention then turns to the LCRG. A brief overview of the research group's work appears first in order to underscore the timeliness as well as the broad scope of its project. The significance of the LCRG within composition studies becomes particularly clear when focusing on three aspects of the group's project that it created in order to enact a Students' Right pedagogical theory: first, the LCRG's strategy for bridging sociolinguistics research on BEV with composition studies; second, the group's decision to make BEV and African American culture subjects of study in the writing classroom; and third, the group's emphasis on prompting teachers to reflect on their attitudes toward racial and linguistic difference. The final section of this chapter attends to reasons why the LCRG's project has escaped disciplinary memory. Recounting this part of the group's history underscores the need for composition scholars to elucidate the political, social, and cultural contexts that influence how professionals or the broader public have interpreted language policies and the professional practices built on them.

Composition's Debate over Language Minorities in the College Classroom

The CCCC adopted the Students' Right resolution in 1972 amid vigorous debate over the purpose of higher education. Civil rights protesters of the 1960s had called for increased access to education for students who, by traditional standards, seemed underprepared for academic work at the university level. The most notable institutional response to these demands came in 1970. During the spring of that year, CUNY adopted a policy that guaranteed entry into one of the university system's eighteen tuition-free colleges for every city resident who earned a high school diploma. This open-admissions policy led to significantly increased enrollment figures, from 174,000 in 1969 to 266,000 in 1975. During this period, Mina Shaughnessy directed the writing program in City College of CUNY's Search for Education, Elevation, and Knowledge (SEEK) program, which offered academic support and instruction for students who entered CUNY through its open-admissions policy. In her landmark 1977 book *Errors and Expectations*, Shaughnessy described how this policy altered CUNY's student population:

> [CUNY] open[ed] its doors not only to a larger population of students than it had ever had before . . . but [also] to a wider range of students than any college had probably ever admitted or thought of admitting to its campus—academic winners and losers from the best and worst high schools in the country, the children of the lettered and the illiterate, the blue-collared, the white-collared, and

the unemployed . . .; in short, the sons and daughters of New Yorkers, reflecting that city's intense, troubled version of America. (1–2)

Shaughnessy observed that the so-called academic losers—the children of the illiterate, blue-collared, and unemployed—brought the most pressing educational issues to the university with them. Their placement exams alarmed many instructors and administrators because their "difficulties with the written language seemed of a different order" from those of other students, so much so that it appeared "even very modest standards of high-school literacy had not been met" (2).

Shaughnessy studied over four thousand of these placement essays written by incoming City College students from 1970 and 1974, and this research informed *Errors and Expectations*. This book classifies the difficulties she saw most often in this writing, provides numerous examples of and analyzes the source of each problem, and presents strategies for teachers to address these issues with students. Shaughnessy's conclusion was that these struggling writers were not "slow or non-verbal, indifferent to or incapable of academic excellence," but rather simply "beginners [who] must, like all beginners, learn by making mistakes" (5). Even more significantly, she explained, many of these students spoke other languages and dialects at home and "never successfully reconciled the words of home and school, a fact which by now had worked its way deep into their feelings about school and themselves as students" (3). But despite their uncertainty about the possible cultural costs of formal education, these students had *chosen* to come to college. They had made it to CUNY, argued Adrienne Rich, poet and former City College writing instructor, having struggled throughout their educational lives to demand their "right to learn and to be treated with dignity" (59).

These rights were largely ignored by English teachers. Many professors believed this influx of students unfamiliar with academic standards of style threatened their sense of professional standing and their traditional modes of writing instruction. Of the scene, Shaughnessy wrote, "Here were teachers trained to analyze the belletristic achievements of the centuries marooned in basic writing classrooms with adult student writers who appeared by college standards to be illiterate" (3). These instructors maintained that the writing produced by these new students did not appear even remotely similar to their traditional notions of appropriate—let alone eloquent—academic writing. Many traditionally minded scholars believed that no type of instructional methods could help these students to become writers when their home languages and their home cultures had already failed them. Shaughnessy lamented the way many writing instructors quickly labeled their open admissions students as "ineducable," "announced to their supervisors (or even their students) after only a week of class that everyone was probably going to fail," and relied on "such pedagogically empty terms as 'handicapped' or 'disadvantaged'" when describing their students' writing difficulties (3–4). In short, CUNY's admissions officers had granted the "academic losers" and the "children of the unlettered" access to college, but many teachers made their own determination that these students truly did not belong among them.

Discussions about how to teach these students extended beyond CUNY and into the field's leading journals, such as *College English* and *CCC*. In these venues, scholars trained in *belles lettres* did not give up on their students so quickly, but many continued to promote a limiting idea about how students should reconcile the words of home and school. J. Mitchell Morse was one of the most outspoken English scholars who sought to rescue students from the effects of what he took to be their linguistically disadvantaged and uncultured home life.

Morse viewed a student's performance in the first-year writing course as an indicator of his or her willingness and intellectual capacity to enter academic culture. He firmly believed that the first rite of initiation into academic culture entailed learning to speak and write *only* Standardized English (SE), the language of "literate society." According to Morse, Black English dialects restricted students' abilities to read, write, and think, let alone to develop the refined critical skills of a liberally educated person. He declared that the ill effects of students' home languages, particularly Black English, had become all too evident to those writing instructors marooned in their classrooms:

> Everybody who has ever corrected freshman themes knows that a limited vocabulary and a limited command of syntax limit the possibilities of thought; and that an inaccurate vocabulary and an unreliable command of syntax often shipwreck thought. Black English . . . lacks the vocabulary and the syntactic resources for thought of even moderate complexity. (841)

Morse argued that African American students would fail college unless they cut ties to their home language. Moreover, African American students' language would ensure they continued to "suffer a real [cultural] deprivation" throughout their lives, because Black English's limited vocabulary and syntactic resources simply would never permit them to appreciate the intellectual value or the aesthetic beauty of written texts (841–42). Morse explained, "People who lack linguistic equipment... are almost helplessly drawn to writing that makes no intellectual demands and offers no disturbing aesthetic stimulation, but affords only a kind of analgesic escape from vacancy" (842). Students who learned SE, on the other hand, could extend their knowledge beyond what they gained through the oral culture of their families and communities. Teachers needed to demand that students replace their BEV with SE to ensure they left the writing course "linguistically equipped" to develop clear, precise thoughts about the world (837).

Interestingly, Morse did not see his teaching approach as being incompatible with claims made by scholars such as Rich that marginalized students had a "right ... to be treated with dignity" (59). Morse believed SE-only pedagogies worked toward socially progressive ends. He saw himself liberating his African American students from their linguistic ghettoes and delivering them into the wider world of ideas. For this reason, Morse believed compositionists had an ethical imperative to teach students to speak and write SE instead of Black English. It was an absolutely necessary—even if somewhat unfortunate—resolution to the conflict between the languages of home and school:

> Unavoidably, with the best of democratic intentions, we ask them to grow beyond their native culture and alienate themselves to their neighbors, friends, and relatives. Unavoidably, with the best of democratic intentions, we ask them to identify with people they have always considered effete impudent snobs. (837)

To underscore his "best of democratic intentions," Morse cited a long list of literate black leaders who "without exception" wrote and spoke in SE, including public officials such as Shirley Chisholm, lawyers such as Thurgood Marshall, revolutionaries such as Huey Newton, and academics such as W. E. B. Du Bois (838–39). Morse asked, "Who among these can't or couldn't or doesn't or didn't write standard English?" (838). Meanwhile, a black leader "who habitually expresses himself in Black English," Morse explained, could attract no more than "a neighborhood following" (839).

He suggested that African American leaders such as Chisholm, Marshall, Newton, and Du Bois achieved no small measure of their success because SE vocabulary and syntax allowed them to communicate precisely and clearly to the American mainstream. Because these skills had enabled leaders to push for political and cultural reform, Morse saw "no contradiction between helping students to become articulate and working for social change" (843). For Morse, though, "becoming articulate" meant learning and using SE only; "working for social change" required alienating oneself from neighbors, friends, and relatives.

Ultimately, Morse and the many others who ascribed to a similar teaching philosophy advocated pedagogies that exacerbated cultural and linguistic conflicts between majority schools and minority students. They distorted the nation's pluralist identity, denying the intellectual legitimacy of minority cultures and languages as resources for strengthening students' analytical and communicative abilities. Morse championed this assimilationist model of education most clearly when he asked students to "alienate themselves from their neighbors, friends, and relatives" and to identify with the "effete impudent snobs" of cultured society (837). With his repeated calls for eliminating students' native dialects in order to promote their social progress and academic achievement, Morse reinforced a definition of *language difference* as *language deficiency* when he claimed that SE alone provided students with the "linguistic keys that would open . . . the world of complex thought and complex beauty" (842). Morse argued that African Americans' language itself should be blamed for their social, economic, and political marginalization. Such a statement helped to reproduce an American educational system that failed to recognize a full range of African American cultural productions and worldviews.

While Morse and other scholars committed to preserving *belles-lettres* argued that the use of Black English thwarted complex thinking, sociolinguists were drawing different conclusions from their systematic study of marginalized dialects of English. Scholars such as Beryl Bailey, Ralph Fasold, William Labov, Walt Wolfram, and Juanita V. Williamson demonstrated through their research that although standardized and nonstandardized English dialects were marked by different surface features, they all operated according to systematic morphological and syntactical patterns. In other words, the members of any given speech community created meaning through language in part by following their dialect's set of internally consistent rules. Sociolinguists documented how BEV users, just like SE speakers, could draw on the dialect's robust vocabulary and syntactical complexity in order to develop clear thoughts and communicate precise meaning.

While many language arts teachers believed that students needed to abandon their Black English dialects in order to learn SE, several sociolinguists built on research demonstrating the morphological and syntactical regularity of oral BEV discourse to develop strategies for teaching African American students how to write SE by analyzing it alongside BEV. Prominent among these scholars was William Stewart, who described his approach as one of teaching Standard English as a Second Dialect (ESD). Stewart suggested that while differences between BEV and SE certainly were functional and structural, they nevertheless were trivial, by and large confined to surface features of the language. Stewart believed that these surface differences led to "cross-dialect interference" when African American students tried to write in SE. Since children internalize the basic behavioral patterns of their first language or dialect by the time they have reached school age, Stewart believed that African American students needed to have the morphological and syntactical rules of BEV and SE made explicit to them. He concluded that if these students could learn to compare and contrast examples of BEV and SE discourse illustrating these different rules and identify where BEV syntax "interfered" when they tried to compose SE, they would be better equipped to develop competencies in written SE. Stewart, then, granted BEV a place in the composition classroom. One must note, however, that he believed attending to this marginalized dialect was useful only insofar as it helped students learn to write SE.

By the late 1960s, a group of African American sociolinguists and compositionists had emerged to argue that such ESD or bidialectalist pedagogies limited the range of what students could envision themselves doing as writers. Ernece B. Kelly made one of the earliest criticisms of compositionists' work relative to dialect difference with her talk at the 1968 CCCC Convention, which she delivered in the immediate aftermath of Martin Luther King Jr.'s assassination. Kelly denounced composition scholars' willful ignorance of Black English and challenged the assumptions on which bidialectalist pedagogies were based:

> Here in Minneapolis we meet to discuss composition. Here we meet to discuss the dialects of Black students and how we can upgrade or, if we're really successful, just plain *replace* them. . . . Why aren't there Blacks here who will talk about the emergence of an image among Blacks which does not permit them to even bother with the question of whether or not the white man understands their dialect? . . . Why aren't there Blacks helping to plan this conference who have access to the papers which deal with the Black aesthetic and its relationship to composition or the Black

image and why it does or does not rest in the anthologies we use or the richness and values of the Black ghetto? (107)

A number of sociolinguists-cum-compositionists echoed Kelly's critique, prominent among them being Geneva Smitherman, James Sledd, and Wayne O'Neil. They maintained that the project to effect bidialectalism constituted an unethical aim for language arts instruction. Sledd argued that even though bidialectalists used the term *dialect difference* to suggest that "correctness" was always relative, they still connoted *dialect deficiency* because, he explained, they only considered students' nonstandardized dialects to be appropriate for uses that middle-class white society granted little intellectual or cultural worth, such as rapping with friends ("Doublespeak" 450–51). Smitherman extended this critique, claiming bidialectalist pedagogies forced students to attend to the relatively insignificant surface features of language. Students thus were effectively discouraged from devoting their full energy and attention to crafting powerful, meaningful prose: "Teaching strategies which seek only to put white middle-class English into the mouths of black speakers ain did nothin to inculcate the black perspective necessary to address the crises in the black community" (*Talkin and Testifyin* 209). These scholars collectively urged compositionists to focus their efforts on teaching students to use writing as a tool for analyzing and producing new knowledge about the world, no matter the dialect. Even more importantly, they envisioned new goals for the composition classroom, such that African American students developed analytical, speaking, and writing skills in their own language that they could use to tackle social problems within their communities and enrich the political and cultural identity of African Americans.

The CCCC's Intervention through Language Policy Work

It was within this context of related debates about open-admissions policies, the intellectual legitimacy of African American students' language practices, and the aims of higher education that the CCCC Executive Committee in 1971 appointed a small committee to draft a policy statement on student dialects in the composition classroom. Melvin Butler chaired the Committee on CCCC Language Statement, and he was joined on the committee by Geneva Smitherman, Adam Casmier, Ninfa Flores, Jenefer Giannasi, Myrna Harrison, Richard Lloyd-Jones, Richard Long, Elizabeth Martin, Elisabeth McPherson, and Ross Winterowd.

Within a year, the committee had drafted the paragraph-long Students' Right to Their Own Language resolution, and the CCCC Executive Committee passed the policy statement in November 1972. This policy crafted an alternative vision for literacy education, one that challenged mainstream society's unwillingness to affirm diverse cultures and languages. The policy statement read as follows:

> We affirm the students' right to their own patterns and varieties of language—the dialects of their nurture or whatever dialects in which they find their own identity and style. Language scholars long ago denied that the myth of a standard American dialect has any validity. The claim that any one dialect is unacceptable amounts to an attempt of one social group to exert its dominance over another. Such a claim leads to false advice for speakers and writers, and immoral advice for humans. A nation proud of its diverse heritage and its cultural and racial variety will preserve its heritage of dialects. We affirm strongly that teachers must have the experiences and training that will enable them to respect diversity and uphold the right of students to their own language. (Committee on CCCC Language Statement 2–3)

With this resolution, the CCCC located the source of marginalized students' problems not within their languages but rather in the power that dominant groups leveraged when labeling nonstandardized languages and dialects inferior to SE. The resolution aimed to embolden educators to transform their pedagogies in ways that challenged this "myth" about languages and defied America's prejudices. Moreover, it encouraged minority students and teachers to claim their linguistic and cultural identities as vital resources for thinking, reading, and writing critically about the world.

The general membership of the CCCC passed the Students' Right resolution by a wide margin at the organization's annual meeting in April 1974, thus making the language statement official organizational policy. Nevertheless, the resolution drew both praise and rebuke. William Pixton, for one, denied that students had a right to their own language. What students did have, he argued, was their "right to the truth"—the truth that BEV is "linguistically different *and* deficient" (252). Allen Smith, meanwhile, criticized the Students' Right policy for the way it seemingly ignored teachers' duty to help students develop the speaking and writing skills needed "to bring one group together with another"

(159). Education scholar Jesse L. Colquit, on the other hand, lauded the resolution's underlying assumption that "while students need to learn the language and culture of the school, the school needs to learn and appreciate the language and culture of the students" (19). While these scholars debated the educational philosophies and pedagogical theories informing the Students' Right resolution, many others expressed their confusion about what the resolution actually demanded of them in the day-to-day of their classrooms. Bruch and Marback go so far in their 2005 collection *The Hope and the Legacy* to suggest "the conversation that surrounded the resolution reflected a public and professional turn away from visionary ideals and abstract ideas," such as equality, difference, and racial justice, "toward practical problems and concrete solutions" (51).

The CCCC, in fact, helped to redirect the conversation this way in 1974. The Committee on the CCCC Language Statement felt that amid the "Student's Right" controversy, too many compositionists had been "forced to take a position on an aspect of their discipline about which they have little real information" (1). The CCCC therefore published a background statement and annotated bibliography in a fall 1974 special issue of *CCC* that pulled together relevant research from composition, education, and sociolinguistics in order to help scholars understand the resolution's theoretical foundations and consider its pedagogical implications. These documents were meant to convince educators to focus "on what the actual available linguistic evidence indicates we should emphasize" in student writing rather than "on what the vocal elements of the public thinks it wants" (1). Reflecting on the committee's work in 1999, Smitherman described more specifically its goal in producing this background statement: "(1) to heighten consciousness of language attitudes; (2) to promote the value of linguistic diversity; and (3) to convey facts and information about language and language variation that would enable instructors to teach their non-traditional students—and ultimately *all* students—more effectively" ("CCCC's Role" 359). Toward these ends, the background document explored such topics as what dialects are and how people acquire them; what it means to say that "dialects differ" and how some dialects are granted more prestige than others; how dialects are related to one's abilities to read, write, and think; and what implications these sociolinguistic insights carry for textbooks, handbooks, standardized testing, and writing instruction. The Committee on CCCC Language Statement suggested throughout the policy statement and background document that research insights from sociolinguistics ideally would help compositionists to invent teaching practices that sparked progressive social change.

In short, the Students' Right policy and background statement advanced the argument that sociolinguistics research called for teachers, administrators, and students to adopt new goals for writing courses. Many linguistic minority students had become so worn down from an overemphasis on seemingly minor aspects of writing (e.g., spelling, vocabulary, grammar, and mechanics) that they felt anxious and hesitant when they approached "formal," school-based writing assignments. This insight mirrored one that Rich had gained through her years teaching basic writing at City College, where she saw many of her students struggle to write formally because they had come to distrust their teachers. Rich explained, "In order to write I have to believe that there is someone willing to collaborate subjectively [as a reader], as opposed to a grading machine out to get me for mistakes in spelling and grammar" (64). The Student's Right background statement tried to convince teachers to reenvision themselves as willing readers, not punitive graders, since students could produce powerful and imaginative prose in any dialect. Teachers were to "concentrate on building up students' confidence in their ability to write" (8), giving them every opportunity, in Rich's words, to "discover that they have ideas that are valuable, even original, and can express those ideas on paper" (67). According to the Students' Right policy, composition courses needed to become spaces where students saw academic work as a means to make sense of their worlds, using writing to shape knowledge, not merely reproduce it. Teachers needed to read students' writing with an eye toward helping them express their ideas more effectively, not more correctly.

The CCCC background statement provided teachers with some pedagogical strategies for respecting students' right to their own language in the writing classroom. These activities and assignments centered on students' analyzing and experimenting with a wide array of linguistic resources. For example, while Morse believed reading materials needed to address minority students' cultural and intellectual deprivation, the CCCC urged teachers to select readings such as John Oliver Killens' *Cotillion* that are "oriented to the experience and sophistication of our students" and that allowed students to see how writers can experiment with different dialects to reflect different characters' social realities (11). Teachers were encouraged to create a variety of writing assignments giving students chances to experiment in similar fashion, writing for different purposes and for different audiences throughout the semester. Students' language choices in these assignments could further support the Students' Right policy by prompting classroom discussion about the "linguistic values and customs" of each student's family and community (4).

The Students' Right policy in effect crafted a new identity for college composition in relation both to other disciplines and to American society. The subject of the classroom shifted from SE grammar and "the belletristic achievements of the centuries" (Shaughnessy 3) to "the totality of language" and "the multiple aspects of the communication process" (Committee on CCCC Language Statement 12). The background statement explained how other fields' limiting ideas about "good" writing effectively narrowed the range of topics that composition courses often addressed:

> Teachers from other fields who view English as a service course, one which will save them the labor of teaching writing, often implicitly define writing as the communication of information within a limited social context. Perhaps when they (and some English teachers) fuss about spelling and usage, they are merely avoiding difficult problems of writing or, at least, avoiding talking about them. . . . Whatever the reason for the complaint, courses which limit themselves to a narrow view of language in hopes of pleasing other departments will not offer a view of dialect adequate to encourage students to grow more competent to handle a fuller range of their language, and thus will defeat their own purpose. (13)

The CCCC believed sociolinguistics research offered "a view of dialect adequate enough" to prompt compositionists to see themselves serving broader social goals instead of other teachers' narrow interests. Compositionists were to aim at expanding students' "range of versatility" such that they could use language to meet different purposes in their homes, in their communities, in their courses, and in their future civic and professional lives (6).

This disciplinary and course goal situated the composition classroom within a wider context, connecting it not only to other classrooms within the university but also to the diverse communities outside the school's walls. As the CCCC declared in its background statement, "Our pluralistic society requires many varieties of language to meet our multiplicity of needs" (5). Forcing students to choose the standardized dialect over their native variety promoted a narrow view of the rhetorical situations to which students might need to or want to respond. Moreover, it reinforced a dominant cultural perspective that viewed usage, grammar, and mechanical conventions as "single-standard etiquette *rules* rather than as *options* for effective expression" (10, emphasis added). The CCCC used the Students' Right policy, then, to persuade compositionists that the purpose of literacy education is not "to erase differences" (2) but to expand all students' linguistic repertoires so they could operate effectively in all types of communication settings.

Having presented the theoretical foundations for its Students' Right resolution, the CCCC nevertheless continued to face charges that it promoted a permissive, *laissez-faire* pedagogy. Even those compositionists who were inclined to support the Students' Right resolution in theory felt that the policy statement and background document did not give them a clear outline of what they should be doing in the classroom. It was amid this discourse about the Students' Right pedagogy that the LCRG used the concept of students' right to their own language as the foundation for its pedagogical response to the changing conditions in CUNY's writing courses. The Brooklyn College-based researchers did exactly what the Students' Right policy called for: they drew on the emerging linguistics research about BEV to transform the composition classroom into a space where African American students' languages and cultures were both subjects of study and resources for critical thinking and writing. The LCRG in effect created a Students' Right pedagogy, giving students new opportunities to reconcile the words of home and school.

The LCRG's Project to Support Language Diversity in the Composition Classroom

The LCRG's founding members, Carol Reed and Sylvia Lowenthal of Brooklyn College and Milton Baxter of the Borough of Manhattan Community College, formed the research group in 1969 to address concerns they had while teaching composition in CUNY's SEEK program.[5] Traditional methods of teaching grammatical correctness frustrated many of the African American students in SEEK. According to Reed, many CUNY instructors, just like Morse, assumed these students made grammatical errors in part because they did not know the rules of SE grammar and mechanics. Teachers therefore gave students "intensive doses of 'more of the same'" (Reed, "Why Black English" 10), namely, repeated exposure—couched as "enrichment"—to the rules of SE grammar and to countless examples of SE prose (Reed, Baxter, and Lowenthal 1).

Reed, Baxter, and Lowenthal questioned this teaching.[6] Having been trained in sociolinguistics, they believed that many African American students' writing reflected "cross-dialect interference." They built on Stewart's work to develop a curriculum grounded on the assumption that students would benefit from having BEV's morphological and syntactical patterns made explicit and learning to identify where aspects of BEV appeared in their efforts to write SE prose (3–5).[7] In 1969, they began to create exercises and writing assignments for a composition textbook that would allow students to learn about the language varieties of their communities as well as how to edit their prose to reflect the SE conventions expected by most teachers in college courses.

The group presented its initial classroom strategies and textbook exercises at several professional conferences, but it was at the 1969 NCTE convention that the group received a big break. Marjorie Martus of the Ford Foundation attended Reed's presentation, and as Reed would later explain, Martus sensed from attendees' enthusiastic responses that all composition teachers needed to know about the LCRG's project (telephone interview, 9 Nov. 2003). Martus encouraged Reed to apply for a foundation grant that could support the LCRG's efforts to develop its textbook manuscript and ultimately publish and distribute it to interested writing programs throughout the United States. Reed, Baxter, and Lowenthal readily accepted this invitation. On 24 March 1970, they submitted a grant proposal to the foundation entitled "A CUNY Demonstration Project to Effect Bidialectalism in Users of Nonstandard Dialects of English."

Ford Foundation officials awarded the research group an initial $64,456 grant to support textbook development, in large part because they agreed with the LCRG that writing teachers needed specific pedagogical strategies to use in their classrooms (Ward 6). The Ford Foundation certainly understood the value of sociolinguistics research on BEV, having already supported Center for Applied Linguistics projects in this area. The LCRG convinced foundation officials that it could—indeed, needed to—translate this research into pedagogical methods in order to help those CUNY instructors who, as Shaughnessy later described them, felt "marooned" in their composition classrooms during the early years of open admissions, with "no studies nor guides, nor even suitable textbooks to turn to" (3).

The LCRG, which grew by 1971 to include Paul Cohen, Samuel Moore, and Jacqueline Redrick, used its Ford Foundation grant money to address this situation on several fronts.[8] First, the group members researched several semesters' worth of their students' writing so they could focus their efforts on addressing only those BEV features that appeared most frequently in students' attempts to write in SE. Second, they developed, piloted, and revised their textbook manuscript for ESD first-year composition courses. Third, the LCRG researchers overviewed their pedagogical methods and textbook manuscript by presenting papers at a variety of conferences, including conventions of the CCCC, NCTE, College Language Association, College English Association, Teachers of English to Speakers of Other Languages, and the Linguistic Society of America. Fourth, the group created a multifaceted approach for preparing educators to teach ethically and effectively to African American students whose writing reflected ESD language-learning situations. And fifth, on the basis of successes in all these other endeavors, the LCRG in 1973 began trying to spark publishers' interest in its textbook manuscript. The sections that follow analyze these various activities in more detail, exploring how the LCRG's efforts to create a progressive composition pedagogy can deepen understanding of what it means to teach in ways that reflect the Students' Right policy.

Bridging the Gap between Sociolinguistics and Composition

As African American scholars who were speakers of BEV, trained in sociolinguistics, and first-year composition teachers, the LCRG researchers were well positioned to develop writing instruction responsive to the language diversity of students entering universities during the early years of open admissions. The group knew writing instructors should hear how sociolinguistics research on BEV could usefully inform their teaching. Just as significantly, the researchers also considered their BEV-speaking students to be an important, interested, and intellectually capable audience for this research. Reed would remark in a 1973 *TESOL Quarterly* article that her students were "ready and willing (if not downright *eager*) to . . . make practical use of an interesting body of knowledge about factors influencing their own linguistic behavior" ("Adapting" 292). The LCRG's grant proposal, along with its textbook manuscript's instructional units on grammar and mechanics, show how the group used sociolinguistics research not only to meet composition instructors' need for methods to teach SE prose[9] but also to get students more engaged in the composition course, building on students' own ideas about what they wanted to learn and do with writing.

The LCRG was clearly indebted to the sociolinguistics research of Stewart, Labov, and Wolfram, which analyzed the systematic nature of

BEV's syntax, phonology, and morphology. The LCRG distinguished its project, though, by tailoring this research to meet the specific needs of writing instructors. The LCRG members felt sociolinguists too often pursued "misdirected priorities in descriptive research," in that they focused their energies too narrowly on identifying and classifying as many features of the spoken BEV dialect as they could (Reed, Baxter, and Lowenthal 8–10). The LCRG researchers instead tailored their descriptions of BEV grammar and syntax to meet the needs of their nonspecialist audience of composition instructors and students.

Just as significantly, the LCRG believed writing instructors would pay closer attention to this research if it presented precise analyses of how students' *speech* specifically influenced their *writing*. Not only did the LCRG acknowledge that spoken standards differed from written standards, but it also wanted teachers to attend only to students' writing habits, not their speech. Being BEV speakers themselves, the researchers believed that when teachers tried to intervene with students' speech, they were effectively telling them to reject a significant aspect of their identities ("Teacher's Manual" 57–59). Therefore, at the outset of their project, the LCRG researchers conducted an exhaustive study of their students' writing. They identified the features of spoken BEV code that appeared most often in their students' attempts to write SE prose (Reed, Baxter, and Lowenthal 8). Through this examination, the LCRG helped teachers to distinguish between those features in students' writing that represented "errors" common to many SE writers, such as the *who/whom* distinction, and those features that resulted specifically from "cross-dialect interference," such as *they/their* distinctions, as in "They are at they mother house," or the zero copula, as in the BEV "He at home now" versus the SE "He is at home" (LCRG, "Teachers' Manual" 24).[10] The LCRG used its research on students' writing, then, to determine what compositionists needed to know about sociolinguistics research on BEV to teach writing effectively to linguistic minority students.

On the basis of these initial investigations into how best to apply sociolinguistics research to composition instruction, the LCRG created contrastive analysis exercises. These materials made up a significant part of the ESD writing instruction found in the textbook manuscript. Half of the units presented grammatical rules for BEV, such as those for subject-verb agreement, negation, and pronoun usage, and juxtaposed them with SE usage rules. In the exercises that followed, students read passages in BEV, as well as some that evidenced hypercorrection, and edited them to meet SE conventions.[11] For example, in a chapter on pluralization rules, students changed BEV usages to their SE equivalents and identified the SE grammatical rules that led them to make the changes. Exercises of this type included the sentence "I know because it has happened to me a few time but I just have to live with it" ("Students' Manual" 115). Given this sentence, students had to distinguish between BEV and SE pluralization rules; in the former, the quantifier *few* signals pluralization, while in the latter, the noun itself, *times*, needs to signal the pluralization.

The LCRG also added nuance to these exercises to stress to students that "correct" SE usage did not determine a writer's effectiveness. This emphasis appears most readily in the textbook manuscript's use of prose passages and poems as materials for contrastive analysis. For example, in a unit on pronoun usage, students first read poems from the Black Arts Movement, Don L. Lee's "The Revolutionary Screw" and "Re-Act for Action" and David Nelson's "Know Yourself." Students then identified where and how each of these poets used reflexive pronouns, such as Nelson's splitting of reflexive pronouns in the lines "Do you know the ugliness of *your still becoming Black self* / Do you know the warm beauty of *your true Black self*" (73–76, emphasis added). Accompanying questions asked students to analyze how each particular usage suited the poet's aim, audience, and message (71–72). These types of exercises emphasized rhetorical effectiveness over grammatical correctness. In so doing, they confirmed students' own perceptions of how language functioned in their social worlds outside of school, where friends and relatives who were lauded for their ways with words commonly "broke" SE grammar rules in order to achieve their communicative goals.

With the systematic ESD approach of their writing textbook, the LCRG researchers contributed to conversations informing the Students' Right policy by articulating specific ways sociolinguistics research on nonstandardized dialects of English could usefully inform writing instruction.[12] Moreover, the LCRG's textbook manuscript made SE conventions a concern only for latter stages of the writing process. Students were taught to write first, recognize areas of cross-dialect interference second, and only then, when editing their drafts, to change these features into the SE grammatical code.

Nevertheless, in certain respects the group's sentence-level translation exercises seemingly reproduced the traditional aims of the composition course. The curriculum characterized SE prose as the "polish" students needed to give their writing in order to meet educators' and employers' expectations for "good" writing. As we will see in the next section, however, the reading materials and writing assignments of the LCRG's textbook manuscript challenged teachers' assumptions about how BEV could invigorate African American students' intellectual work.

Valuing the Black English Vernacular in Composition Classrooms

As the previous section illustrated, the LCRG aimed "to effect bidialectalism in users of nonstandard dialects of English"—to quote its grant proposal title—by creating exercises to improve students' abilities to write SE. With its emphasis on contrastive-analysis exercises and "translation" between BEV and SE, the LCRG's textbook manuscript did indeed lead students to view SE writing as *the* medium for academic work. In fact, the LCRG researchers made the very distinction Sledd criticized when, in the textbook manuscript's introduction, they explained to students that SE represented a formal style of language appropriate for school, job applications, and addresses to professional groups, while the BEV of their communities was most suitable for talking with family, rapping with neighbors, or writing letters to friends (16). Through statements such as this one, along with the repeated emphasis on moving from BEV rough drafts to SE final copies, the LCRG's textbook manuscript reproduced traditional requirements for the first-year composition course, whereby teachers demanded SE proficiency from students to grant them credit for the course.

While the LCRG's project does share many similarities with those bidialectalist pedagogies, in other significant ways it defies easy categorization with those focused solely on the surface features of white, middle-class English. Student-centered research projects as well as culturally relevant writing assignments and reading materials from the textbook manuscript suggest the LCRG's project pushed students and teachers to analyze and work with language at deeper levels than just its surface features. These aspects of the LCRG's pedagogy challenged what Reed called the "compulsory miseducation" that African American students endured through traditional curricula, which taught them to devalue BEV and consider African American communities as verbally "impoverished" ("Adapting" 294).

Indeed, several aspects of the LCRG's textbook manuscript show the group believed that the composition course needed to account more fully for the lived experiences, worldviews, and languages of African American students. To work toward these ends, the LCRG created research projects through which students treated BEV as a legitimate object of inquiry in the writing classroom. In one such project for their own courses, the LCRG's SEEK students used tape recorders to chronicle effective BEV speech in their communities (Reed, Baxter, and Lowenthal 18). Along with these tapes, the LCRG's students composed ethnographies in which they identified the wide range of linguistic strategies and interpersonal behaviors that BEV speakers used to communicate meaning (Reed, telephone interview, 7 December 2003). Such class projects pushed the LCRG's students to produce more substantial work than they would within bidialectalist courses. Rather than "seek[ing] only to put white middle-class English into the mouths of black speakers" (Smitherman, *Talkin and Testifyin* 209), the LCRG enabled its African American students to compose academic research that addressed an important issue facing their communities. Specifically, the LCRG incorporated data from students' tapes and ethnographies into the textbook manuscript (Reed, Baxter, and Lowenthal 18), thus enabling the student-researchers themselves to help improve literacy education for African Americans.

The LCRG's textbook manuscript also gained students' interest by centering discussions and writing assignments on their own experiences with language difference in their schools and in their communities. For example, the first essay assignment asked students either to analyze how they "change [their] speech for different occasions" or to narrate situations in which they "have to talk 'uppity'" (15). The research group effectively linked the classroom to students' social worlds, as these essay assignments allowed students to discuss their own ideas and attitudes toward language diversity. Moreover, these prompts encouraged students and teachers to grapple with the politics of language use that bidialectalist pedagogies often left unexamined.

Reading materials in the textbook manuscript likewise countered the widespread perception that African American students came to school from linguistically deprived communities. The LCRG offered students a wide range of readings to illustrate that BEV has "its own continuum" of rhetorical styles, ranging "from the street to the pulpit" ("Teachers' Manual" 23). For this reason, the textbook manuscript included toasts by poet and jazz musician Gil Scott-Heron,[13] raps by Frankie Crocker and Lou Rawls, excerpts from the autobiographies of Malcolm X and Billie Holiday, a student essay responding to public criticism of CUNY's open-admissions policies, articles from African American newspapers, recipes from soul food cookbooks, and poems from the Black Arts Movement, such as Helen King's "Reflections of a 69th Street Chicago Pimp after Reading a Really Good Black Poem."

The LCRG also devoted over twenty textbook pages to instruction on African American narrative styles. Readings in this section were followed by comprehension questions asking students to make links between BEV use and African American worldviews. In one example, students read "The Fall," an African American toast in which the protagonist narrates his exploits of lawlessness and, even after being jailed, boasts, "I hope the game [on the streets] is still the same / when I finish up next fall" ("Students' Manual" 354). Questions followed asking students to analyze various aspects of the toast, including "Are there special speech acts [in the toast] characteristic of Black delivery style?" and "In what ways does the toast represent a 'blatant disregard and even contempt for white cultural norms'?" (355). By giving such materials physical space within its textbook manuscript, the LCRG answered Kelly's call for compositionists to deal with "the richness and values of the Black ghetto" (107). The LCRG's textbook manuscript helped students to move beyond bidialectalist pedagogy's sole focus on making their academic writing "formal." These reading materials and analytical prompts gave students opportunities to learn about the many powerful rhetorical patterns and strategies African Americans use to create distinctive language traditions.

Through these types of materials, the LCRG reinforced the need for compositionists to understand and respect the social contexts within which students learned and used BEV. The LCRG textbook manuscript linked language and culture in this way to redress how most English-language arts curricula ignored the variety and complexity of black worldviews and, in turn, devalued many African American cultural forms (Reed, "Adapting" 294). To be sure, there were teachers who included in their syllabi texts by prominent African American writers such as Richard Wright, Gwendolyn Brooks, and James Baldwin. The LCRG argued, however, that such courses too often narrowly taught students to evaluate African American writers' prose and poetry according to traditional conventions of style and to analyze these texts' characters with reference only to Eurocentric social values and worldviews (LCRG, "Teachers' Manual" 20–23).[14] The LCRG instead shaped compositionists' ideas about the linguistic politics of writing instruction by showing how teachers' best intentions to value BEV in the classroom would be meaningful only if teachers and textbooks valued the social contexts of BEV use as well.

Prompting Teacher Reflection on Racial and Linguistic Difference

The LCRG's project was evidently well-received by teachers. Samuel Moore sent this message to the Ford Foundation following his presentation at the 1972 CCCC convention: "Because [my] presentation outlined methods and gave examples of actual materials designed to attack the problem effectively, much interest was generated in what we are doing here at Brooklyn College." Nevertheless, the LCRG knew the discipline's assumptions about linguistic diversity would not change if teachers viewed these activities and assignments simply as more efficient means for ridding students' writing of BEV. Indeed, as the Students' Right policy explained, "the training of most English teachers concentrated on the appreciation and analysis of literature" (Committee on CCCC Language Statement 1), creating situations in which teachers might be more likely to snap up classroom activities like the LCRG's that addressed this language "problem" without also reflecting on their assumptions about the purpose of the composition course. The Students' Right policy for this reason demanded that teachers "have the experiences and training that will enable them to respect diversity and uphold the right of students to their own language" (3). Toward similar ends, the LCRG created a teacher's manual, tutorial sessions for preservice educators, and workshops for in-service compositionists to address how normative ideas about race, language, and the aims of education informed dominant approaches to writing instruction. With these various activities, the LCRG expanded its pedagogical focus to include teaching teachers, not just students. Their aim throughout was to heighten teachers' awareness of how their practices in linguistically diverse classrooms were shaped by social attitudes concerning cultural and linguistic difference.

The LCRG teacher's manual prompted teachers, particularly white SE-speaking instructors, to reflect on how acknowledging BEV use in the classroom necessarily changed the relationship between students and teacher. The researchers emphasized this fact in the manual's introduction. Here the group discussed the rationale and methodology for its course and also answered ten common questions teachers had about BEV in general and its role in the classroom in particular. Among the most significant questions were these three: "What attitudes can be found in the black community regarding BEV?" (39–46); "Are BEV and SE mutually intelligible?" (61–63); and "Must a teacher be fluent in BEV in order to use a bi-dialectical approach?" (59–60). The LCRG responded to these questions but then asked teachers to see that even better answers could emerge from their interactions with students. To foster these relationships, the LCRG created the textbook manuscript's essay assignments, described in the previous section, for which students wrote about their everyday experiences with language. Such writing projects not only enabled students to research their communities but also helped teachers to learn about their students. The teacher's manual also included many similar open-ended discussion questions meant "to tap the students' intuitions about their dialect" (30). As the LCRG explained, "The students, therefore, are the primary sources of BEV data, and the teacher—in recognition of this—ought to gain an appreciation of BEV from them as much as from the curriculum materials presented in the manual" (30).

Framing the teacher's manual this way encouraged teachers to position themselves as students of BEV too, open to learning from their own students' language practices. In so doing, the LCRG strategically troubled many teachers' desire to enter the classroom feeling they knew all there possibly was to know about the subject of language learning. While the LCRG certainly used sociolinguistics research to build a theoretical foundation for compositionists' approaches to language diversity, its teacher's manual nevertheless asked instructors to see that social interaction and reflection across racial and linguistic difference was how meaningful knowledge about BEV could be created.

The LCRG set up small, controlled environments for such cooperative learning and reflection through a partnership with Brooklyn College's School of Education. The research group arranged collaborative learning sessions that paired upper-division education majors with BEV-speaking students enrolled in the LCRG's composition courses (Reed, Baxter, and Lowenthal 25–30). In some respects, these sessions seemed to reinforce the narrower version of bidialectalist pedagogies, as the preservice teachers helped the SEEK students to revise their essays and edit them into SE using the grammatical concepts they were learning in the textbook manuscript. Other activities, however, allowed the composition students and education majors to learn more about language practices in African American communities. For example, in some sessions the pair read toasts. The pair would first edit these toasts to reflect conventions of SE, but then, just as the composition students did in the textbook manuscript exercises, the group would discuss how these toasts commented on America's mainstream cultural norms and how specific narrative techniques helped the storyteller to make his or her point (Reed, telephone interview, 7 December 2003). Such activities encouraged both the first-year composition students and the education majors to explore the interconnectedness of African American language practices and worldviews.

In addition to these weekly tutorials, all participants met with Fred Hill, an educational administrator with a background in sensitivity training and behavior therapy. Hill facilitated discussions and reflections on how power, race, and language affected interactions in these tutoring sessions (Reed, Baxter, and Lowenthal 28–29). Collectively, these tutorials and discussions deepened the preservice teachers' understanding of African American linguistic traditions and heightened their sensitivity to their students' rhetorical sophistication and critical sensibilities. Just as significantly, by arranging these sessions, the LCRG offered both future teachers and current SEEK students opportunities to explore their attitudes about racial, ethnic, and linguistic differences and to reflect on how these beliefs influenced the learning atmosphere in college.

In its workshops for CUNY instructors, meanwhile, the LCRG prompted a more thorough interrogation of how composition curricula were too often grounded on discriminatory assumptions about the value of nonstandardized dialects. As the group explained in its teacher's manual, English language arts instruction promoted the "general tendency in American society to assimilate divergent cultural and linguistic heritages into a kind of homogeneous mainstream culture, to the exclusion, in particular, of the culture in which BEV is found" (22). The LCRG used its workshops to help teachers realize that they should not focus instruction solely on BEV's linguistic features but needed also to explore the cultural contexts—the spaces, the audiences, the values, the content—that shape BEV, rather than relegating it "to the status of 'street language'" (22). Similarly, as Baxter suggested in his 1976 *College English* article "Educating Teachers about Educating the Oppressed," the LCRG helped CUNY instructors to recognize BEV as an entire communicative system, complete with gestures, body language, and intonation patterns that speakers and listeners used to create meaning (680). The LCRG's workshops provided a space for helping teachers, many of whom came from different linguistic and cultural backgrounds than their students, to understand and interpret the various tools their students often used to communicate ideas. This emphasis throughout the CUNY workshops encouraged instructors to recognize the range of cultural and interpersonal elements they needed to attend to in creating meaningful language-learning situations for linguistic-minority students.

Given these aims, the LCRG devoted significant portions of the workshop to the difficulties and demands of introducing the textbook manuscript and BEV within the composition classroom. The researchers knew that African American SEEK students had endured twelve years of what Reed called "indoctrination" to the belief that they had no significant linguistic heritage ("Adapting" 294). Workshop participants thus were warned that many BEV-speaking students would resist acknowledging their language in the college classroom, particularly when white teachers tried to use the textbook manuscript. Reed explained, "The student will most likely resent the teacher's calling attention to what he regards as an embarrassing deficiency. He will most likely be wont to suspect racist motives, interpreting his teacher's intent as some subtle new attempt to trap him into admitting what he secretly suspects is proof of his linguistic inferiority" (294–95). Since there was potential for student resistance, the LCRG used the workshops to suggest strategies for introducing the ESD curriculum. For example, they suggested teachers assign books such as Edward T. Hall's *The Silent Language* and Robert A. Hall Jr.'s *Linguistics and Your Language* to help students appreciate the concepts of cultural and linguistic relativity (295–96). An even stronger strategy, discussed earlier, came from the LCRG researchers' own SEEK classrooms; teachers could begin courses with student ethnographies on language practices in their communities, underscoring their commitment to making BEV and African American culture significant subjects of study in the composition classroom. The LCRG repeatedly emphasized—in its teacher's manual, in its published articles, and in its workshops—that how teachers introduced the BEV-centered curriculum, as well as how they engaged students' responses to this approach, would greatly affect students' motivation to do the intellectual work the course demanded of them.

The LCRG's work in teacher-training anticipated the fact that many compositionists would respond to the Students' Right policy by focusing solely on the question "What do I do?" The research group understood that sociolinguistics research and classroom exercises alone would not push educators to affirm BEV's relevance to students' writing and academic inquiry. The teacher's manual, tutoring programs, and workshops consequently became spaces in which the LCRG cultivated habits of self-awareness and self-reflection within composition teachers. The workshops in particular were well-attended, with the names of prominent scholars such as Mina Shaughnessy, Patricia Laurence, and Kenneth Bruffee appearing on workshop sign-up sheets the LCRG filed in its annual reports ("LCRG-CUNY Teacher-Training"; Bruffee). Letters written to the LCRG by workshop participants suggest many teachers found these experiences essential for their professional development. For instance, Elaine Avidon, course coordinator for Herbert H. Lehman College, wrote in April 1971, "One of our faculty members participated in your workshop this past weekend at the Conference on English in the Community Colleges. It was clear to her after listening to you, and it's clear to us after listening to her, that we need to hear more about your work in Black English." The following month, Manette Berlinger of Queensborough Community College echoed these same thoughts in a letter to Reed: "I am writing first to tell you how really good your workshop was at the Technology Conference last May 9, and second to ask your advice about implementing some of your ideas at Queensborough." Rose Sealy, community liaison representative for Brooklyn College's Education Department, wrote a letter on 31 May 1972, thanking Reed for making a presentation to graduate students in her vocational development course: "The student response was overwhelmingly favorable and the interest generated continued well beyond that class period." Sealy also thanked Paul Cohen and Bonnie Cottman for their presentations to those undergraduate preservice teachers who were entering their tutoring partnerships with the LCRG's first-year composition students. "All three presentations," Sealy noted, "have helped to kindle faculty interest in the inclusion of facets of the LCRG's program in the Teacher Training program in general and the experimental School Community Teaching-Learning Centers program in particular."

These programs heightened teachers' awareness of how normative assumptions about race and language shaped their interactions with students. They also prepared educators to teach students not only to recognize but also to value and build on the language resources they brought to the classroom. More importantly, these programs allowed instructors to envision how their interactions with students across linguistic difference transformed their understanding of sociolinguistics research and the aims of writing instruction.

"Back-to-Basics" in the Debate over Curriculum Reform

As its period of annual funding from the Ford Foundation drew to a close in June 1974, the LCRG researchers had already enjoyed numerous successes. Colleagues had given them good feedback about their teacher-training programs. Many students noted in course evaluations that the

LCRG course was "better than any other writing course" they had ever taken ("Student Course-Evaluation"). And linguist Beryl Bailey, head of Hunter College's Black and Puerto Rican Studies Program, concluded her 1972 review of the LCRG's textbook manuscript with this assertion: "This project represents the serious efforts of a responsible and energetic group of researchers to fill a breach in the new dimensions which Open Admissions has thrust upon higher education in New York City" (5). On the basis of these positive evaluations, the LCRG circulated revised drafts of its textbook manuscript and teachers' manual to external reviewers as well as six commercial publishers, including Harcourt-Brace Jovanovitch, Prentice Hall, and Houghton Mifflin, as well as the Center for Applied Linguistics.

At the same time the LCRG pushed to publish its materials and reach a broader audience, however, a highly charged public discourse constricted mainstream ideas of productive and appropriate literacy education. Although not the first to do so, Merrill Sheils issued the most visible warning of a literacy crisis with her now infamous 1975 *Newsweek* cover story, "Why Johnny Can't Write." In this article, Sheils alerted readers that statistics measuring literacy in the United States were declining each year, and she made a specific argument about the source of these problems, implicitly targeting the CCCC Students' Right language policy. Sheils strategically juxtaposed examples of college students' tangled, sentence-fragmented prose with passages from the CCCC document. In so doing, she encouraged readers to equate affirming students' different languages with ignoring—even deeming irrelevant—well-established standards of correctness, all in the name of making every student feel welcome in school. She explained:

> The point is that there have to be some fixed rules, however tedious, if the codes of human communication are to remain decipherable. If the written language is placed at the mercy of every new colloquialism and if every fresh dialect demands and gets equal sway, then we will soon find ourselves back in Babel. In America... there are too many people intent on being masters of their language and too few willing to be its servants. (65)

Sheils conflated ungrammatical, incoherent prose with urban nonstandardized dialects to force a specific conclusion: the new students of open admissions, through their demands for culturally relevant education, had wrestled away teachers' authority to impose objective standards; corrupted the integrity of writing instruction for all students;

and, ultimately, cheapened the significance of a college degree. In his reading of Sheils's work, John Trimbur suggests that as she lamented the blurring of lines separating "masters" from "servants," Sheils tried to reassert literacy's traditional authority to "draw lines of social distinction, mark status, and rank students in a meritocratic order" ("Literacy" 279). Given this implicit argument, one can see that to Sheils and other critics, Students' Right pedagogies like the LCRG's represented academic permissiveness in the name of improving minority students' self-esteem.

A "back-to-basics" educational movement built on this belief that colleges no longer instilled American values of hard work and discipline. This discourse intensified criticism of the LCRG and its work. The ministers, politicians, businessmen, and parents who led the grassroots back-to-basics movement saw the literacy crisis as evidence of a more widespread social decline illustrated most prominently in the civil disturbances of the 1960s (Brodinsky 522). The back-to-basics supporters in particular believed the civil rights movement's demands for equal access had been translated into student demands for a light work load and easy credits. Central to the back-to-basics movement's vision for restoring significance to U.S. education was a sternly disciplined, teacher-centered pedagogy; academic criteria, not social criteria, as the basis for promotion through the curriculum; and the elimination of experimental and innovative programs in favor of textbooks that provided frequent drilling and promoted traditional social values (Shor 78–79). The Scholastic Aptitude Test (SAT) even came to reflect the influence of back-to-basics reform. Amid clamor about declining SAT scores, testing officials in October 1974 added a thirty-minute section to test students on their knowledge of SE grammar (Parks 196–97).

This emphasis on SE and the movement toward educational "basics" directly affected the LCRG. Its textbook manuscript seemed to confirm critics' belief that teachers had lowered their standards of "good" writing to accommodate students' nontraditional literacies. Emphasizing basic SE grammar and standardized testing instead, critics argued, would reinstate clear-cut measures of quality and reestablish literacy's ability to ensure that hard-working students could achieve economic and social status.

Some English teachers in the CUNY system made similar arguments about the need for professors to reclaim authority from students and reinstate rigorous writing standards. For instance, in a 1974 *CCC* article, Joam Baum of CUNY's York College exhorted her colleagues to quit using "textbooks and workbooks that strain for relevancy and slick contemporaneity" (295). Echoing Morse, Baum argued this approach would not solve open-admissions students' writing problems because these students were "not underprepared in feeling, but in thinking" (295). She demanded that publishers recommit to producing "slim essential monographs" that covered issues in logic and academic forms, which in Baum's opinion were "the particular demonstrated needs" of open-admissions students (295).

Baum labeled her ideas as "traditional, even reactionary" (294), given that she called for removing politics from writing instruction. Her argument in effect characterized pedagogies as misguided, even uninformed, when they allowed students to write about their social worlds and in the languages they used to negotiate everyday life. In so doing, she, like many others, ignored the theoretical foundations on which scholars such as the LCRG researchers were working. Moreover, she failed to acknowledge a significant assumption that informed both the LCRG's pedagogy and the CCCC Students' Right language policy: "traditional" approaches to writing instruction had done a disservice to most African American students in the first place.

Given this controversy sparked by Sheils and fueled by the back-to-basics movement's causal analysis that culturally relevant pedagogies led to declining educational and social values, publishers were sufficiently alarmed about the potential marketability of the LCRG's textbook manuscript. In a letter to Martus at the Ford Foundation, Baxter explained that every publisher the group contacted was unwilling to publish the textbook manuscript "in these unstable economic times" because they sensed there was "a 'limited' market for curriculum materials addressed to an all-black audience." Meanwhile, Allene Grognet, publications director of the Center for Applied Linguistics, predicted that "the sales potential of these books could be fairly large, but not through the regular educational channels." She believed they could be used most widely in alternative sites of education such as adult education, vocational retraining, and church and community-action schools. This characterization of the LCRG's textbook manuscript as material for "alternative" education underlined the pervasiveness of the normative educational philosophy. Quite simply, concentrated attention to the languages and literacies of African American students was not viewed as central to the university's academic mission. No less significant were bottom-line concerns. Publishers might have been able to sell large quantities of textbooks to these alternative markets, but they were not the mainstream—and hence, more profitable—markets that publishers value most.

When Richard Wright and Walt Wolfram, both sociolinguists affiliated with the Center for Applied Linguists, reviewed the textbook manuscript in June 1974, they expressed similar concerns about how students and teachers might react to the textbook manuscript's attention to BEV. They recommended changes that would narrow its focus to teaching students to write SE. Wright in particular felt "the heavy usage of Black pride materials" needed to be eliminated because it encouraged BEV-speaking students "to 'be themselves' while living in ignorance of the role/function of language in the larger world community." Moreover, he felt that "with all the glorification of BEV through poetry, narratives, etc., the student might come to wonder exactly what the course is all about." The textbook needed to focus more narrowly on "the teaching [of] and sensitivity to SE," he argued, and to include far more models of SE prose. Wright called for the LCRG to condense its discussion of BEV and the politics of dialect difference into a preface, whereas in the LCRG's draft these ideas were at the heart of most readings, comprehension questions, and writing assignments. Wright felt that if the preface contained the textbook manuscript's sole efforts "to win converts to a more humanistic view of BEV," the body chapters would be free to focus on the business at hand in first-year composition, namely, teaching SE, the standard of correctness students would need to meet to open "linguistic avenues to wider audiences, both nationally and internationally."

The LCRG maintained that publishers' and sociolinguists' predictions about the textbook's likely reception were unjustified. The researchers repeatedly told Ford Foundation officials that these evaluations were never confirmed with classroom observations of the textbook manuscript being used in pilot courses. Indeed, Richard A. Lacey, the foundation's program officer for the LCRG's project, noted, "Although [the LCRG] invited publishers to visit classes, publishers' representatives have tended to rely on their own or outside professional opinions of the worth of their materials without seeing firsthand the work of the group with students at Brooklyn College and Manhattan Community College" (Memo to Martus, 29 July 1974). Were reviewers to have observed students and teachers using the textbook manuscript in CUNY classrooms, they might have perceived a disconnect between Wright's assertions and the ideas guiding the LCRG's approach. For example, whereas Wright felt the LCRG needed to teach linguistic-minority students not to "liv[e] in ignorance of the role/function of language in the larger world community" (1), the essay prompts and discussion questions in the textbook manuscript allowed students to explore what they already knew from their everyday experience—language skills could be leveraged to create greater social and economic opportunities, but they could also be used to accentuate differences and promote discrimination. Moreover, the LCRG knew such discussions did not distract students from the "real" work of learning SE grammar but instead were central to helping them prepare to negotiate the demands they undoubtedly would face throughout their academic and professional careers.

In order to contradict publishers' and reviewers' assessments about the reception and effectiveness of the textbook manuscript, the LCRG presented Ford Foundation representatives with end-of-semester evaluations written by both students and teachers who had used the ESD materials in their courses. These documents showed that even those SEEK students who initially resented having to take a writing course for BEV speakers eventually left the semester feeling proud of their language and their communities ("Student Course-Evaluation"). On the basis of its findings as well as its disagreements with reviewers, the LCRG refused to surrender editorial control of its project. The researchers wanted to ensure the textbook manuscript continued to focus on both SE *and* BEV as a means for making composition classrooms into spaces where students and teachers examined the connections between language, culture, and power.

Ultimately, the LCRG never overcame these public and professional perceptions that BEV's presence in the classroom drained educational resources and hastened the decline of academic standards. The Ford Foundation, in its highly visible position, felt pressured to dissociate itself from a project that the mainstream press would characterize as threatening the values and standards of public education. Consequently, in an 18 July 1974 letter to the LCRG, Lacey stated that the Ford Foundation could no longer "justify continued involvement" in its project, "especially given the increased national attention recently directed to the problems you have addressed." The Ford Foundation discontinued funding the LCRG on 30 June 1974, just months before the CCCC would articulate the pedagogical implications of the Students' Right to Their Own Language resolution in its fall 1974 special issue of *CCC*. Lacey of the Ford Foundation ultimately concluded that the researchers "were tackling a terribly important problem without enough horses" (Memo to Martus, 12 July 1974).

The pressures preventing publication of the LCRG's textbook manuscript complicate our common assumptions about why the Students' Right ideal never materialized into widespread classroom practice.

Present-day compositionists tend to think that no theoretically based pedagogical projects were developed in the Students' Right era, or if they were created, they just weren't effective. The LCRG's project proves otherwise. The textbook manuscript went unpublished because of resistance to the LCRG's efforts to reconcile what Min-Zhan Lu describes as the "discrepancy between the academy's account of what student writers can/should be allowed to do and the student writers' counter accounts of what they can do/are interested in and capable of doing" ("Composing" 18). Back-to-basics reformers restored faith in authoritarian pedagogy and narrowed many publishers' and teachers' visions of what linguistic-minority students needed to learn in writing classes. This political and social conservatism shaped the material conditions of 1970s writing instruction in ways that affect how we see the Students' Right policy today.

The LCRG's project shows us the Students' Right era was not long on theory but short on praxis. As Reed argued at the 1981 CUNY Association of Writing Supervisors Conference, the racially charged analyses of a literacy crisis led many teachers to become "timid and fearful of any curriculum materials" focusing on dialect differences ("Back" 9). The market for the textbook manuscript effectively shrank, "successfully stifling efforts to disseminate new and effective teaching strategies to English teachers in inner-city classrooms across the country" (9–10). Back-to-basics discourse characterized racial and ethnic minority students as unmerited beneficiaries of CUNY's open-admissions policies. Many professors, reviewers, textbook publishers, and political commentators agreed. As a result, they paid no attention to the LCRG's aim to teach African American students to write SE academic prose. Instead, the group's "heavy usage of Black pride materials" and its valuing of BEV's presence in the classroom fueled fears that innovative educators had allowed the "new" African American students of open admissions to be masters, not servants, of their language and their education. This controversy undoubtedly contributed to the LCRG's failure to publish its textbook manuscript, leaving the discipline of composition with no published history of the LCRG's work.

The Students' Right Policy's Disciplinary Legacy

Through its textbook manuscript, teacher's manual, and training workshops, the LCRG created a composition course in which students could enact their right to their own language. Despite the project's significant breadth, however, the absence of the group's work in composition histories speaks volumes about the imperative, in Smitherman's words, to "publish—or your ideas perish" (personal interview, 26 March 2004). Certainly, the LCRG's project met pressing disciplinary needs, a fact underscored by the Ford Foundation's substantial monetary support as well as feedback the researchers received from colleagues. Ultimately, though, the group's efforts to strengthen composition's commitment to linguistic diversity were dismissed by publishers concerned with managing bottom lines amid feverish back-to-basics discourse. Since the researchers could not effectively respond to the fears of administrators, teachers, and publishers, the LCRG's textbook manuscript remains unpublished, and the ideas it advanced remain unaccounted for in present-day work on linguistic diversity in composition in general and the history of the Students' Right language policy in particular.

The way in which another form of basic writing pedagogy gained a foothold at CUNY during this period further underscores how political conservatism sealed the fate of the LCRG curriculum. As can be seen in the previous section, back-to-basics discourse successfully juxtaposed the university's standards of academic excellence with seemingly political pedagogies like the LCRG's that countered the miseducation of minority students. Bruce Horner's analysis of the material and institutional conditions of CUNY's early open-admissions years shows how compositionists, already marginalized within CUNY, ensured their institutional existence in the face of this discourse. Specifically, compositionists argued they would prepare SEEK students to fit into the academic system rather than challenge the narrow definition of "academic excellence" that functioned to make higher education an exclusive community ("Discoursing" 207–8). As Horner suggests, compositionists reinforced their argument by teaching students basic writing "skills" and focusing their research efforts on developing, in Shaughnessy's words, "more efficient and challenging ways of teaching grammar and mechanics" (qtd. in Horner 209).[15] Basic writing pedagogy survived, Horner argues, because it preserved the back-to-basics movement's distinction between academics and society's political and economic concerns.

In some respects, the LCRG's project fit this dominant approach to writing instruction, for half of the textbook manuscript crafted a more efficient approach for teaching BEV-speaking students to write SE prose. However, because the textbook manuscript's reading materials, writing assignments, and research projects brought linguistic and racial politics into the composition classroom, more widespread adoption of the LCRG's project could have threatened the already tenuous position of CUNY's writing programs. Horner's analysis illustrates how material and institutional conditions enabled one pedagogy and research agenda among many to secure a dominant position within the discipline, thereby effectively narrowing the range of what scholars and teachers were able to see as possible within basic writing classrooms. Recovering the history of the LCRG's project fortifies Horner's claim that material, institutional, and political conditions affect our theoretical and pedagogical visions for enabling students to do critical intellectual work.

Within this conservative atmosphere, the LCRG project's chance for survival may also have been lessened by the group's focus on curricular reform to the exclusion of policy and advocacy work addressing other factors that affect marginalized students' participation in higher education. Certainly, the LCRG's emphasis on curriculum reform was essential, given the dominant focus at CUNY on developing "more efficient and challenging ways of teaching grammar and mechanics." The research group reinvigorated public education's democratic values as it helped linguistic- and racial-minority students to deepen their knowledge about their linguistic heritages and, in so doing, develop an intellectual base that traditional education had systematically denied them. As Mary Soliday argues in her study of the politics of remedial education, however, progressive pedagogical projects open themselves to conservative critiques when, much as the LCRG did, scholars only address the cultural conflict that marginalized students face as they work their way into the academy. While Soliday acknowledges the significant insights gained through such analyses, she nevertheless warns they can also serve the purpose of critics who argue that Open Admissions students and the remedial instruction developed for them perpetuate low standards and drain the university's resources (105–6).

Soliday's work, then, suggests ways to see how the LCRG's project could have been strengthened. Their arguments for curriculum redesign could have been coupled with analysis of how other material conditions affected students' access to campus, textbooks, and the time and space needed for academic work, as well as how public under-funding of higher education exacerbated these difficulties curtailing open-admissions students' access to college. As Valerie Kinloch argues, to talk of students' right to their own language "is also to talk of the redistribution/ reallocation of and access to literacy resources for all students" ("Revisiting" 88). The LCRG did focus on African American students' need for access to culturally relevant—and more effective—educational materials, but its sole focus on curricular reform allowed back-to-basics supporters to sidestep discussions about the politics and economics of education. These critics were free to attack curricular projects such as the LCRG's that seemed to favor social promotion over academic integrity.

As composition scholars attend to students' material concerns, they also must better understand how the group's textbook manuscript, the CCCC Students' Right policy, and journals from this era created a limited representation of what Smitherman calls "the linguistic-cultural complexity of the composition classroom" ("CCCC's Role" 369). The almost exclusive attention to African American students and BEV in these materials signals that future recovery work needs to account for the presence of other students who faced linguistic and ethnic discrimination in open admissions classrooms. Victor Villanueva, for one, has prompted compositionists to begin talking about the language politics of the Students' Right era in broader terms than just *Standardized English* and *African American Language*. Consider his description of growing up in Williamsburg and Bedford-Stuyvesant, just blocks from the Brooklyn College campus:

> I was born in Brooklyn. Raised there with Black kids and Asian kids and one Mexican kid and Boricuas. My first language was Spanish; my first English was the English of the neighborhood, Black and Spanglish, or even a Black Spanglish. When I was 15, the family moved to California. I've been in the West (except for two years in Kansas City and trips abroad) ever since—with Mexican kids, Chicano kids, vato kids, pachuco kids, Indian kids, Asian kids, Black kids, and White kids. And the nonsense that Ricans have to endure in New York is the same nonsense that all the other kids of Color endure. (qtd. in Smitherman and Villanueva, Introduction 1)

Part of the motivation for revisiting the Students' Right resolution, then, is to understand it as a language policy that championed the linguistic rights of *all* marginalized students and promoted the value of *all* forms of linguistic diversity. Archival research and oral histories of the Students' Right era should look to account more fully for the Puerto Rican, Dominican, Cuban, Mexican, Jamaican, Japanese, Chinese, and Native American students whose presence in composition classrooms of the 1970s has been elided in our disciplinary histories.

As mentioned in the introduction to this chapter, the LCRG's grant proposals in fact stated that the researchers created the ESD curriculum for both African American and Puerto Rican students who spoke

BEV. The textbook manuscript and teacher's manual, however, focused exclusively on African American language practices and cultures. It is unclear whether, and if so, in what ways, the LCRG prompted students to investigate how Puerto Rican and African American cultures intersected and diverged in the communities where students lived. Future work in recovering pedagogical projects submerged by dominant educational discourses of the 1970s could help us to understand more precisely how *Black English Vernacular* might have functioned as a blanket term that elided other forms of cultural and linguistic difference in college classrooms.[16] Such studies would direct compositionists' attention to the specific educational pressures that faced linguistic-minority students from Latino, Asian American, Caribbean American, Native American, and rural white communities whose language varieties have not been valued in the academy. Just as importantly, analyses of how Students' Right-era compositionists and sociolinguists responded to this range of language diversity can encourage present-day scholars and teachers to reimagine the discipline as one with a history of engaging, learning from, and drawing upon multiple language traditions.

Recovering the history of these projects gains special importance given recent efforts in composition to reinvigorate the Students' Right policy. In the preface to their 2009 edited collection *Affirming Students' Right to Their Own Language: Bridging Language Policies and Pedagogical Practices*, Jerrie Cobb Scott, Dolores Straker, and Laurie Katz suggest that "it is quite timely to . . . examine the progress we have made in the pedagogical arena" with respect to the Students' Right theory (xviii). The CCCC Language Policy Committee similarly argued that English language arts educators, many of whom still feel inadequately prepared to address the learning needs of linguistic-minority students, must be trained to understand and use "the last quarter century's advances in research on language and linguistic diversity" ("Language Knowledge" 18–22, 33). The fate of the LCRG's project demonstrates the need for "progress" in the pedagogical arena and "advances" in research on linguistic diversity to be considered more broadly than by our discipline's customary measure of publication. Historical investigations such as this one should lead scholars to reconsider the widespread doubt among compositionists that "the words of the [Students' Right] resolution have been anything more than empty" (Bruch and Marback, "Critical" xiii). These studies can also problematize the common perception, as Smitherman characterizes it, that the Students' Right resolution failed to bring change because "it was informative in terms of theory [but] . . . did not go far enough in praxis" ("CCCC's Role" 365). As this chapter shows, the LCRG researchers applied theory in a variety of ways. The textbook manuscript materials respected students' nonstandardized dialects, emphasized the rhetorical histories behind students' languages, and enabled students to build upon their linguistic resources in order to negotiate the demands of academic writing. The teacher-training workshops and teacher's manual prompted writing instructors to explore how their attitudes toward racial and linguistic difference had been shaped by social norms and how these attitudes in turn influenced their expectations of students' work.

This study of the LCRG therefore asks compositionists to view the Students' Right policy in a new light, as a heuristic scholars have used and continue to use for inventing ethical and productive responses to linguistic diversity. The Students' Right resolution and background documents surely have never been mistaken for an annotated syllabus telling teachers how to work through each class period and assignment. But as this chapter shows, the theory of the Students' Right to Their Own Language policy has prompted teachers to listen to students' experiences with and ideas about language, to enable students to begin creating their own scholarly identities through researching and writing about the languages of their communities, and to negotiate the institutional and political resistance to positioning marginalized dialects, languages, and cultures at the center of the composition curriculum.

And there are other important, yet largely ignored, projects from the Students' Right era that scholars would do well to recover. For example, the Psycholinguistics Project Staff of the Chicago Board of Education developed a curriculum in the late 1960s and early 1970s that taught basic reading to African American students through a bidialectical approach that paired "Everyday Talk" and "School Talk" versions of stories. Equally as important, however, this project aimed to strengthen students' positive attitudes about themselves, their schools, and their communities through the use of culturally relevant reading materials. Moreover, this curriculum created space, both in the pages of the textbooks and within planned classroom activities, for students to tell stories in their own language as a means of both analyzing their language patterns and learning to translate them for other audiences. The three-book *Bridge* reading program coauthored by Gary Simpkins, Grace Holt, and Charlesetta Simpkins and published by Houghton Mifflin worked along similar lines. It helped African American students learn to read by first working with materials written in BEV and then "bridging" this literate knowledge to situations where they were reading materials written in SE. Unlike the LCRG, Simpkins and Simpkins conducted an extensive, controlled study of 540 African American students that demonstrated the effectiveness of the *Bridge* readers. Among these students, ranging from seventh to twelfth graders, those who used the *Bridge* readers showed "significantly larger gains" on the reading comprehension sections of the Iowa Test of Basic Skills (237). Even with this statistical validation of the *Bridge* program's effectiveness in helping students to learn to read SE, Houghton Mifflin dropped the project after several teachers and parents complained that the readers were diverting students' energy and attention from the task of acquiring SE (J. Rickford and A. Rickford 113). John R. Rickford and Angela E. Rickford note, however, that "we have yet to see a detailed elaboration of the reactions to the *Bridge* reading program," suggesting that there is much to be learned from a focused study of not only "who railed against it" but also "who presented the program to each of these respondents, in what way, and whether opportunities for them to respond to the criticisms were provided and exploited" (115). Equally important for composition scholars would be an archival study of the unpublished instructor's manual of activities and classroom assignments that Geneva Smitherman, Elisabeth McPherson, and Richard Lloyd-Jones compiled for the CCCC. This manual was meant to help teachers begin putting the Students' Right policy into practice, but Smitherman reported that CCCC leadership rejected it in 1980 ("CCCC's Role" 366). As with the present chapter's study of the LCRG, historical analyses of these Students' Right-era textbook projects would provide significant insight by detailing the instructional practices and pedagogical theories at the heart of these texts as well as analyzing the material and discursive pressures that have relegated such projects to the margins of composition studies' disciplinary histories.

Indeed, the history of the LCRG as well as these other projects should inform our contemporary efforts to reinvigorate the Students' Right policy. In recent years, the work of a number of compositionists (Kinloch; Scott, Straker, and Katz; Gilyard and Richardson; Ball and Lardner; Aguilera and LeCompte) has demonstrated ways to translate the theory of the Students' Right policy into present-day pedagogical practices. As Kinloch rightfully contends, "We need to revisit the *Students' Right* resolution in responding to the changing landscape of our classrooms, discourse communities, and profession so as to not misrepresent organizational statements and resolutions as decade-specific only" ("Revisiting" 87). Kinloch makes a vitally important argument here for rereading the Students' Right language policy through a contemporary lens in order to invent pedagogies that are responsive to current disciplinary theories as well as national and local educational pressures and student groups. Nevertheless, historical analysis can and should complement these efforts. It leads scholars to attend more carefully to how material, institutional, and political contexts have affected previous pedagogical advances and, as a result, have shaped contemporary readings of the CCCC's original 1974 Students' Right resolution. The lessons to be learned from such historical study can help scholars and teachers join Smitherman, Villanueva, Gilyard, Richardson, Ball, Lardner, Kinloch, and others in creating sustainable projects to reform teacher-training and situate linguistic and cultural diversity at the center of rhetoric and composition studies.

2 THE CCCC NATIONAL LANGUAGE POLICY
REFRAMING THE RHETORIC OF AN ENGLISH-ONLY UNITED STATES

> What is it that has made a society out of the hodgepodge of nationalities, races, and colors represented in the immigrant hordes that people our nation? It is language, of course, that has made communication among all these elements possible. It is with a common language that we have dissolved distrust and fear. It is with language that we have drawn up the understandings and agreements and social contracts that make a society possible.
> —S. I. Hayakawa, "One Nation . . . Indivisible?" 1985

> The National Language Policy is a response to efforts to make English the "official" language of the United States. This policy recognizes the historical reality that, even though English has become the language of wider communication, we are a multilingual society. All people in a democratic society have the right to education, to employment, to social services, and to equal protection under the law. No one should be denied these or any civil rights because of linguistic differences. This policy would enable everyone to participate in the life of this multicultural nation by ensuring continued respect both for English, our common language, and for the many other languages that contribute to our rich cultural heritage.
> —CCCC, "The National Language Policy," 1988

SPEAKING IN 1985, FORMER U.S. SENATOR S. I. HAYAKAWA WARNED that a language crisis threatened America. While Merrill Sheil's 1975 "Why Johnny Can't Write" drew attention to the presence of "street" dialects of English in the 1970s classroom, Hayakawa argued that the nation's most pressing linguistic problem one decade later had become languages other than English that were infiltrating public life. He claimed that public institutions had gone too far in tolerating people who only speak and read non-English languages, from schools with their bilingual education programs to government agencies with their provisions of bilingual voting ballots, bilingual signs, and bilingual forms. These bilingual services were a problem, he argued, because they allowed people to believe they could participate in U.S. public life and claim a full American identity even as they retained strong linguistic and cultural ties to their local minority communities. In reality, Hayakawa explained, this tolerance of other languages only divided the nation. Communication among all U.S. citizens required a single language; without one, a society could not be unified. Sure enough, Hayakawa observed, misunderstandings, disagreements, distrust, and fear were increasing between those people who did speak English and those who did not. Hayakawa proposed an English Language Amendment to the U.S. Constitution that would make English the nation's only public language and, he believed, unify and strengthen the nation once again.

With its 1988 National Language Policy, the CCCC engaged this debate over language diversity in the public sphere. The CCCC National Language Policy registered the organization's opposition to the English-only movement of the 1980s, but it did so by highlighting how composition scholars held values about social unity, democratic freedoms, and national identity in common with Hayakawa and his English-only supporters, political and cultural conservatives, and, indeed, a large segment of the American public. The National Language Policy, however, asked scholars, teachers, and community leaders to consider how these values could be revitalized through efforts not to restrict but rather to foster greater linguistic diversity in U.S. public life. With this language policy, the CCCC presented an alternative vision of how language use could inform the national identity. Just as significantly, the National Language Policy asked compositionists to see themselves not only as scholars and teachers but also as citizens who could provide greater leadership in public debates about language policy and linguistic diversity.

Guiding the CCCC's interventions in the English-only debate was the CCCC Language Policy Committee (LPC), formed in 1987 and chaired by Geneva Smitherman, who brought significant language policy experience from her service on the Committee on CCCC Language Statement that drafted the 1974 Students' Right resolution. The committee's initial work involved assessing the implications of English-only laws both for linguistic minorities and, significantly, for English teachers. Committee members drafted the National Language Policy and an accompanying brochure, and they wrote and spoke in various forums to educate fellow compositionists and community leaders about a policy alternative to English-only. From this initial focus on how an English-only policy would affect public life and how composition teachers could provide leadership in language policy debates, the LPC added new dimensions to its National Language Policy-inspired work through the turn of the twenty-first century. The committee still kept track of language policy debates at the national and state level, but it also expanded its focus to include composition pedagogy, exploring ways that teachers could revise the goals and practices of literacy education to more actively promote language diversity.

Drawing on archival materials as well as texts published by LPC members, this chapter explores scholars' understanding of the National Language Policy and analyzes the significance of the committee's work for the field of composition studies. These archival materials document various activities that the LPC performed to engage the English-only debate, promote multilingualism as a public good, and redirect composition studies' approach to linguistic diversity. Studying these materials clarifies the specific function that language policy statements perform for organizations such as the CCCC and for scholars working in their local institutions. Equally as important, this archival study also illustrates the need to assess the influence of language policy statements such as the National Language Policy across a longer period of time rather than just within their immediate rhetorical situation. The LPC's work encourages scholar-teachers to view language policies not as isolated statements but rather as texts that prompt actions to extend the policy's reach and weave its values into the daily practices of schools, government institutions, and community agencies. The National Language Policy, like other language policies such as the Students' Right resolution, did not bring sweeping and immediate changes to the discipline or to public policy making. Nevertheless, archival materials suggest that it has served as a guide to action for research, publication, training, and teaching that has incrementally brought about disciplinary change over the course of two decades.

Unlike the Students' Right resolution, though, the National Language Policy focused composition scholars' attention on a language policy debate that carried just as much importance for social services and political activity in local communities as it did for language arts teaching.

The LPC in this way positioned the CCCC as a civic institution that could challenge restrictive language policies not only inside but also outside the composition classroom. As Smitherman would note in 1987, the National Language Policy was meant to fill a "language leadership vacuum" ("Lessons" 30) in public debates on English-only laws and to craft an alternative vision of what democratic communities could look like within the United States.

The organization's alternative visions of national identity and communal values become particularly clear as one reads the language policy within the context of the conservative political rhetoric of the 1980s from which the English-only movement emerged. Indeed, to understand language policies of the 1980s, one needs to know about these specific contexts and political conversations because the English-only debate was permeated by discourses on individual freedom and responsibility, cultural cohesion, and national identity. Analyzing how the LPC negotiated the social, political, and cultural discourse of Ronald Reagan's presidential era forces us to recognize that language policies are just as much about addressing the "public attitudes and political values" (Marback 14) concerning linguistic, cultural, and national identity as they are about detailing specific strategies for managing the languages that people learn and use in schools and the larger society. In short, the CCCC National Language Policy aims to persuade composition scholars to assume both professional *and* civic duties. But more than simply deepening understanding of this language policy itself, examining the National Language Policy and the LPC's work within the context of the Reagan presidency and the English-only movement expands ideas about the history of composition studies. This investigation defines the discipline's history not just in terms of what teaching practices composition scholars have created or what theoretical schools they have developed but also how they have responded to public debates on literacy education, linguistic rights, and language policies.

To make this argument, this chapter first situates the National Language Policy within the social, political, and cultural contexts from which it emerged. It examines how Reagan-era political discourse revitalized American rhetorical commonplaces concerning individual freedom and self-help, communal responsibility, and independence from governmental interference, and how, in turn, these values shaped public perceptions on social welfare, immigration, and education policies. The chapter then analyzes how the rhetorical strategies of the English-only movement built on this conservative discourse and articulated a strong link between the English language and U.S. national identity. After relating the events that triggered the CCCC's response to the English-only movement, the chapter moves in the final section to discuss how the LPC crafted the National Language Policy to create a civic identity for the CCCC, positioning the organization as a leader in public debates about language policy and linguistic diversity. The National Language Policy offered a role for compositionists in creating greater opportunities for language minorities to contribute to U.S. public life and changing many Americans' attitudes about learning second and third languages. This chapter considers both the LPC's work in the immediate moment of the 1980s English-only debate and its long-term project to teach composition scholars how they can help to bring about the organization's vision for a multilingual public sphere. Indeed, this analysis of the National Language Policy and the LPC's work demonstrates why debates and policies dealing with non-English languages must be seen as vital to composition studies' own mission, for supporting linguistic minorities and building a greater commitment to multilingualism can also reinvigorate the discipline's commitment to teaching students a range of reading, listening, speaking, and writing skills they need to participate in American democracy as well as the larger international community. The chapter then concludes by exploring how the National Language Policy's argument for the CCCC to operate as both a professional and civic body connects to contemporary concerns inside composition studies.

President Reagan's Mission to Empower Individuals and Restore National Pride

Ronald Reagan took office in 1981 as Americans' confidence in their nation sagged. The energy crisis of 1979, combined with a stagnant economy marked by double-digit inflation, skyrocketing interest rates, and high unemployment led many people to believe the nation's standard of living was stuck in irreversible decline. And the United States' defeat in Vietnam, the Soviet Union's invasion of Afghanistan, and the Iranian Hostage Crisis seemed to signal the declining status of the United States in the international military and political arena. In a 15 July 1979 speech, President Jimmy Carter noted the nation's "crisis of confidence," one marked by "the loss of a unity of purpose for our nation" (Carter). Christopher Lasch similarly observed that by 1979, "a mood of pessimism in higher circles [had] spread through the rest of society as people [lost] faith in their leaders" (17).

Reagan skillfully channeled these frustrations in his presidential campaign and eventual landslide victory over Carter. Reagan sought to revive Americans' faith in the greatness of their nation and restore "the traditional values of family, work, neighborhood, peace, and freedom" (White 4). Central to Reagan's vision of American identity was his belief, echoing John Winthrop's 1630 proclamation, that the United States was "a city on a hill," a unique nation providentially divined to lead the world by "upholding the principles of self-reliance, self-discipline, morality, and—above all—responsible liberty for every individual" (Reagan, "Announcement"). Reagan believed the nation could restore its confidence and reclaim its national identity if it committed to these principles once again. As John Kenneth White notes, Reagan's appeals to traditional values such as self-discipline, family and religious morals, liberty, freedom, and patriotism proved to be persuasive not because they were "nice-sounding platitudes" but rather because they created "romantic visions that voters [sought] to emulate in their own lives." "Consequently," White adds, "most want[ed] reassurances from their political leaders that such dreams [could] be made real" (5).

Reagan provided this reassurance. He expressed faith that local communities had the desire, the talent, and the confidence to make the country great again. Reagan believed this potential had simply been squashed by big government. This set of colossal federal institutions, he argued, was disconnected from Americans' day-to-day lives. In the November 1979 speech announcing his presidential candidacy, Reagan promised to be a "leader who will unleash [Americans'] great strength and remove the roadblocks government has put in their way" ("Announcement"). Reagan explained to American voters that freeing individuals from government interference would empower them to fulfill their civic, professional, and personal goals. Once this yoke was lifted, individuals would be free to compete for advancement up the social and economic ladder, and their efforts would put the United States back on the path toward an ever-rising standard of living. Throughout the 1980s, then, Reagan championed individual responsibility instead of entitlement programs and promoted personal solutions rather than big government interventions. These rhetorical commonplaces came to guide many conservative political and cultural leaders as they argued about how to make America great again.

For example, Reagan's faith in individual initiative and responsibility led him to criticize federal entitlement programs. Welfare programs such as food stamps and Aid to Families with Dependent Children did not work, he argued, not only because the government had become a costly and inefficient provider of social services but also because such programs undermined traditional American values ("Announcement"). In other words, Reagan blamed both the provider and the recipients of entitlement programs. Big government failed America by not motivating individuals to compete in the workforce and marketplace; welfare recipients failed their fellow citizens by not working hard for an honest wage. In his second State of the Union address, Reagan emphasized the great number of people who cheated and took advantage of federal "entitlement" programs that had simply grown too large: "Virtually every American who shops in a local supermarket is aware of the daily abuses that take place in the food stamp program, which has grown by 16,000 percent in the last 15 years" (Reagan, "Address," 26 January 1982). Reagan's social and economic policies reinforced a belief that big government provided too many services to effectively oversee its own operations and, more importantly, too many incentives for poor Americans to stay unemployed.

A key aspect of Reagan's plan to improve the national economy and restore American identity was to replace big government solutions with calls for more private responsibility. Reagan withdrew federal funding from "wasteful and discredited government programs," signing into law in August 1981 a bill that reduced spending for entitlement programs by $44 billion over a three-year period. As he withdrew these federal funds, Reagan sought "to mobilize the private sector . . . to bring thousands of Americans into a volunteer effort to help solve many of America's social problems" (Reagan, "Address," 26 January 1982). By 1986, Reagan's welfare system had taken many financial and logistical responsibilities away from big government and placed them in the hands of community-based organizations (Reagan, "Address," 4 February 1986). While he rhetorically packaged his welfare policies in terms of "public responsibility," Reagan effectively undermined any public responsibility to ensure economically and politically marginalized peoples had an equal opportunity to participate fully in public life. Instead, Reagan's welfare policies not only targeted big government as one source of the problem but also cast economically marginalized Americans as being in need of moral improvement, eliminating government programs as a way to force individuals to become more self-reliant and self-disciplined.

Reagan's position regarding immigration policy, another pressing issue during his presidency, also played out this theme of individual enthusiasm, energy, and creativity as key to revitalizing the nation.[1]

As he stressed the "individual" nature of American identity, however, Reagan defined the "immigrant experience" in a way that demanded immigrants adopt a particular relationship to both their home country and the United States. Reagan presented this image of the U.S. immigrant in his speech at the Statue of Liberty Centennial Celebration in 1986. Once again invoking Winthrop's "city upon a hill," Reagan described this "city" as one destined "to be found by a special kind of people from every corner of the world, who had a special love for freedom and a special courage that enabled them to leave their own land, leave their friends and their countrymen, and come to this new and strange land to build a New World of peace and freedom and hope" ("Remarks"). Reagan here emphasized the "special courage" immigrants needed to leave their land, their family, their friends, and their nation behind. Significantly, though, Reagan repeated the word "leave" in a way that implied immigrants needed to cut ties with the political and cultural ideologies of their homelands and adopt only dominant American values, no matter how emotionally difficult, unnecessary, or impractical such actions might have been.

In defining the U.S. immigrant experience this way, Reagan sustained mainstream Americans' faith that the United States was a nation where everyone enjoys freedom and equality of opportunity. Just as important, he set up immigrants to be judged as worthy Americans to the extent that they committed themselves wholeheartedly to the "American" way of life. This commitment required immigrants to leave behind the concerns of their homelands or ethnic communities and to make decisions in terms of what was best for the American citizenry as a whole. In short, this faith in the assimilation narrative pressured immigrants to participate in public life on terms that the majority culture had set for it, which during the 1980s meant demonstrating an unwavering U.S. patriotism and a commitment to leading one's family and communal lives according to middle-class, European American values.

Reagan maintained that U.S. schools had a significant responsibility to instill this common American identity in the nation's youth. In his 1989 farewell address, Reagan admitted that of all the progress the nation made during his eight years in office, he was proudest of "the resurgence of national pride that I called the new patriotism" ("Farewell"). Reagan nevertheless warned that American schools and families needed to commit to ensuring the younger generation felt this same national pride. "Our spirit is back," he explained, "but we haven't reinstitutionalized it." Schools, families, neighbors, and even the popular culture industry, he argued, needed to "teach history based not on what's in fashion but what's important—why the Pilgrims came here, who Jimmy Doolittle was, and what those 30 seconds over Tokyo meant." He continued, "If we forget what we did, we won't know who we are. I'm warning of an eradication of the American memory that could result, ultimately, in an erosion of the American spirit." From Reagan's perspective, U.S. schools had ignored their responsibility to teach "what's important" in favor of teaching "what's in fashion."

Several conservative political commentators went a step further to explicitly name the force they believed was diverting schools' energy and attention from this central responsibility: multiculturalism. Schools had succumbed to the multicultural education movement, they argued, and begun catering to immigrants and ethnic and linguistic minorities. E. D. Hirsch Jr. argued in his 1987 *Cultural Literacy: What Every American Needs to Know* that school officials and teachers had bought into multicultural education's belief that "the traditional literate materials that used to be taught in the schools" are "class-bound, white, Anglo-Saxon, and Protestant, not to mention racist, sexist, and excessively Western" (21). He maintained, however, that the multicultural curriculum hurt students because it did not help them master the "shared national vocabulary" (134), information that one needed to know to enter the culturally literate mainstream. Even more important, Hirsch warned, by giving priority to multicultural education over the "traditional literate materials" of mainstream society, schools encouraged students to form stronger allegiances with their ethnic, linguistic, or religious communities than with the larger national community.[2] Most problematic for Hirsch in this regard was bilingual education. He believed multilingualism "enormously increased cultural fragmentation, civil antagonism, illiteracy, and economic-technological ineffectualness" (92). In short, multilingualism and bilingual education distracted schools from their mission of ensuring a "civil peace" grounded in a uniquely American set of traditions, values, and opinions (92–93).

Reagan and Hirsch not so indirectly attacked a multicultural education that critiqued how dominant national narratives engrained European American cultural values in public life. Whereas multicultural education aimed at "understanding, engaging, and transforming the diverse histories, cultural narratives, representations, and institutions" that produce social inequality and discrimination (Aronowitz and Giroux 198), Reagan and Hirsch tried to preserve the national identity by using school to teach a single version of U.S. history, one they believed would revive people's faith in America's divine providence to lead the world. In so doing, political conservatives of the Reagan era defined the "citizenry" not as a collective that continually dialogued about the nation's domestic and international commitments but rather as a people who, when freed from the yoke of big bureaucracies such as educational administrations, revered and worked to preserve a fixed national identity. Significantly, these themes of national identity, of freeing the individual from out-of-touch big government and big educational institutions, and of promoting self-sufficiency would become rhetorical emphases for the English-only movement in its campaigns for a national language policy.

The English-Only Campaign for a National Language and Culture

As Reagan entered the White House in 1981, S. I. Hayakawa, then a U.S. senator from California, was introducing legislation to the U.S. Congress that, like many of Reagan's policies, aimed at reuniting the nation and renewing its democratic ideals. Hayakawa, also a linguist and former president of San Francisco State University, warned his fellow representatives and the public of "an unhealthy development": Hispanics sought "to maintain—and give official status to—a foreign language within our borders" (21). Hayakawa echoed Reagan's critique of big government and anticipated Hirsch's critique of American schools as he drew attention to how bilingual education and bilingual social services threatened the cohesion of U.S. society. To restore the damage done by this "linguistic division" (21), Hayakawa introduced Senate Joint Resolution 72, officially titled "A joint resolution proposing an amendment to the Constitution of the United States with respect to proceedings and documents in the English language." This law would have declared English to be the official language of the United States and would have restricted the federal government's ability to "make or enforce any law which requires the use of any language other than English" ("Proposed" 112). This resolution was cosponsored by ten other legislators but never voted on by the 97th Congress.

Undeterred, Hayakawa retired from the Senate in 1983 and intensified his efforts to persuade the nation that an English Language Amendment (ELA) to the U.S. Constitution could "dissolv[e] distrust and fear" among the citizenry (15). Hayakawa cofounded the lobbying group U.S. English in 1983. Responding to Reagan's call that local communities needed to defend American values when big government failed them, U.S. English targeted the state level as the space for winning "legal protection" for the English language (Crawford, Editor's Introduction 1). By 1986, two other organizations, English First and the American Ethnic Coalition, had also formed to lobby in favor of an ELA.[3]

The English-only movement scored its first substantive victory in the California primary that year. Seventy-three percent of voters there supported Proposition 63, which became Article III, Section 6 of the California State Constitution. This law was intended "to preserve, protect, and strengthen the English language" ("State Official Language Statutes" 134). It granted state legislators the power to "take all steps necessary to insure that the role of English as the common language of the State of California is preserved and enhanced," and it gave California residents standing to sue the state in order to enforce this law (134).

The English-only movement continued to gain momentum through 1988, when voters in Colorado, Florida, and Arizona passed ELAs to their state constitutions. On one hand, the Colorado and Florida measures were simply one-line declarations that "English is the official language of the State" (qtd. in Combs 132). On the other hand, Arizona's Proposition 106, which passed by fewer than eleven thousand votes, a margin slimmer than one percent, imposed restrictions on language use. Arizona's law bluntly stated, "This State and all political subdivisions of this State shall act in English and no other language" (qtd. in Combs 152). Education scholar and language policy activist Mary Carol Combs argued that many of the Arizona voters who supported Proposition 106 likely did so not "because of its punitive language" but rather "because they hoped to reify its imagined benefits" (146), particularly the common American culture they believed could be restored through the unifying power of a common language. National lobbying organizations such as U.S. English played a significant role in shaping public debate about these ballot initiatives. U.S. English's Legislative Task Force contributed $158,774 (98 percent of the budget) to support the Arizonans for English Only group's broadcast and print advertising campaign (140).

The English-only movement's campaigns in support of California, Colorado, Florida, and Arizona's ELAs resonated with conservative discourse about how the nation could restore its core identity. Indeed, the English-only movement's rhetorical strategy proved to be successful when it drew on two themes popularized by Reagan: one, the power of individuals to make the nation better if big government institutions got out of their way, and two, the need for schools to bond the nation with a common set of cultural values.

The English-only movement's attack on bilingual education in particular resonated with Reagan's rhetoric of the civic disservice done by big government. Hayakawa described the U.S. Department of Education and bilingual educators as groups focused more on expanding their political influence than on helping linguistic minority students to acquire English language skills they needed to enter public life. Hayakawa argued that educational institutions, like all forms of big government, operated unaware of the individual aspirations of the parents and students they were supposed to serve:

> The new U.S. Department of Education, established during the Carter administration, was eager to make its presence known by expanding its bureaucracy and its influence. The department quickly announced a vast program with federal funding for bilingual education, which led to the hiring of Spanish-speaking teachers by the thousands. . . .
>
> "Bilingual education" rapidly became a growth industry, requiring more and more teachers. Complaints began to arise from citizens that "bilingual education" was not bilingual at all, since many Spanish-speaking teachers hired for the program were found not to be able to speak English. But the Department of Education decreed that teachers in the "bilingual" program do not need to know English!
>
> Despite the ministrations of the Department of Education, or perhaps because of them, Hispanic students to a shocking degree drop out of school, educated neither in Hispanic nor in American language and culture. (18)

Hayakawa's brief history of bilingual education purposefully emphasized its origins in the Carter administration and in the 1970s, a period that Reagan persuaded many Americans to see as one in which big government mismanaged the nation's affairs. Hayakawa added to this argument by defining bilingual education as an "industry," a monolithic enterprise unable to lead communities because it was far removed from the day-to-day concerns and needs of parents and students.

Hayakawa's narrative also bolstered the conservative argument that by failing parents and students, schools had compromised the nation's cultural identity and political strength. He maintained that it was through classes taught in English that immigrants learned "the social imperatives of being an American, the attitudes and customs that shape the American personality, the behavior that makes a good American citizen" (qtd. in Baron 56). Hayakawa left no doubt that it was the Department of Education and bilingual educators who limited linguistic-minority students' opportunities to improve their educational, professional, and civic lives. Given this failure of leadership, voters needed to intervene. By adopting an ELA, voters would force schools to conduct classes in English only and help linguistic minorities to assimilate. Hayakawa suggested that a vote for English-only laws was a vote for strengthening the nation's common culture and a vote for ensuring each individual's opportunity to acquire the skills—namely, speaking and writing English—that would allow her or him to exercise political and economic freedom.

Linda Chávez, who served as president of U.S. English in 1987 (before resigning one year later), expanded the English-only movement's rhetorical strategy to target not only the bilingual education industry but also big government.[4] Chávez had significant governmental experience, working as staff director of the U.S. Commission on Civil Rights from 1983 to 1985 and later chairing the National Commission on Migrant Education from 1988 to 1992, and she blamed big government for creating barriers—in the form of bilingual services—that discouraged linguistic minorities from participating fully in U.S. public life. Chávez accused Latino political leaders in particular of trying to prevent their constituents from learning English and advancing socially and economically. Chávez and her fellow English-only supporters viewed proficiency in English as the key asset Latinos needed to acquire in order to enter U.S. public life and achieve their individual aspirations.

Chávez argued in her 1991 book *Out of the Barrio* that Latino politicians limited their constituents' opportunities for advancement by steadfastly refusing to abandon the civil rights model of social and economic assimilation. Whereas previous generations of immigrants eagerly assimilated, she explained, "the entitlements of the civil rights era encouraged Latinos to maintain their language and culture, their separate identity, in return for the rewards of being members of an officially recognized minority group" (5). These government policies, Chávez argued, led Latino leaders to create "a perverse standard of success" whereby "to succeed at the affirmative action game, Hispanics had to establish their failure in other areas," such as education and employment (433). Chávez, then, compounded Hayakawa's claim that "advocates of Spanish language and Hispanic culture are not at all unhappy about the fact that 'bilingual education,' originally instituted as the best way to teach English, often results in no English being taught at all" (19).[5] Both Chávez and Hayakawa portrayed Latino leaders who advocated for bilingual services as self-serving politicians, opportunists who worked to "succeed" in the eyes of the community by bringing home government handouts and affirmative action favoritism. To Chávez and Hayakawa, these politicians were the ones "failing"—failing constituents by impeding their efforts to acquire the language skills they needed to pursue their individual dreams and achieve social and economic progress. Echoing Reagan's arguments on social policy, Chávez in particular argued that providing "entitlements" created disincentives for self-improvement. ELAs, she argued, would redefine "success" in ways that truly empowered individuals and reinvigorated the nation's values of equal opportunity and honest work.

By taking up this rhetorical and political agenda, U.S. English supporters rendered the complexity of linguistic minorities' lives—the complexity of learning English, the complexity of enacting one's commitment to national and communal identities, the complexity of advancing in society—in simple terms. Chávez argued that once big government got out of people's way and disincentives for self-improvement were removed, individuals would take the initiative to learn English. Interestingly, this perspective on "entitlements" and "handouts" as government interference, coupled with the belief in personal responsibility and the perception of education as a monolithic industry, allowed English-only supporters to avoid discussing the material conditions that affected how linguistic minorities could go about learning English. The only barriers to learning the language that groups such as U.S. English acknowledged were the bilingual resources that allowed them to go about their daily lives without needing to acquire English. For this reason, English-only advocates made the passage of ELAs their major goal. They focused solely on taking away non-English language resources rather than also providing additional support for English-language learning.

In its fight against a big government seemingly unconcerned with preparing students for their civic and professional duties, English-only supporters called on teachers to challenge the educational bureaucracy's demands for bilingual education and to do right by the children in their classrooms. Richard Rodriguez made one of the more prominent statements against bilingual education in his 1982 *Hunger of Memory*. Rodriguez argues in this memoir that bilingual education misleads linguistic-minority students because it promises them that they can acquire the language of public life in America even as they retain allegiances to their heritage cultures. By recounting his painful experiences learning English—and assuming a public identity—in an immersion setting, Rodriguez argues that bilingual education provides too much of a disincentive for enduring this painful, but ultimately necessary, transition:

> Without question, it would have pleased me to hear my teachers address me in Spanish when I entered the classroom. I would have felt much less afraid. I would have trusted them and responded with ease. But I would have delayed—for how long postponed?—having to learn the language of public society. I would have evaded—and for how long could I have afforded to delay?—learning the great lesson of school, that I had a public identity. (19)

Rodriguez's story proved persuasive to many English-language arts educators. He assured teachers that while the process of learning English in this way was difficult, such difficulty was absolutely necessary. Students had an "obligation" "to speak the public language of *los gringos*" (19), and teachers had the obligation to require it of them. Indeed, Rodriguez's descriptions of his own teachers reassured educators they should not waver in their demand that students use the majority culture's public language:

> Fortunately, my teachers were unsentimental about their responsibility. What they understood was that I needed to speak a public language. So their voices would search me out, asking me questions. Each time I'd hear them, I'd look up in surprise to see a nun's face frowning at me. I'd mumble, not really meaning to answer. The nun would persist, "Richard, stand up. Don't look at the floor. Speak up. Speak to the entire class, not just to me!" But I couldn't believe that the English language was mine to use. (In part, I did not want to believe it.) I continued to mumble. I resisted the teacher's demands. (Did I somehow suspect that once I learned public language my pleasing family life would be changed?) Silent, waiting for the bell to sound, I remained dazed, diffident, afraid. . . .
>
> Weeks after, it happened: One day in school I raised my hand to volunteer an answer. I spoke out in a loud voice. And I did not think it remarkable when the entire class understood. That day, I moved very far from the disadvantaged child I had been only days

earlier. The belief, the calming assurance that I belonged in public, had at last taken hold. (19–22)

Rodriguez's description of his teachers as being "unsentimental" about their responsibility to teach the nation's public language appealed to many teachers precisely because they longed to feel as if they were helping the "disadvantaged child."

Indeed, *Hunger of Memory* confirmed for many English language arts teachers that an ELA was necessary to remind schools of their responsibility—and students' obligations—to U.S. society. Rodriguez's argument also resonated with educators because of their shared belief that the ability to speak and write English would free linguistic minorities to participate in public life. In turn, these teachers felt a responsibility to focus on teaching students the grammar and structure of Standardized English only. Trudy J. Sundberg expressed this viewpoint in a 1988 op-ed letter to *English Journal* ("Case"). Sundberg argued that English teachers' responsibilities were best fulfilled through English-language immersion classes, since they most enabled "limited- and non-English-speaking Americans . . . to enjoy the rights of full participation in society" ("Responses" 85). Like many teachers, Sundberg took the goal of the English language arts class to be preparing students for public life. She believed English teachers should focus solely on providing linguistic-minority students with the skills and knowledge of the public culture. Given what she saw as a clear distinction between public and private languages, Sundberg, echoing Rodriguez, argued that demanding linguistically disadvantaged students to speak, listen, read, and write in English only was a necessary step toward saving these children. Through this difficult work, teachers would help to strengthen America, wresting control of their lives away from government bureaucracies and educational administrators and reinforcing the nation's identity as a land of equal opportunity.

As this brief overview suggests, the English-only movement's rhetorical strategies drew upon discourse about reclaiming the national identity in the face of big government's efforts to erode a common culture. Groups such as the CCCC that attempted to counter the English-only movement, then, entered a rhetorical terrain that was already populated by discourses that created "romantic visions" (White 5) of American ideals of individual opportunity and freedom. The CCCC would engage in this struggle over definitions of American values by creating an alternative rhetorical framework for talking about what strong communities and individual opportunity looked like.

The Language Policy Committee's Strategy to Neutralize the English-Only Movement

As political and cultural conservatism came to dominate the national mindset, leaders in the field of English studies initiated dialogue about the discipline's role within U.S. society, particularly in terms of challenging dominant ideas about how the English language defined the national identity. In 1981, NCTE president William Irmscher wrote to CCCC chair Lynn Troyka urging her organization to create a new language policy statement that would correct what he saw as the Students' Right resolution's "limited historical reach" (qtd. in Parks 210):

> [A] new statement might try to describe an increasingly complex situation in this country that concerns foreign languages. The chauvinistic attitude of most Americans toward other languages poses an obstacle to respect for speakers of other languages and an accommodation of their language needs to the national scene. The language problem has acquired new dimensions since 1972. CCCC should now address the new decade in an informed way. We need a statement that reflects both an idealistic and realistic assessment of the language situation in this country. (qtd. in Parks 211)

Irmscher spoke to the political and cultural work that a new language policy could do. This language policy would accentuate certain disciplinary concerns, broadening composition studies' view to consider not only speaking, reading, and writing in English but also the entire range of linguistic practice in all language varieties throughout the United States. This new language policy would also present a new way of talking about the nation's "language situation," covering both current language practices as well as people's attitudes toward different language users and the effects these attitudes have on linguistic minorities. Moreover, Irmscher suggested that a new language policy could energize public debate on linguistic diversity by providing both a realistic and idealistic picture of what the nation's language situation could be.

Before responding to the nation's "increasingly complex language situation," however, the CCCC Executive Committee decided first to assess this situation and determine whether a professional response was indeed needed. The CCCC Executive Committee voted in 1981 to form the Committee to Study the Advisability of a Language Statement for the 1980s and 1990s (Parks 211–12), a committee chaired by Harold Allen and including among its members Milton Baxter, formerly of the

Language Curriculum Research Group, and Richard Rodriguez, who as I just noted above, was on his way to becoming an outspoken critic of bilingual education.

This committee passed the buck down the educational line. Its final report failed to build on the progressive vision for the CCCC first proposed in the Students' Right resolution. Calling for "full professional action on a front wider than that of CCCC," the committee pinned the greatest responsibility on elementary and secondary teachers to foster more respect for linguistic diversity and students' right to their own languages (qtd. in Parks 225). In short, it positioned those "new dimensions" of "the language problem" (Irmscher, qtd. in Parks 211)—ones concerning languages other than English—outside the scope of the CCCC's concerns and responsibilities. In dismissing Irmscher's call, the committee reinforced the status quo in the field of college-level rhetoric and composition, eschewing the need for more informed approaches to linguistic diversity in the classroom and in the community. Moreover, it failed to articulate either an idealistic or realistic vision of how the organization could operate within an ever more linguistically diverse society.

Some composition scholars believed that the Committee to Study the Advisability of a Language Statement's 1981 report compromised the CCCC's mission. Smitherman, for one, observed in 1987 that the organization's lack of initiative through the first part of the decade created a "language leadership vacuum" into which moved "reactionary and counter-progressive forces and movements" ("Lessons" 30). Indeed, as we saw earlier in this chapter, Reagan's presidential rhetoric revitalized conservatism at the start of the decade, and "counter-progressive movements" such as the English-only campaign made significant strides during the subsequent five years. These counter-progressive movements made their way into English teachers' conversations about language education. Hayakawa published a brief column entitled "Why the English Language Amendment?: An Autobiographical Statement" in the December 1987 issue of *English Journal*, and Sundberg echoed his arguments while connecting them to pedagogical concerns in her letter that appeared in the journal's March 1988 issue. In the same December 1987 *English Journal* issue that ran Hayakawa's piece, Victor Villanueva described how Rodriguez delivered his featured speech at the 1986 NCTE Conference and received "an enthusiastic, uncritical acceptance, marked by a long, loud standing ovation" ("Whose Voice" 17). And as Lynn Bloom would report in 1999, the "Aria" chapter from *Hunger of Memory*, the essay in which Rodriguez makes his most overt critiques of bilingual education, was reprinted twenty-three times in textbooks and anthologies over the course of two decades after its initial 1980 publication in *American Scholar*. All of this evidence suggests, then, that the "counter-progressive" English-only movement with its anti–bilingual education stance undoubtedly affected many teachers' approaches to writing instruction.

Aware that the CCCC had all but ignored the encroachment of conservative discourse and policies on language diversity, Smitherman and other politically oriented members of the organization reacted promptly when California passed Proposition 63 in 1986, which aimed to "preserve, protect, and strengthen the English language" ("State Official" 134) and sent a negative message about the place of language diversity in California's communities and schools. Smitherman and the CCCC Progressive Composition Caucus saw a role for the CCCC to play in the public debate on language policy issues, given its position as "the leading professional organization dealing with language and literacy" (CCCC, Annual Business Meeting minutes, 21 March 1987, 5). The caucus submitted a motion for the CCCC's 1987 annual business meeting that called for the organization's leaders to appoint a committee, chaired by Smitherman, that would "articulate the issues and formulate and implement strategies to educate the public, educational policy-makers, and legislatures" about the dangers of English-only legislation (5). This motion was passed by the CCCC membership, and by 22 November 1987, the CCCC Officers Committee had approved the formation of the LPC. The CCCC Executive Committee authorized $3,000 for the LPC's initial work (CCCC Officers' Committee, Meeting minutes, 21 March and 22 November 1987), and Smitherman recruited Elizabeth Auleta, Thomas Kochman, Elizabeth McPherson, Guadalupe Valdés, Jeffrey Youdelman, and Ana Celia Zentella to serve with her on the committee.

To fill the "language leadership vacuum" in national debates about linguistic diversity and language education, the LPC pursued four types of activities, which are briefly outlined here and then expanded upon below. First, the LPC composed the National Language Policy, which committed the CCCC to helping create a society that accommodated multiple languages within the public sphere. Second, the LPC educated CCCC members about the English-only debate, helping them to see why the issue concerned their discipline and how they could work in their classrooms and their communities to promote multilingual language learning. Third, the LPC tried to shape political and public opinion on English-only laws by contacting community leaders and media outlets. And fourth, the LPC networked with other professional and civic organizations to combat the English-only movement and promote an alternative policy that called for material support to help all citizens learn multiple languages.[6]

The central focus of the LPC's work, of course, was drafting the National Language Policy. Seven years after Irmscher's call in 1981 for "both an idealistic and realistic assessment of the language situation in this country" (qtd. in Parks 211), the CCCC envisioned a U.S. society in which multiple languages were widely used within the public sphere. The National Language Policy, which the CCCC Executive Committee and general membership unanimously adopted as the organization's official policy in 1988, reflected a proposal that Smitherman generated in the conclusion of her 1977 *Talkin and Testifyin* (240–41) and outlined in greater detail at Howard University's Black Communications Conference in 1984 (Smitherman, "Mis-Education" 114–15), the same year that a U.S. Senate subcommittee held hearings on four proposed ELAs. Each document advocates an English-*plus* policy that emphasizes the need for all people in the United States to learn and use multiple languages.[7] The National Language Policy statement in particular has the expressed goal of "enabl[ing] everyone to participate in the life of this multicultural nation by ensuring continued respect both for English, our common language, and for the many other languages that contribute to our rich cultural heritage." Toward these ends, the National Language Policy calls for the political and material support of three different types of programs, namely English language, heritage language, and second language education. These distinct educational programs were each highlighted in the policy's "three inseparable parts":

1. To provide resources to enable native and nonnative speakers to achieve oral and literate competence in English, the language of wider communication.
2. To support programs that assert the legitimacy of native languages and dialects and ensure that proficiency in one's mother tongue will not be lost.
3. To foster the teaching of languages other than English so that native speakers of English can rediscover the language of their heritage or learn a second language. (CCCC, "National Language Policy" 2)

The LPC's creation of this policy was significant in part because it did more than simply critique the English-only ideology. Instead, it helped both composition professionals and the wider public to imagine what a policy alternative to English-only legislation could look like. To elaborate this vision, the LPC also created a brochure that explained the historical and theoretical contexts for both the policy and the organization's opposition to the English-only movement (CCCC Language Policy Committee, "Outline/Draft").

The LPC did not stop with the National Language Policy brochure in its efforts to educate rhetoric and composition scholars about the English-only issue. The committee also worked to counter the "common sense" assumption expressed by Sundberg that English teachers should support an ELA because this legislation promotes the idea of everyone learning English. To carry out this educational effort, LPC members presented a double session at the 1988 CCCC convention. In this panel, Jeffrey Youdelman and Elizabeth Auleta analyzed the ideological motivations of the English-only movement, while Guadalupe Valdés and Elizabeth Baldwin described how English-only legislation would affect college-level language arts education. Geneva Smitherman, Ana Celia Zentella, and Thomas Kochman provided context and detail to help fellow composition scholars understand the CCCC National Language Policy, and Elizabeth McPherson and James Stalker rounded out the panel as they helped audience members develop their own ideas about how to enact this policy both inside their classrooms and within their communities (CCCC Language Policy Committee, Program Proposal).[8] The LPC also composed supporting materials such as bibliographies for scholars who wanted to introduce the National Language Policy and the organization's campaign against the English-only movement at regional conferences ("Interim Report #1" 5). And finally, the LPC proposed the creation of a background statement to accompany the National Language Policy as a special issue of *CCC*, much like the one that appeared with the Students' Right resolution in the journal's fall 1974 issue (CCCC Language Policy Committee, "Revised Draft: Background Document"). The LPC's proposed outline for this background statement suggests that it would have addressed the following types of topics: the "social and cultural implications" of English-only and English-plus; lessons from other nations about the relationship between "cultural diversity and political unity"; information about language variation and change and the relationship between language and cognition; and implications of the National Language Policy for testing and evaluation, classroom teaching, and the teacher's civic identity ("Revised Draft").[9] Unfortunately, this background statement was never fully developed or published. Nevertheless, its outline highlights what the LPC believed that composition scholars needed to know more about in order to understand how the English-only movement conflicted with college-level rhetoric and composition scholars' goals for student learning in the classroom and for meaningful participation in the public sphere.

In addition to this educational effort within the discipline, the LPC also filled the language leadership vacuum by going public with the National Language Policy and working to shape political and popular opinion on linguistic diversity in the United States. The LPC drafted letters and fact sheets for NCTE and CCCC members to use in contacting legislators and newspapers, and it initiated contact with media outlets to focus their attention on the need for an English-plus policy (CCCC Language Policy Committee, "Interim Report #1" 4–5). Additionally, the committee brainstormed ideas for developing a video on English-only legislation and the National Language Policy that would target the lay public, and it sketched proposals to state humanities councils for support of similar types of public-oriented projects and programs on language diversity issues (5). While these latter projects, like the background statement, never became realities, the LPC's plans suggest that it saw the CCCC membership not just as teacher-scholars but also as public intellectuals and civic leaders who could prompt community dialogue about linguistic diversity and language policy.

The fourth and final move by the LPC was to amplify these efforts to "go public" in its opposition to the English-only movement by networking with like-minded professional organizations and advocacy groups. The LPC believed that linking with groups such as the NCTE's Commission on Language, the Linguistic Society of America, the Center for Applied Linguistics, and the National Council for Black Studies would create opportunities for fertile exchange that could help the LPC "to formulate mechanisms and strategies for educating legislators, educational policy-makers, and the lay public about language learning, the rich heritage of American English, and the implications and consequences of legislative proposals for 'English-only'" (CCCC Language Policy Committee, "Interim Report #1" 2). For similar reasons, Smitherman extended the CCCC's reach beyond academia by representing the organization within the English Plus Information Clearinghouse, or EPIC. EPIC was established in 1987 through a coordinated effort by the National Immigration, Refugee, and Citizenship Forum and the Joint National Committee for Languages. More than fifty organizations, including the CCCC, signed onto EPIC's "Statement of Purpose," which denounced the English-only movement and promoted multilingualism for all Americans (English Plus Information Clearinghouse). EPIC hoped, through the sheer number of its participating organizations, to counter the perception that only a handful of self-interested organizations and professions opposed English-only legislation.[10]

After initiating these four types of activities over a six-year period, the LPC ceased formal work for a brief time in 1993 and 1994, in part because the CCCC Officers Committee expressed concern that the LPC did not have an active charge. Nevertheless, the CCCC Executive Committee asked Smitherman to keep it abreast of current developments in the English-only movement (CCCC Officers Committee, Meeting Minutes, 15 March 1994, 7). She filed periodic reports to the Executive Committee, and she also submitted formal requests to reconvene the LPC so it could enhance the CCCC's leadership position in public debates about language diversity in literacy education. In March 1995, the LPC was reconstituted. One of its first activities was to gain a rich portrait of English teacher-scholars' knowledge of and attitudes toward language policy and linguistic diversity.[11] To do so, the LPC conducted a survey of CCCC and NCTE members that would help the committee to strategize how it could heighten awareness of the National Language Policy and the Students' Right resolution and show teachers how to use these documents to guide their teaching and public advocacy for literacy education. This survey ultimately shaped the LPC's 2003 collection *Language Diversity in the Classroom: From Intention to Practice*. This book, edited by Geneva Smitherman and Victor Villanueva, explored ways to change classroom practice and teacher training to foster greater respect for linguistic diversity and promote students' and teachers' use of their diverse languages and literacies as resources for learning.

The three sections that follow consider the LPC's activities over this sixteen-year period (1987–2003) in order to highlight three important aspects of language policies and activity that surrounds them. This study underscores the disciplinary significance of the National Language Policy in terms of how it situates topics and activities seemingly peripheral to the CCCC's work—laws concerning the language that federal and state governments use, instruction in languages other than English—squarely inside the organization's set of concerns. Examining the National Language Policy also reveals the rhetorical nature of language policies, as it drew on commonplaces circulating in political and cultural discourse but reworked these themes to challenge English-only arguments and propose an alternative vision of how to unify a linguistically diverse nation. Even as this analysis draws out the rhetorical nuance of the National Language Policy itself, however, it also underscores the limits of reading the CCCC's language policies in isolation. Indeed, archival and published materials documenting the LPC's activities over the fifteen-year period after it wrote the National Language Policy demonstrate that language policy work must involve more than just drafting and publishing a policy statement. The three-part analysis that follows, then, should help to deepen our understanding of the National Language Policy and our awareness of the work necessary to implement language policies in professional and civic life.

Revitalizing the Nation's Core Values through Public Multilingualism

Even as the LPC tried to combat "counter-progressive movements" and their conservative policy proposals, it worked with the same rhetorical commonplaces of individual ingenuity, communal cooperation, and political unity on which Reagan and the English-only movement relied. At the same time, the LPC composed the National Language Policy to reimagine how language use relates to the ways these values play out in American life, challenging the English-only movement's ideas about how linguistic minorities could participate in U.S. society. At issue were the spaces where people should use English and other languages as well as the ends toward which these languages should be put to use. English-only advocates did acknowledge that the United States needed more "foreign" language skills, but they reinforced dominant ideas about where and how these languages could be used: outside the nation's borders to help America succeed within the international economy. Supporters of the English-only movement believed that the presence of "foreign" languages within the nation's borders, particularly in public spaces, fractured what once was the entire populace's collective identification with a common national identity. For English-only activists, unifying the public required linguistic conformity. When a person spoke English, that signaled a willingness to cut ties with ethnic or cultural communities and commit fully to the nation's ideals; only when every individual in the nation made the choice to speak English could Americans trust one another and truly appreciate the range of individual experiences and the diversity of cultures that made the country great. The English-only argument was grounded on an assumption that the majority culture alone should determine where, how, and for what purpose minority groups participate in public. The LPC used the National Language Policy to propose a different vision of public language use, one in which conformity was not forced onto individuals but rather multilingualism was allowed to flourish in ways that simultaneously reshaped and strengthened U.S. civic and cultural life.

Like English-only supporters, the LPC understood that the public good gets formed through community interaction, but it proposed a different idea of what this interaction could look like. Both English Language Amendments and the National Language Policy rested on the belief that linguistic minorities had a responsibility to participate in public life beyond their ethnolinguistic communities in order to help address concerns in their neighborhoods, cities, and nation. Unlike Rodriguez and his "unsentimental teachers," however, the CCCC policy did not demand that minorities cut ties with their linguistic communities, nor did it put the onus for public participation solely on language minorities by demanding they first learn English before entering civic life. Instead, in a section of its policy brochure entitled "What You Can Do," the LPC called on scholars, teachers, and public leaders to "strive to include all citizens of all language communities in the positive development of our daily activities" (CCCC, "National Language Policy" 5). The National Language Policy did not provide specific examples of actions that would promote this inclusion. One can imagine, though, that an obvious strategy would be to facilitate multilingual dialogue in public arenas, such as composing and designing texts for multiple language groups and recruiting, training, and deploying translators for community forums and events. Equally important, however, would be finding ways to persuade linguistic minorities that their time, energy, insights, and even monetary contributions were needed to improve the community and the nation.

Ultimately, the National Language Policy was meant less as a text to prescribe activities and more as a means to change public ideas on linguistic minorities. With the section title "What You Can Do" along with the phrases "include all citizens" and "positive development," the policy evoked Reagan-era commonplaces of communal responsibility and national unity, but it encourages readers to see this unity resulting not from forcing linguistic conformity but rather from sustaining a collective effort to ensure that everyone could contribute to improving their cities, states, and nation. Whereas English-only supporters believed the presence of non-English languages in public spaces signaled a community's decision to turn its back on America, the National Language Policy promoted a vision of civic dialogue in which people's cultural and ethnolinguistic experiences usefully informed their sense of American identity and their definitions of the "common good."

The National Language Policy's particular understanding of communal responsibility extended to its call for all Americans to learn multiple languages. Even as it acknowledged the fact that "English has become the language of wider communication" in the United States, the National Language Policy pledged the CCCC both to support programs for linguistic minorities that "ensure that proficiency in one's mother tongue will not be lost" and also "foster the teaching of languages other than English" so that monolingual English speakers can develop bi- or multilingual skills. This latter aspect of the CCCC policy is critical. As John Trimbur argues in his 2006 essay "Linguistic Memory and the Politics of U.S. English," the National Language Policy's support for multilingualism has been interpreted too narrowly by composition scholars, many of whom see the policy simply "affirming the linguistic rights of minority language groups to use their own language as they see fit" (586). As Trimbur notes, the National Language Policy instead promotes a vision of U.S. society in which "all citizens . . . become capable of communicating with one another in a number of languages, code-switching as appropriate to the rhetorical situation" (587). Rather than just promoting English teaching to help linguistic minorities acquire the common linking language, and rather than just promoting efforts to bring linguistic minorities into public discussions by translating their speech and writing into English, the LPC promoted widespread multilingual competence as the most just way to create more opportunities for linguistic minority groups to participate in public life. The CCCC policy, in other words, redefined the United States' language problem not as linguistic minorities' inability to speak, write, or read English but rather as the monolingual majority's inability to speak, write, or read any languages other than English.

In its policy brochure, the LPC emphasized three supporting reasons for why the nation needed to promote the "learning [of] second and third languages by all Americans" (CCCC, "National Language Policy" 5). For one, the brochure claimed, a greater number of multilingual Americans would help to "unify diverse American communities" (5). This statement in part suggested that expanding the number of linguistic tools each person could use would necessarily enable more communities to talk with one another and understand their common interests. Just as important, however, the CCCC policy brochure also seemed to promote the view that developing a number of widely used public languages, not just English, would signal the political and cultural majority's willingness to share in the difficult work of learning another language well enough to use it to communicate with others. This willingness would signal the majority's empathy for linguistic minorities as well as respect for their languages and its significance for their personal, civic, and professional lives. In this way, then, the National Language Policy played on the Reagan-era commonplace of unity to suggest diverse communities could be unified by such empathy and respect, strengthening linguistic minorities' trust that their contributions to public activities were both valued and necessary.

The second reason the National Language Policy brochure gave for promoting multilingualism for all Americans was so the nation could "participate more effectively in worldwide activities," a claim that echoed Reagan's faith that individual initiative and creativity would restore America's greatness. The CCCC policy here seemed to align with English-only leaders such as Hayakawa who conceded that any ELA needed to ensure that "foreign" language education would not be eliminated (but who did not also concede, it should be noted, that bilingual education should be preserved as well). But whereas English-only supporters emphasized the economic benefits of foreign language skills, the LPC members proposed new criteria to guide decisions about what second and third languages Americans should learn. In her 1987 *College English* essay "'Lessons of the Blood': Toward a National Public Policy on Language," which she used to heighten the exigence for the National Language Policy, Smitherman called on educators, school administrators, and policy makers to create more opportunities for students to learn "language[s] spoken by persons in the Third World," particularly Spanish, the language that predominated life in the western hemisphere (31). Reading the National Language Policy through the lens of Smitherman's argument to emphasize learning Third World languages underscores the policy's goal of a multilingualism built not on economic interests but rather the desire to correct what she called the "narrow provincialism emanating from a world superpower" (33). Smitherman's writing, then, further clarified the policy's vision of creating a multilingual U.S. populace able to "participate more effectively in worldwide activities" (CCCC, "National Language Policy" 5). This multilingualism, the policy suggested, could heighten citizens' awareness of countries it had long ignored or profoundly shaped in negative ways.[12] In addition, it would also create a public more in tune with the political views and social activities of immigrants and language minorities whose personal and professional experiences had been profoundly shaped by the United States' relationship with their home countries.[13]

Thus, the National Language Policy redirected Reagan-era concerns for America's position within the world to focus on deepening citizens' sense of empathy and openness to learning rather than reasserting national greatness.

This ability to learn from linguistic minorities within the United States and marginalized communities throughout the world also spoke to the argument in the National Language Policy brochure that developing multilingualism among all Americans would "enlarge our view of what is human" (5). In taking up this argument, the National Language Policy once again challenged English-only discourse. Hayakawa claimed that he and other English-only supporters "rejoice in our ethnic diversity, which gives us our richness as a culture," but he nevertheless maintained that Americans could only create "a unique and vibrant culture" from this ethnic diversity if they all spoke the same language (19). The National Language Policy promoted a different perspective on how a richly diverse culture could be fostered and sustained with its suggestion that multilingualism could help to "enlarge our view of what is human." The policy itself does not elaborate on this phrase, but when reading it in conjunction with Smitherman's argument for more Americans to learn Third World languages, the passage seems to emphasize the importance of being able to listen to marginalized groups' stories and talk with them about their experiences in their native languages; of looking past assumptions to explore how and why a person's self-identity forms in relation to the nation or an ethnolinguistic community in a particular way; and of learning to recognize common values and aspirations that connect people across cultural and linguistic differences. Moreover, while English-only supporters promoted linguistic conformity as a means to ensure everyone's commitment to the nation-state, the National Language Policy brochure here suggested that multilingualism could help the political and cultural majority to better understand how and why a linguistic minority's experiences often influence the ways they fashion and carry out an "American" identity.

As these three reasons for promoting multilingualism illustrate, the National Language Policy and its accompanying brochure redirected Reagan-era rhetorical commonplaces of communal cooperation, individual responsibility, political and cultural unity, and the United States' international preeminence toward the ends of imagining a multilingual public sphere. While the English-only movement believed that communities could only come together if minorities helped themselves and learned English, the CCCC saw possibilities for unifying diverse communities within America and forging new international relationships if every person within the country accepted the responsibility to learn more than one language. Indeed, creating a new rhetorical framework for talking about the nation's identity and its linguistic practices served as the National Language Policy's primary purpose. But as the following section illustrates, the LPC did more than just envision how the nation could best incorporate minorities into public life. It also made sure that the policy and related documents highlighted the absolute necessity of providing the material and political support to ensure its particular policy vision of national multilingualism could become a reality.

Attending to the Material Needs of Language Learners

The LPC used the National Language Policy and related documents to refute the English-only movement's arguments about what motivated and what enabled people to learn new languages. As we saw in the analysis of Hayakawa, Chávez, and Rodriguez, English-only advocates claimed that the (seeming) prevalence of bilingual education and bilingual services allowed non-English speakers to feel comfortable living their lives using only their native languages. They suggested that government provisions of bilingual services lowered linguistic minorities' motivations to learn English, to contribute to the national economic and political process, and to commit to advancing themselves in society. In short, they argued, the accessibility of services in linguistic minorities' native languages kept them from realizing the value of learning English. English-only activists defined the ideal condition for learning English as one in which "support" meant the majority culture demanded English only, a sort of tough love that would spur on linguistic minorities to push themselves and learn the language. Thus, their English-only policies sought to remove bilingual texts and services as a means to create conditions that would motivate people to "pay the price" of entering fully into public life—learning English.

The LPC challenged these assumptions, as it focused attention on the material conditions affecting how people learn languages and how they put these language skills to use in meaningful ways. The first of the National Language Policy's three parts did not state that all people simply needed more encouragement to learn English. Instead, it asserted that the CCCC, the government, and the public must commit to "provid[ing] resources" that would enable all people—native and nonnative speakers alike—"to achieve oral and literate competence in English, the language of wider communication" (CCCC, "National Language Policy" 1). Pointing to the language-learning needs of all people, not just those who possess limited proficiency in English, was significant because it called for materially supporting a comprehensive, long-term approach to English language learning, one that enabled citizens to develop not only basic literacies for functioning in day-to-day life but also advanced literacies that could allow them to contribute to "the positive development of our daily activities" (5).

The LPC's emphasis on funding language education was important because many Americans mistakenly believed that a vote for English-only legislation was a vote for funding English language education (Crawford, "What's behind Official English" 175). Indeed, English-only leaders often ignored the fact that many linguistic minorities could not get into English-language classes even when they tried. For example, in November 1986, the English-only movement was successfully leading the campaign to pass Proposition 63 and, in so doing, to send a message that it believed would motivate everyone to learn English. At the same time, more than forty thousand people in Los Angeles were on waiting lists for English-language courses (Woo). To clarify voters' misconception about the relationship between ELAs and funding for English courses, the LPC explained in its policy brochure that "laws making English the official language do nothing to increase the number of [English] classes, nor do they teach a single person English" (CCCC, "National Language Policy" 3). The LPC used another text to make this statement more directly to educational policy makers. In a 1988 letter to school superintendents and federal and state legislators drafted by the LPC and signed by then-CCCC chair Andrea Lunsford, the committee reminded them that English-only laws do nothing to provide one more course, one more teacher, or one more textbook for the thousands of people who were on waiting lists for English classes (CCCC Language Policy Committee, Letter from CCCC Chair).[14]

The LPC expanded this discussion about educational support by illuminating an equally significant yet often ignored way that material conditions influence English-language learning. In her 1987 *College English* article, Smitherman argued that while English-only advocates believed laws forbidding bilingual services would motivate language minorities to learn English, people's motivations for learning the nation's dominant language actually were influenced by a broader range of concerns, including economic and political justice. She maintained that for many students from historically marginalized groups, motivation to learn

Standardized English comes from perceiving genuine opportunities to use the language in personally, publicly, and professionally significant ways. "Acquisition of the language of wider communication," Smitherman wrote, "must provide entrée to power and resources, or there is little reason for indigenous populations to adopt it" ("Lessons" 34). Here she applied pressure to Hayakawa's arguments about where individual initiative to learn English comes from. She also added an important dimension to the LPC's explanation of what people could do to ensure that linguistic minorities' "basic human rights are preserved" (CCCC, "National Language Policy" 5). While the National Language Policy brochure mentioned the need to "provide education, social services, legal services, medical services, and protective signing for linguistic minorities in their own languages" (5), Smitherman's article added that the community had a responsibility to help marginalized people integrate socially and economically into the wider community.

By making this particular argument, the LPC used the policy to recast the work of composition scholars. Creating genuine opportunities for language use meant compositionists needed to undertake political and social activities that extended beyond their classroom teaching. In particular, Smitherman called on compositionists to work "on the political front" with other social and political advocacy groups, such as those addressing poverty and unemployment, "to ensure rewards from language and literacy for America's working and UNWORKING classes" ("Lessons" 33–34). English teachers, she believed, had a responsibility to integrate their expertise on language and literacy with community efforts for social and political justice. The LPC prioritized this type of work because it believed that creating greater access to language courses would only be worthwhile if the community acted on its responsibility to improve the material and social conditions that would motivate people to learn English. Moreover, attending to language learners' material conditions served to critique the literacy myth underlying the English-only movement's main argument, namely, that learning English was *the* ticket minorities needed to enter the nation's social and economic mainstream.

These different ideas about the public's "obligation" to linguistic minorities also informed the divide between English-only advocates and the LPC on how to handle classes that teach people languages other than English. Hayakawa, Rodriguez, and others argued that maintaining heritage languages was a matter of private, not public, concern. For example, U.S. English made this statement in its "Guiding Principles":

"The rights of individuals and groups to use other languages and to establish *privately funded* institutions for the maintenance of diverse languages and cultures must be respected in a pluralistic society" (U.S. English 145, emphasis added). In this way, English-only supporters implied that heritage languages were appropriate for private but not public spaces within the United States.

The LPC targeted this public disinvestment in education for linguistic minorities and called for the public to fund educational opportunities for *all* Americans to learn second and third languages. As the previous section demonstrated, the National Language Policy advanced the argument that multilingualism aligned with widely supported goals of public education. Achieving these ends, the policy explained, required the CCCC and the public both to support programs that enabled people to maintain proficiency in their first language and to "foster the teaching of languages other than English" so that native English speakers had opportunities to acquire a second or third language (2). Thus, while the English-only movement did acknowledge people's "right" to use languages other than English inside U.S. borders, it relegated these languages to private situations and the foreign language classroom. The National Language Policy, on the other hand, called for bringing heritage language learning and heritage language use into public spaces rather than private studies. Echoing the Students' Right resolution of a decade earlier, the policy brochure suggested that declaring a language appropriate only for "private" use would create linguistic and cultural stigmatization for students. "When students cannot use their strengths," the National Language Policy brochure explained, "they experience alienation and failure" (3). For this reason, the brochure encouraged compositionists to help bring marginalized languages into the public realm, encouraging immigrants to pass on their native languages to their children and to use these languages "in the company of other Americans of differing backgrounds" (5). The LPC also argued in the policy brochure for heritage language learning in particular to be a matter of public concern and to be supported with public funds because it "expands students' learning opportunities," allowing them to diversify their linguistic repertoires and develop rhetorical skills for participating in a variety of cultural, political, and professional spaces rather than narrowing their language skills to one standardized variety (3).

As with Smitherman's *College English* article, LPC member Ana Celia Zentella pursued a research agenda that buttressed the National Language Policy's call for public support of multilingual education. Zentella's work challenged the English-only argument that heritage language learning could in fact be supported and even grown solely through family efforts and other "private studies," an argument that not only encouraged disinvestment in linguistic-minority students' overall education but also oversimplified public ideas about language learning. The English-only debate motivated Zentella to understand the conditions that enabled or prevented students from acquiring and maintaining heritage languages. Her 1997 monograph *Growing Up Bilingual: Puerto Rican Children in New York* focused in part on the reasons why family and other "private" efforts were not always enough to promote heritage-language learning and maintenance among children. She wrote,

> There is little awareness of what it takes to raise children in the US so that they end up with a command of two languages. Most caregivers are satisfied if children understand enough Spanish to behave appropriately. Almost no one insists that Spanish be spoken in certain settings or with certain speakers. The expectation is that exposure to grandmothers will ensure fluency in Spanish, and that English is learned in schools and on the block. But grandmothers with limited years of formal schooling cannot teach children to read and write standard Spanish, and since most of them understand English and do not insist on being addressed in Spanish, grandchildren may get little practice in speaking Spanish. (285)

Zentella's research suggested that the English-only movement's plan to relegate heritage language instruction to private studies was really just an effective way to ensure that students developed little rhetorical proficiency in their home languages.[15] Reinforcing the argument made by the National Language Policy nine years earlier, Zentella concluded that the entire nation, not just smaller linguistic communities, had compelling reasons and even a responsibility to provide material and social support for heritage language and bilingual education.

Of course, these arguments for communal responsibility in creating appropriate conditions for heritage language and multilingual education conflicted with political conservatives' frustrations with "big government" and increased public spending. Indeed, not only did English-only supporters believe that removing bilingual services would motivate people to learn English, but they also argued that it would no longer waste the public's money on immigrants and language minorities who simply had to work harder to achieve their language-learning goals. The LPC, on the other hand, saw the language policy as a matter of justice, a principle worth striving to enact since it was one of the nation's founding principles. One sees in the National Language Policy, the LPC's letter to schools officials and political leaders, Smitherman's article, and Zentella's monograph a concerted effort to highlight the political, economic, and social gains the entire populace could enjoy when the language policy was embedded within a larger policy effort to ease the transition of linguistic minorities and immigrants into the life of the larger community.

The National Language Policy's call for changing the material conditions for language learning in the United States, then, was a second critical aspect of its work, drawing necessary attention to how a multilingual public sphere could become a reality. Through the policy statement, the accompanying brochure, and other related texts, the LPC continually reinforced its claim that a National Language Policy should address not only language use and education but also a broad range of social and economic concerns that affect people's ability to access language classes, to put languages to meaningful use, and to contribute to the overall well-being of themselves, their families, and their communities and nation. Echoing Smitherman's opinion in her 1987 *College English* article, the National Language Policy and its accompanying brochure called for rhetoric and composition scholars to be civically engaged, providing public leadership aimed at improving the social, cultural, and political environments that influence students' literacy development. The National Language Policy obliged scholars to work in schools and within local political networks to help make multilingual learning a national educational project and to create opportunities for students to use many different languages in public spaces.

Inventing a Pedagogical Theory of the National Language Policy

The LPC's immediate concerns in the late 1980s were to counter the English-only movement and persuade compositionists and the broader public that building a greater public commitment to multilingualism would reaffirm the nation's ideals. The LPC was dissolved for a two-year period in 1993 and 1994, as the CCCC Officers Committee believed that efforts to monitor the English-only movement "could be accomplished outside of a committee" (CCCC Officers Committee, Meeting Minutes, 15 March 1994). Smitherman wrote a letter to the CCCC Executive Committee on 9 March 1994, arguing that "there is still a real need for [the LPC] to exist," not only to monitor the English-only movement but also to further "explain the CCCC [National] Language Policy and demonstrate its value." Indeed, as Harvey Daniels explained in the preface to the NCTE Commission on Language's 1990 collection *Not Only English: Affirming America's Multilingual Heritage*, the need remained to address many composition scholars' concerns about working in linguistically diverse classrooms. Daniels observed that many teachers had developed troubling ideas about the relationship between English-only policies and the English language arts classroom. He explained, for instance, that many teachers believed English-only laws would not affect their work inside the classroom since they already taught English, not foreign languages or bilingual education (Daniels, "Preface" viii). Moreover, many English teachers believed it was in their best interest to support English-only legislation because it added even greater weight to the work they did in teaching English to all people, both native and nonnative speakers alike (viii). These beliefs informed teaching practices that denied students opportunities to use their language resources as a foundation for English learning. In this way, such beliefs also created negative classroom climates that further alienated linguistic-minority students. The presence of such beliefs inside the profession undoubtedly fueled Smitherman's drive to bring back the LPC.

Her arguments proved to be persuasive. By 1995, the LPC had been reconstituted by the CCCC Officers Committee, and as Smitherman had promised, it set about demonstrating the National Language Policy's value. Significantly, however, the LPC took a long-term approach to this work. It undertook a substantial project to better understand the sources of teachers' ideas about language and linguistic diversity and to use these findings to develop strategies for implementing the values at the heart of the National Language Policy into composition pedagogy. In taking up this work, the LPC would ultimately produce a variety of texts that incorporated the National Language Policy into the field's research agenda, teacher-training programs, curricular initiatives, and day-to-day teaching activities. Committee members created a proposal for an extensive survey of composition teachers, generated a report based on that survey that highlighted teachers' attitudes toward and knowledge of language diversity, and produced an essay collection that directly addressed these attitudes and deepened teachers' knowledge such that they could better help students draw on their diverse literacies as resources for learning. The scope of the LPC's work reflects the committee's understanding that shifting the intellectual foundations of the profession required not simply a to-do list of classroom activities but rather a sustained effort to probe the attitudes and deeply held beliefs about diversity, language learning goals, and teacher responsibility that inform pedagogical norms.

It must be noted that in several early outlines and drafts of the National Language Policy brochure, the LPC did discuss pedagogical strategies for asserting the legitimacy of students' native dialects and languages. Specifically, the LPC recommended in these drafts that teachers make students' languages and language-learning experiences an explicit topic for classroom discussion and student research. The LPC also encouraged teachers to respond to students' writing in ways that would build their confidence in the cultural value and communicative potential of their home languages. For example, one early draft of the brochure suggested that teachers foster discussion with students about "how children acquire their mother tongue," "what motivates [people] to learn other languages and dialects," and how "social and cultural forces... have shaped and changed language" (CCCC Language Policy Committee, "Outline/Draft" 4). This draft also asked teachers to create an atmosphere of respect for students' home languages and dialects by "respond[ing] to and evaluat[ing] students' speaking and writing in light of [their] own humane understanding of language and current linguistic research" (4). As we have already seen, however, the final draft of the National Language Policy and its accompanying brochure focused solely on engaging and redirecting rhetorical commonplaces the English-only movement used to support its call for linguistic conformity.

This decision to edit the teaching discussion out of the National Language Policy brochure in part seems to reflect the committee's belief that the situation called for asserting a civic identity for the CCCC and working to fill the "language leadership vacuum" in public policy debates (Smitherman, "Lessons" 30). This policy statement and brochure offered a different way of talking about how America's linguistic identity could revitalize the nation's ideals. But the LPC's choice not to explicitly discuss the pedagogical implications of the National Language Policy in the brochure does not mean the committee members were ignoring the need to address teachers' classroom concerns.

The situation facing the LPC was that its appeals for a "humane understanding" of language ran into those teachers who, as Rodriguez described them, "were unsentimental about the responsibility" to demand that students speak and write in English only (19). For these teachers, a "humane pedagogy" was one in which they enforced an English-only policy in the classroom so that students "learn the language of public society" and use it with "assurance" (19, 22). Victor Villanueva, who joined the LPC when it was reconstituted in the mid-1990s, interrogated this pedagogical stance in a 1987 *English Journal* article. Here he argued that Rodriguez's romanticized descriptions of his teachers problematically allowed other teachers to feel comfortable in their decisions to ban native languages and dialects in the classroom. Villanueva believed that Rodriguez's story appealed to many teachers because in it the "complexities of the minority are rendered simply—not easy—but easily understood" ("Whose Voice" 19). As such, Villanueva argued, Rodriguez's narrative permitted teachers to feel as if they understood not only the difficult decision students faced but also the right choice for students to make: sacrifice their home languages in order to learn English and gain a public identity. Villanueva's insights underscored the fact that the LPC needed to do more than simply provide teachers with a list of classroom activities that would promote language diversity. Instead, the committee had to probe the sources of teachers' knowledge of and attitudes toward nonstandardized languages. This self-examination would be a first step toward helping teachers reimagine their classrooms as spaces where students developed a range of rhetorical and linguistic skills they could use to negotiate the varying and sometimes conflicting cultural demands from families, communities, schools, and jobs.

Archival evidence reveals how the LPC used the National Language Policy as just the first piece in a long-term strategy for transforming teachers' "humane understanding" toward linguistic diversity and writing pedagogy. To create a stronger foundation for building a National Language Policy-inspired pedagogy, the LPC proposed in 1995 to conduct a survey that would "tap into [English language arts educators'] socially constructed knowledge about language matters" (CCCC Language Policy Committee, "Proposal" 1). More specifically, the committee wanted to learn what teachers knew about the relationship between language and culture, where they acquired this knowledge, and how they put this knowledge to use in the classroom. The LPC explained to the CCCC Executive Committee that gaining this insight would help them know what strategies they needed to develop and where they needed to implement them in order to transform English language arts education into a cornerstone of a national multilingual pedagogy (2).

LPC members conducted the survey from 1996 to 1998, and as they analyzed their data they identified the types of knowledge and training that teachers needed to create classrooms that fostered multidialectical and multilingual literacies. As it presented its key findings in the 2000 *Language Knowledge and Awareness Survey* report, the LPC noted that two-thirds of NCTE and CCCC members had not heard of the Students' Right resolution or the National Language Policy. This lack of awareness manifested itself in two significant ways. First, theories of language diversity had not been incorporated into most teacher-training programs, even as 95.5 percent of respondents said that teachers should take a course on this topic (12). Second, those teachers who had not received training on the specific topics of African American English or American dialects tended to believe that the aim of the writing course, particularly for students from nonstandardized language backgrounds, should be to learn Standardized English only (12). In the conclusion of its report, then, the LPC argued that implementing a National Language Policy-inspired pedagogy in part required developing training programs for both secondary and postsecondary English teachers that would allow them to study relevant social and regional dialects and introduce them to pedagogical strategies for teaching English as a Second Language (ESL) and Standardized English as a second dialect (ESD). The LPC also explained that training programs needed to give teachers opportunities to make explicit their attitudes toward the role of nonstandardized languages in students' lives as well as to heighten their awareness of how their attitudes toward students' languages—attitudes they might display either overtly or covertly—influenced teachers' practices and students' performances in the writing classroom.

True to its word in the 1995 proposal (2), the Language Policy Committee applied the survey results to help develop strategies for using the National Language Policy to reshape rhetoric and composition pedagogy. These strategies appeared in the 2003 essay collection *Language Diversity in the Classroom: From Intention to Practice*, coedited by Smitherman and Villanueva. This book features essays written by eight current members of the LPC. Grounded in knowledge they gained through the LPC survey, the authors develop strategies for countering the English-only impulse guiding many teachers' practice and for incorporating the values at the heart of the CCCC's language policies into college-level writing classrooms and teacher-training programs. Elaine Richardson's essay examines the survey data in detail to better understand how teachers' raced, classed, gendered, and generational backgrounds likely influence how they respond to nonstandardized dialects and other languages in the composition classroom, and she concludes this fine-grained analysis with an invitation to "deeper reflection as we consider what we as a profession can do to improve the delivery of services to the diverse students (including White ones) who enter our classes"

("Race" 63). In response to this invitation, essays by Arnetha Ball and Rashidah Jaami' Muhammad as well as Gail Okawa describe how to conduct teacher-training courses that give participants opportunities to deepen their knowledge about nonstandardized language varieties and to reflect on the source of their attitudes toward these languages. Kim Brian Lovejoy, meanwhile, focuses more explicitly on composition pedagogy as he presents a thorough description of various reading and writing assignments that ask students to explore linguistic varieties in their cultures as well as to experiment with different dialects in their own writing. Significantly, *Language Diversity in the Classroom* crafts a holistic approach to improving writing pedagogy in the spirit of the Students' Right resolution and the National Language Policy, an approach that reflects the committee's findings about the links between teacher knowledge, attitudes, and practices.

The *Language Knowledge Awareness Survey* report and the *Language Diversity in the Classroom* book help us to reenvision the National Language Policy not as an answer to all of teachers' pedagogical problems but rather as a text that prompts teachers to reflect on and even reform the values that guide their pedagogies. Viewing the LPC's work over two decades reframes our perspective of the National Language Policy as a text meant to prompt teaching innovations and political activity over the long term rather than as a short-term fix for broken pedagogical practices.

Moreover, the LPC's long-term effort to outline a pedagogy that builds linguistic diversity underscores the fact that English-only laws would carry important consequences for English language arts classrooms. While the National Language Policy encouraged teachers to envision themselves as civic leaders within their communities, as agents of change working to prepare "everyone to participate in the life of this multicultural nation" (CCCC, "National Language Policy" 1), the other materials created by the LPC, particularly the *Language Knowledge and Awareness Survey* report and the *Language Diversity in the Classroom* volume that resulted from it, performed a different rhetorical function, namely, helping teachers to understand why English-only laws threatened composition classrooms and how they could encourage students to develop rhetorical competence not just in Standardized English but also in a variety of linguistic registers and languages. Scholars, then, should not read the National Language Policy alone. Instead, they should consider how all of the LPC's documents worked together to transform the rhetoric and composition classroom from a space where students learn English only to one where students develop critical awareness of how multiple languages and dialects do in fact reshape and reinvigorate the national identity.

Asserting the National Language Policy's Efficacy for Present-Day Composition Studies

The CCCC National Language Policy did not stop the English-only movement at the state level, as twenty-eight states now have a law declaring English as their official language. The National Language Policy did not radically change conservatives' minds about what linguistic minorities must do in order to prove they are committed to America and its ideals. And although the U.S. Congress has never passed an ELA, it also has never adopted legislation that actively promotes multilingualism in the United States. All that being said, this archival study of the National Language Policy and the LPC's work does give us new ways to read the policy and understand its significance for the field of rhetoric and composition.

Reexamining the National Language Policy within its original political and social context reveals a rhetorical strategy for engaging in language policy debates that relies on identifying with opponents' ideas about what the nation's common good should be. The policy acknowledged the conservative values and beliefs that inform many people's support of the English-only movement, but at the same time it reimagined how these ideals could truly come to life in a multilingual society. This approach to countering the English-only movement stood in contrast to those of composition scholars writing in the late 1980s who focused on exposing nativist, racist, and xenophobic elements of the English-only movement. The work of Vivian Davis, Elliot Judd ("Federal"), and James Sledd ("Anglo-Conformity"), among others, argued that the English-only movement's rhetorical strategy simply appealed to citizens' base emotions. Davis, Judd, and Sledd charged the English-only movement with presenting a dangerously simplified view of where society's problems came from and how they could best be resolved. This chapter's analysis of Ronald Reagan, E. D. Hirsch, S. I. Hayakawa, Linda Chávez, Richard Rodriguez, and others does indeed support these claims, particularly in terms of how the United States is envisioned as a "shining city on the hill" where cultural, ethnic, and linguistic identities that differ from white, middle-class social norms can and must be erased if this "city" is to survive.

What this chapter's reading of the National Language Policy also reveals, however, is a different analytical and rhetorical strategy from the one pursued by Davis, Judd, Sledd, and others. The CCCC policy is grounded on the assumption that many people who support the English-only movement do so because of what they perceive to be their good intentions of helping immigrants and minorities succeed and contribute to public life. Indeed, as one could see in Richard Rodriguez's *Hunger of Memory* or Trudy Sundberg's 1988 letter in *English Journal*, even several English teachers supported the English-only policy for what they believed to be professionally and civically ethical reasons. Many backers of the English-only movement, in other words, simply would not recognize themselves in representations that portray ELAs as the work of racists or nativists. The rhetorical strategy employed by the LPC instead tried to open up space for acknowledging shared values of individual freedom, communal responsibility, and national unity while also proposing a different vision of how the nation's civic life could be revitalized. The LPC's work shows its efforts, through a variety of texts, to continually discover new ways to talk persuasively about linguistic minorities participating more fully in U.S. public life.

As part of this rhetorical effort, the LPC challenged and redirected public support for ELAs by presenting an actual policy alternative. The National Language Policy did not spell out specific details on how to create a multilingual public sphere, but it did draw attention to three types of educational programs—English language, heritage language, and second language education—that had to be politically and fiscally supported in order for this goal to be achieved. The CCCC's policy alternative focused on actively creating opportunities for people to learn languages. This approach stood in sharp contrast to the English-only movement's focus on taking away services as a means to motivate people to learn English as well as the Reagan administration's political strategy to erode governmental support in the name of promoting individual and communal responsibility for solving social problems. In proposing a specific English-plus alternative to English-only policies, the LPC highlighted the need for those fighting for language rights to do more than simply disparage ELAs.

A related lesson from this study is that the National Language Policy envisioned roles for composition scholars outside of the classroom, positioning them as civic leaders who could guide public debates about language policy, linguistic diversity, and literacy education. As the LPC acknowledged the financial and political support needed to make its policy vision a reality, it situated the struggle for language rights within the larger political effort to ensure greater economic and social justice for marginalized groups within the United States. Through texts such as its letter to legislators and school superintendents as well as Smitherman's 1987 *College English* essay, the LPC exposed the literacy myth on which the English-only argument and the Reagan administration's social policies were founded, namely, the belief that hard work—such as learning English—alone could help people to access the economic and political mainstream. As Smitherman noted, much work needed to be done to ensure that linguistic and ethnic minorities could participate fully in U.S. public life. Through activities like formally registering the CCCC as a member of EPIC, the LPC aligned compositionists with groups fighting for civil, economic, and social justice for marginalized groups, such as the American Jewish Congress, Caribbean Education and Legal Defense Fund, Chinese for Affirmative Action, Disciples of Christ, Haitian Refugee Center, IRATE (Coalition of Massachusetts Trade Unions), Mexican American Legal Defense and Educational Fund, and the New York Association for New Americans. Indeed, while the National Language Policy brochure called on compositionists to "strive to include all citizens of all language communities in the positive development of our daily activities" (CCCC, "National Language Policy" 5), these affiliations and many other aspects of the LPC's work made it clear that a host of social and economic issues needed to be addressed to help linguistic minorities live in situations where they could reasonably devote time and energy toward working with fellow citizens to solve community, city, state, and national problems. The LPC's activities, in other words, underscore the fact that any language policy must attend to more than just language issues.

At the same time that this study of the National Language Policy and the LPC highlights the need to engage larger political and economic struggles for marginalized communities, including linguistic minorities, it also speaks to the need for social activist groups to pay attention to language issues. The LPC rightly argued that there can be no democratic justice without linguistic justice. The National Language Policy brochure explicitly stated that preserving basic human rights required providing "education, social services, legal services, medical services, and protective signing for linguistic minorities in their own language" (5). Just as important as preserving these basic human rights, however, was preserving people's civil right to participate in the nation's political life in whatever language would allow them to confidently express their ideas. The

LPC, in other words, underscored the fact that while compositionists must attend to the material and the political realities facing linguistic minorities, social activist groups must attend to language rights. An ELA, just like discriminatory economic and social policies, would isolate linguistic minorities and further diminish the cultural majority's understanding of marginalized groups' political and social needs as well as the contributions they can and do want to make in public life. While English-only policies reinscribed a notion of democracy in which linguistic and cultural conformity was needed to ensure national unity, the National Language Policy rested on a belief that national unity can be strengthened by expanding opportunities for all citizens to dialogue across lines of linguistic difference, especially by teaching more Americans to listen, read, speak, and write the languages of political and cultural minorities. Social activists need to see how ensuring peoples' right to use heritage languages or other nonprivileged language varieties in public spaces, and creating environments in which they can indeed do so, can help propel linguistic minorities to contribute to efforts at solving local and national problems.

This chapter also prompts us to rethink how we assess the National Language Policy, challenging a common perception that the policy, in Bruce Horner's words, "attracted little attention" ("Students' Right" 41) and had little influence on the field of composition studies. Because one of a language policy's primary rhetorical functions is to provide a framework for future action, it needs to be understood in relation to the other texts and other activities that accompany and follow from it, especially when such projects take a long time to develop or do not explicitly name a specific policy as an influence. The analysis in this chapter adopts a longer view that accounts for the multifaceted nature of the LPC's effort to implement the National Language Policy into the field's mission and daily activities. The range of archival and published materials documenting the LPC's work demands that scholars not isolate the National Language Policy when arguing whether or not it was a successful document. The policy should be read alongside the LPC's other texts and within the longer time period of the committee's work in order to understand how a language policy statement can shape the teaching philosophy, research activities, and even civic engagement of rhetoric and composition scholars.

In many ways, this long-term perspective on the 1988 National Language Policy and the LPC's work over the fifteen years following its initial publication simply underscores the long stretches of time needed to process new perspectives on language diversity. Scholars need time and opportunities to explore a language policy's implications for the discipline and the broader public and to invent new research projects, teaching and teacher-training practices, and civic leadership activities that reflect the values underpinning these language policies. Indeed, Smitherman has adopted a similar perspective when assessing the Students' Right resolution. Writing in 1999, she maintained that the 1974 resolution's influence could be seen in the National Language Policy. This latter text, she argued, reflected the fact that compositionists' "sociolinguistic and political maturity about language rights issues" had evolved over the fourteen years they had to consider and grapple with the Students' Right resolution since its initial publication (369). Viewing the National Language Policy from a similar long-term perspective asks one to consider not simply whether or not the language policy brought immediate changes in public debate on English-only policies but also how the text brought the topic of multilingualism into rhetoric and composition's range of disciplinary concerns, an influence that has manifested itself in a paradigm shift in the field's research, teaching, and service projects dealing with language diversity. Texts such as Horner, Lu, and Matsuda's 2010 edited collection *Cross-Language Relations in Composition*, research projects such as Damián Baca's work on Mestiz@ scripts, and Michelle Hall Kells's explorations of Tejano code-switching, pedagogical interventions such as Jaime Mejía's and Daniel Villa's efforts to help students strategically use Spanish language varieties in their writing, and curricular innovations such as Emily O. Wittman's creation of a translation studies course for all undergraduate English majors do not explicitly name the National Language Policy as an influence, but their attention to multilingual communication practices reflects a paradigm shift in the field's publication and teaching practices that can be traced in part to the CCCC policy.

Adopting this long-term perspective in assessing the National Language Policy allows one to understand the policy's significance not only for composition's research and teaching missions but also for scholars' engagement in present-day language policy debates. During the past two decades, English-only laws have not often won when challenged in the court of law, but the English-only movement has garnered much greater support in the court of public opinion. Many present and pressing political controversies, particularly those surrounding immigration policy, have further deteriorated the climate of respect for language diversity in U.S. society.

To appreciate how the social and political atmosphere for the nation's ethnolinguistic minorities has become negatively charged, one can look to the controversy centered on a Spanish-language version of the U.S. national anthem, entitled "Nuestro Himno" ("Our Anthem"), that was released during the 2005 congressional debate on immigration policy.[16] Critics expressed outrage at the singing of the U.S. national anthem in a language other than English (Wides-Munoz). Senator Lamar Alexander, a Republican from Tennessee, went so far as to propose a resolution "giving senators an opportunity to remind the country why we sing our National Anthem in English" (qtd. in "Sen. Alexander to Introduce"). Alexander echoed the same concerns Senator Hayakawa had expressed two decades earlier, stating:

> We Americans are a unique nation of immigrants united by a common language and a belief in principles expressed in our Declaration of Independence and our Constitution, not by our race, ancestry or country of origin. We are proud of the countries we have come from, but we are prouder to be Americans. (qtd. in "Sen. Alexander to Introduce")

For Senator Alexander, one's use of a language other than English signals that person's choice to affiliate with his or her ethnolinguistic community and necessarily to make oneself an outsider to the common culture that the senator wants to preserve. Moreover, Senator Alexander sees one's decision to use non-English languages, like the singers do in "Nuestro Himno," as a statement to reject the principles of justice, freedom, and equality uniting all Americans. Here, then, Senator Alexander defines an American civic identity in "either/or" terms: one either strengthens America by learning and using English, or one rejects a true American identity by speaking some other language.

This concern with preserving the seemingly intimate connection between the English language and the values expressed in America's treasured political texts manifested itself again in H.R. 997, the English Language Unity Act of 2009. In addition to declaring English to be the nation's official language, this legislation also aimed to "avoid misconstructions of the English language texts of the laws of the United States" ("English Language Unity Act of 2009"). The text of H.R. 997 suggested that such measures were needed in order "to provide for the general welfare of the United States." Whereas the National Language Policy is grounded on a belief that national unity can be forged across linguistic difference, the English Language Unity Act seeks to reinscribe a narrow view of how citizens can carry out the nation's democratic principles in their daily lives.

And most recently, Arizona has begun targeting teachers who speak English with an accent. In April 2010 Arizona's education department began evaluating instructors who teach English to nonnative speakers, auditing them "on things such as comprehensible pronunciation, correct grammar, and good writing" (Jordan). Adela Santa Cruz, director of Program Effectiveness in the Arizona Education Department's Office of English Language Acquisition Services, explains that teachers whose language skills are deemed to be inadequate are assigned to classes to help them improve their English, including in some instance an accent-reduction course. If teachers' grammatical or pronunciation skills don't sufficiently improve after such linguistic retraining, then school districts must decide either to fire the teachers or reassign them to classes where they would not be working with English-language learners. Santa Cruz claims that the policy protects students' interests, stressing that evaluators only pinpoint teachers' accents "when pronunciation affects comprehensibility" (Jordan). Miriam Jordan of the *Wall Street Journal*, however, suggests that some evaluations seem to have blurred the line between a teacher's ability to communicate effectively with students and his or her ability to speak "unaccented," grammatically correct English. Jordan notes, "State auditors have reported to the district that some teachers pronounce words such as violet as 'biolet,' think as 'tink' and swallow the ending sounds of words, as they sometimes do in Spanish."

This current policy's focus on teachers' accents and pronunciation is particularly discriminatory in light of an earlier English-only education policy instituted in 2000, when voters passed a ballot initiative requiring that school instruction be conducted only in English. Hundreds of teachers whose first language was Spanish had been hired by the state in the 1990s to teach bilingual education, but as Jordan explains, after the 2000 English-only educational policy was put in place, many of these teachers were forced to switch from teaching their subjects in Spanish to teaching them in English. Ultimately, Arizona's current policy relies on a belief that a teachers' inability to speak unaccented English—in reality, a teachers' inability to speak English without a Spanish accent—makes him or her a poor model for students learning English as well as a poor teacher. Ultimately, however, this policy also sends a negative message to students and parents about the value of the languages they bring to the classroom and the cultural and linguistic identities they should look to cultivate (or repress) as they make their way through school.

The National Language Policy puts these types of issues, ones related to multilingualism in both schools and society, on rhetoric and composition's disciplinary map. More importantly, under Geneva Smitherman's leadership, the LPC compelled composition scholars to recognize a civic component to their professional identities and provide greater leadership in public debates over language policy. The language-related anxieties expressed by Senator Alexander, the English Language Unity Act, and Arizona's policy against teachers with accents, among others, show that the need for this language leadership still exists. The CCCC National Language Policy can guide scholars in their efforts to articulate a vision of how the nation's democratic ideals can be revitalized through a greater public commitment to linguistic diversity.

3 THE DEFENSE DEPARTMENT'S NATIONAL SECURITY LANGUAGE POLICY
COMPOSING LOCAL RESPONSES TO THE UNITED STATES' CRITICAL LANGUAGE NEEDS

> The Secretary of Defense . . . wants his young soldiers who are on the front lines of finding these killers to be able to speak their language and be able to listen to the people in the communities in which they live. That makes sense, doesn't it, to have a language-proficient military—to have people that go into the far reaches of this world and be able to communicate in the villages and towns and rural areas and urban centers, to protect the American people. We need intelligence officers who, when somebody says something in Arabic or Farsi or Urdu, know what they're talking about. That's what we need. We need diplomats—when we send them out to help us convince governments that we've got to join together and fight these terrorists who want to destroy life and promote an ideology that is so backwards it's hard to believe. These diplomats need to speak that language.
> —President George W. Bush, 2006

SPEAKING BEFORE THE 2006 U.S. UNIVERSITY PRESIDENTS' SUMMIT on International Education, President George W. Bush unveiled the National Security Language Initiative, which put $114 million toward efforts to improve language education as a means to secure the nation. This initiative aimed to expand the number of Americans mastering what military and intelligence officials have labeled "critical-need" languages, particularly Arabic, Chinese, Russian, Hindi, and Farsi. Throughout his speech, President Bush described foreign language education as a means to protect the United States in the short-term by "defeating [terrorists] in foreign battlefields so they don't strike us here at home." He also explained how foreign language education could protect the country in the long term by helping to "defeat this notion about . . . our bullying concept of freedom," as learning the languages of other countries and cultures could be a way "to reach out to somebody" and let that person "know that I'm interested in not only how you talk but how you live."

President Bush's National Security Language Initiative is one piece of an emerging, post-September 11 national security language policy that proposes to develop multilingualism in more U.S. citizens. In one way, such a policy challenges English-only legislation, as it proposes that U.S. students learn to communicate in multiple languages rather than in Standardized English only. In other respects, the national security language policy is based on troubling notions about language, identity, and the pedagogical aims of language arts teaching. The Modern Language Association (MLA) has initiated several activities in response to this policy debate, proposing alternatives to a language policy based solely on military concerns. Even though this language policy ostensibly pertains only to foreign language education, English-speaking scholars working in rhetoric and composition studies should also put this policy on their disciplinary map. Engaging this debate can invigorate the professional and civic commitments articulated in the CCCC's own language policy statements, for the emerging national security language policy stands to influence language arts education, students' literacy practices, and their concept of civic action. At a more fundamental level, this language policy debate also demands composition scholars' participation because it involves questions about who defines the nation's language needs and how language arts education should aim to meet them.

As the two previous chapters suggest, the field of composition studies has already developed theoretical and pedagogical frameworks for promoting multidialectalism and multilingualism in the United States. These frameworks, however, were constructed as challenges to government policies and teaching practices explicitly concerned with English, specifically, policies and practices that would make Standardized English *the* language of communication in the U.S. public sphere and in its classrooms. The CCCC published the National Language Policy in 1988 as a counterstatement to the English-only movement, calling for composition scholars to encourage all U.S. citizens to learn and use multiple languages as a means to "unify diverse American communities" and "enlarge our view of what is human" (5). More recently, scholars such as Bruce Horner, John Trimbur, Suresh Canagarajah, Min-Zhan Lu, Gail Hawisher, Cynthia Selfe, Paul Kei Matsuda, and Anis Bawarshi have focused their efforts on just this type of work, advocating for and exploring ways to redesign U.S. composition instruction so that students develop writing proficiency in multiple languages, not just Standardized English only. In *Cross-Language Relations in Composition*, a 2010 essay collection to which these scholars contributed, Horner argues that "students need to learn to work in their writing within, on, among, and across a variety of Englishes and languages" ("From 'English Only'" 3). Defining the goal for literacy education in this way suggests that while the visions outlined in the Students' Right resolution and National Language Policy have not been realized, these documents continue to serve as significant prompts to theoretical and pedagogical invention.

While composition scholars have responded to various manifestations of English-only policy in the United States, the present debate about a national security language policy provides another opportunity to transform language practice and literacy education in ways expressed by the Students' Right resolution and the National Language Policy. Rhetoric and composition scholars, as well as applied linguists working in English departments, could use the present language policy debate to coalesce with foreign language scholars and linguistic-minority community leaders to promote, design, and implement multilingual language arts programs that advance the goals of linguistic human rights (Skutnabb-Kangas 496–505) and greater civic dialogue between linguistic minorities and the monolingual English-speaking majority. The change from the presidential administration of George W. Bush to that of Barack Obama makes this language policy debate no less pressing, as national security, international diplomacy, and education have remained high-priority items on the federal government's agenda. Compositionists can work with foreign-language scholars at their schools and in organizations such as the MLA to advocate for implementing this policy in ways that, in the words of the CCCC National Language Policy, "include all citizens of all language communities in the positive development of our daily activities" (5).

As they created this national security language policy, President Bush, high-ranking U.S. Department of Defense (DOD) officials, scholars at the Defense Language Institute, and several congressional leaders were motivated in part by retired Israeli general Arie Amit's 2002 warning that the United States would not win its global war against terrorists unless it understands "their language, their literature, and their poetry" (qtd. in Porter 4).[1] The emerging language policy provides financial resources to motivate schools to refocus their programs on these languages and these literatures. Rhetoric and composition scholars should not deny the significance of national security needs as part of what a multilingual society should be able to address. This chapter, however, analyzes the effects that follow from framing a national language policy in ways that tightly link "language instruction" to "national security." This chapter also draws on the Students' Right resolution and National Language Policy to envision ways that the emerging national security language policy could better attend to the political, social, and cultural needs of marginalized language communities within U.S. borders.

With this purpose in mind, this chapter first analyzes the policy debate concerning a national security "language crisis," highlighting in particular how several DOD documents, President Bush's National Security Language Initiative, and congressional legislative proposals presented designs for a national educational infrastructure grounded in definitions of foreign languages as military tools. The chapter then moves from critique to action as it builds on the analysis in chapters 1 and 2. This chapter demonstrates how to read the Students' Right resolution and National Language Policy as texts that prompt invention of local-level strategies that rhetoric and composition scholars can pursue—designing research assignments that ask students to explore linguistic diversity and language policy, collaborating with their colleagues in foreign language departments, and writing institutional policy at their colleges and universities—to shape the emerging national language policy so that it promotes multilingualism as a means of dialoguing to understand and resolve differences rather than translating to infiltrate and defeat enemies.

Defining the Military's "Critical Language Needs"

The U.S. military began to identify a national security "language crisis" as it increasingly faced new types of post–Cold War threats, particularly from terrorist groups. Historian Clifford Porter of the Defense Language Institute, the U.S. military's primary language school,[2] published a white paper in 2002 outlining the language-related dimensions of combating terrorism and other forms of "asymmetrical warfare" (1), which involves surprise and deception rather than conventional, direct applications of military force. Such terrorist forces are not "strictly organized military units," like those the United States could more easily track behind the Iron Curtain during the Cold War, but rather are "less-predictable enemies that may or may not fight on conventional battlefields and hide in the hinterlands of the world where the languages spoken are rarely studied in the Western world" (1–2). The asymmetrical nature of the Global War on Terrorism, argues Porter, demands that the military invest in developing its human resources rather than sophisticated satellites and weapons: "When the enemy is unconventional, hiding with civilian populations and motivated by an ideology that targets civilians, the foreign language capability of intelligence and special operations assets is one of the critical tools to unlocking the secrets of the enemy in his hiding places" (3). Moreover, Porter explains, while satellite technologies and global positioning systems can help the U.S. military to know where enemy forces might be located, these and other technologies cannot tell U.S. commanders "how the enemy thinks from the strategic to the tactical levels of war" (1). DOD officials realize that such insight must instead come through learning the languages and understanding the cultures of principal actors in terrorist networks.

For U.S. military and intelligence officials, the terrorist attacks of 11 September 2001 illustrated the severity of the national security "language crisis" in the DOD and related agencies such as the Central Intelligence Agency (CIA) and the Federal Bureau of Investigation (FBI). Inquiries into those terrorist attacks led to suggestions that the government's insufficient language resources contributed to its inability to anticipate and prevent the attacks. Several reports, including one published by the 9/11 Commission, warned that the military and intelligence communities did not have enough linguists and translators on staff to sustain a full-scale counterterrorism effort (National Commission 78, 92). The U.S. General Accounting Office (GAO) similarly found that at the FBI, "shortages of language-proficient staff have resulted in the accumulation of thousands of hours of audiotapes and pages of writing material that have not been reviewed or translated" (14). In this same January 2002 report, the GAO concluded that the army did not have "the linguistic capacity to support two concurrent major theaters of war, as planners require" (15). The 9/11 Commission Report, of course, levels its critique primarily at interagency communication problems within the U.S. intelligence community, but it also implies a direct relationship between the U.S. military and intelligence communities' language resources and the security of the American people. In short, the 9/11 and GAO reports encourage readers to imagine key terrorist communications lost and buried under mountains of undeciphered messages at the DOD, FBI, and CIA.

Examining the Military's Linguistic Readiness

These government findings led DOD leaders to examine the military's language situation, and from these studies military leaders identified two primary factors fueling this language crisis, one dealing with the military itself and the other originating in U.S. schools. The first reason concerns the military's language policy in terms of both attitudes toward and management of foreign-language skills. Several DOD self-studies revealed that a narrow understanding of "language skills" and "language needs" has long been engrained in U.S. military culture. DOD officials noted in the 2004 *National Security Strategy* report that in many instances, U.S. combatant commanders think about the military's language needs solely in terms of linguists who translate intelligence-related texts. These commanders, the report concludes, "lack understanding of the multiple dimensions of language capability" they could deploy while planning and executing military operations (qtd. in U.S. Dept. of Defense, *Defense* 2004, 14).[3] Moreover, U.S. command structures have been based on a deep-rooted bias in the military culture that does not regard language competencies as "warfighting skills" (U.S. Dept. of Defense, *Defense* 2005, 3). Because of this lack of understanding and bias, the military has not listed language skills and cultural knowledge as important qualifications for officers seeking assignment to combatant commanders' staffs. In turn, the military has not prioritized language education in its officer training programs. Equally significant, combatant commanders have ignored opportunities to give greater voice on their planning staffs to personnel who already hold relevant language abilities, especially foreign area officers, who possess a unique combination of combat skills; deep knowledge of a region's culture, politics, and economics; and advanced proficiency in speaking, listening, and reading at least one foreign language in a wide range of military, diplomatic, and civic contexts (Science Applications 17–19).

The U.S. military's difficulties in Afghanistan and Iraq have brought to light the effects of limited language and cultural knowledge in planning military operations. A 2004 DOD report notes that senior leaders and planners in Afghanistan and Iraq "cite the lack of qualified language professionals and regional experts as a major shortcoming . . . in initial planning for combat and contingency operations, for the execution of the combat phase, and for post-combat reconstruction and stabilization efforts" (U.S. Dept. of Defense, *Defense* 2004, 29–30). The implications of these shortcomings are clear. When DOD officials and U.S. combatant commanders do not understand all that "language competence" entails and hold deep-rooted biases against language skills, their evaluations of the military's combat readiness do not fully account for its (in)ability to work with coalition forces and to forge common ground and resolve differences with local government officials, military and business leaders, and civilians.

A second contributor to the U.S. national security "language crisis," federal officials contend, has been the field of language arts education itself. The nation's geopolitical and cultural interests have long shaped the infrastructure of U.S. foreign-language education such that a majority of students learn Western European languages such as French, German, and Spanish (Watzke 39–52) rather than Arabic, Dari, Pashto, Farsi, and other languages spoken and written by peoples where the U.S. military has initiated conflict in recent years. In his remarks at the 2004 States Institute on International Education in the Schools, Undersecretary of Defense for Personnel and Readiness David S. C. Chu expressed his disappointment that, according to a 2002 MLA study, "Less Commonly Taught Languages" comprise only 12 percent of all U.S. college-level language enrollments ("Meeting" 5).[4] Chu criticized colleges and universities because these numbers signal their "lack of instructional capacity" in DOD "investment languages": Arabic, Chinese, Farsi, Hindi, Korean, Russian, Turkish, and other central Asian languages (6). While statistical increases in Arabic, Chinese, Hindi, and Tagalog instruction were "heartening," Chu noted these enrollment figures were mostly for introductory courses (6). The DOD, he argued, needs both high schools and colleges to create sustained courses of study in these languages. Chu warned that if language scholars "stay this course" and do not shift their attention to the DOD's critical-need languages, "a large proportion of our American youth will not be prepared for the very different environment in which we find ourselves" (7). Whereas the Students' Right resolution and National Language Policy commit scholar-teachers to promoting multilingualism as a means of enabling greater civic participation by linguistically marginalized groups, Chu maintains that language educators have a responsibility to their students and to the nation to ensure language education builds the nation's security-related language resources. In short, the CCCC language policy statements are, in Smitherman's words, "weapons which language rights warriors can wield against the opponents of linguistic democratization" ("CCCC's Role" 373). Chu, on the other hand, sees the nation's schools as spaces for building new types of foreign-language skills, weapons the U.S. military can wield against the opponents of Western democratization and capitalist expansion.

Having identified these two factors contributing to the national security "language crisis," the DOD offered corresponding strategies for resolving the crisis through language policy. The first strategy involves instituting a new language policy for the DOD, one that better identifies and addresses the military's language needs. Undersecretary Chu assembled a team to create the *Defense Language Transformation Roadmap* that could "transform the way [the DOD] value[s], develop[s], and employ[s] language and regional expertise" (U.S. Dept. of Defense, *Defense* 2004, 6). Finalized in January 2005, the *Roadmap* recognizes foreign-language skills as important tools in military operations. The *Roadmap*, for example, calls on DOD leaders to generate a complete list of the military's language needs for particular missions and personnel roles and to devise an index that measures the military's level of readiness in terms of its language capabilities for specific operations (U.S. Dept. of Defense, *Defense* 2005, 5). It is not immediately clear how the authors of the *Roadmap* expect, at least in the short term, combatant commanders to gain a robust understanding of what foreign-language competence entails and why and where it is specifically needed within operations being planned. Nevertheless, the *Roadmap* does demand that "deep understanding of the cultural, political, military, and economic characteristics of a region must be established and maintained" on every combatant commander's staff (U.S. Dept. of Defense, *Joint Vision 2020* 23; qtd. in Science Applications 8). DOD leaders believe that officers with regional knowledge and linguistic skills must be assigned to combatant commanders' staffs. Doing so, they argue, can improve commanders' ability to understand security situations from a variety of cultural perspectives.

Consistent with its aim to change the DOD's implicit language policy, the *Roadmap* does not stop at the commanders' staff. Instead, it calls for language skills to be deployed strategically throughout the entire military. Toward this end, the *Roadmap* suggests creating tests to identify the kinds and levels of language competence that all U.S. military personnel possess, and it charges U.S. military leaders with deploying these personnel in positions that allow them to use, and thereby maintain, these skills in their day-to-day military activities (11–12). The *Roadmap* tasks the Defense Language Institute with accelerating the pace at which military language professionals develop high-level competencies in reading, listening, and speaking critical-need languages; designing language education courses tailored to military professionals needing lower levels of language proficiency; and developing the institutional capacity "to respond rapidly to emerging language training requirements" (11–12). And finally, the *Roadmap* calls for the DOD to create a plan for recruiting heritage-language speakers and other students who possess "critical need" language skills (6). Ultimately, the *Defense Language Transformation Roadmap* aims to remake the DOD's language policy, proposing actions that will cultivate a new attitude toward foreign language skills in U.S. military culture.

As the DOD *Roadmap* advocates for a change in military leaders' perception of foreign language skills, it crafts a new design for the U.S. armed forces in which commanders deploy language skills as strategically as they do new war-fighting technologies. The *Roadmap* attends to the fact that the U.S. military's language needs extend beyond training personnel to translate intelligence documents, interrogate prisoners of war, or conduct covert operations. Indeed, the *Roadmap* suggests that infusing a deeper linguistic and cultural understanding into all levels of the military can improve its ability to operate effectively with various multinational coalitions and in concert with different government agencies and international organizations.

The *Defense Language Transformation Roadmap*, then, constitutes a new language policy for the U.S. military, one that sees the organization making conscious attempts to develop, manage, and use its pool of foreign language skills. This language policy complements DOD leadership's vision for the twenty-first-century U.S. military, one that gains as much advantage through its personnel's brainpower as through its technological superiority. In short, U.S. military leaders believe the key to waging war more effectively requires not simply creating more technologically sophisticated weaponry but rather gathering, analyzing, and applying information more efficiently (U.S. Joint Chiefs of Staff 20). The DOD language policy fits into this vision, then, as it aims "to ensure the right [language] skills are developed" that enable U.S. military personnel "to shape events, to respond rapidly, and to operate globally" in the twenty-first century (U.S. Dept. of Defense, Office of the Undersecretary 29).[5] Underlying the military's language policy, however, is a belief that there are right and wrong languages for schools to develop and right and wrong ways for these linguistic skills to be deployed—namely, toward the ends of meeting the U.S. military's current needs in its fight against terrorism.

Laying Claim to the Nation's Existing Language Resources

The DOD's *Roadmap* highlights the route along which the military must travel to resolve the national security language crisis, but DOD officials contend that on-ramps must be built to bring U.S. schools and colleges along, as well. They maintain that a broader, nationwide effort is needed to develop language resources that can adequately secure the United States. The DOD tried to initiate this endeavor by convening the "National Language Conference: A Call to Action" in June 2004. This conference, cohosted by the University of Maryland's Center for Advanced Study of Language,[6] brought together various stakeholders in the language policy issue, such as foreign-language scholars from both the secondary and collegiate levels, including Rosemary G. Feal of the MLA, Martha Abbott of Fairfax County (VA) Public Schools and the American Council on the Teaching of Foreign Languages, and Dana Bourgerie of Brigham Young University's National Flagship Program in Chinese; private companies that provide language and localization services, such as Venturi Technology Partners and World Learning for Business; leaders from federal agencies such as the Departments of Justice, Homeland Security, Labor, and Health and Human Services; and the corporate sector, such as Rick Lazio, CEO of the Financial Services Forum, and Bernhard Kohlmeier, director of Product Integration for Microsoft. The DOD brought together these various groups in hopes of creating a national security language policy that would unite the federal government, the private sector, and the nation's schools in a coordinated effort to develop the U.S.'s resources in "critical need" languages.

A significant aspect of the National Language Conference proved to be differences in how presenters defined "the nation" and its "critical language needs." Several presenters argued that a national language policy must account for a variety of cultural, social, and political concerns both abroad and in the United States. Some federal representatives, for example, attempted to expand definitions of the nation's language needs to recognize non-English-speaking citizens' claims to equal access and civil rights as well as to address the general lack of cultural understanding and empathy for linguistic minorities. For example, Marijke van der Heide described the Justice Department's insufficient pool of translators for federal trials. Samuel Mok, meanwhile, outlined how the Labor

Department could benefit from more bilingual employees to service Limited-English Proficiency small-business owners and workers, and Deena Jang underscored the Department of Health and Human Services' desire to recruit more heritage-language speakers into the medical field in order to remove cultural and linguistic barriers that limit many citizens' access to the health care system. These federal representatives argued that a national language policy should acknowledge the existence of linguistic minority communities in the U.S. and conceive of the nation's needs more broadly than the military proposed.

Undersecretary Chu and U.S. Representative Rush Holt, on the other hand, used their conference presentations to define the military's language needs as the nation's sole pressing language need. Both men described the nation as a citizenry unsafe at home because of the military's language shortfall in overseas theaters of war. In his opening address, Representative Holt argued that the September 11 terrorist attacks on U.S. soil occurred because vital intelligence gathered in foreign countries had been "lost in translation" (1). Chu, meanwhile, explained that while "national security and national interest could once be discussed in terms of physical borders and cultural boundaries, it is indisputably no longer so. National security concerns take us from the streets of Manhattan to the mountains of Afghanistan and to the resort cities of Bali" ("Influence" 3). Although Chu collapsed a distinction between U.S. language needs *here* inside the United States and *there* in other countries, both he and Holt talked about the nation's language needs in terms of understanding a "foreign" element inside what seems to be America's politically, culturally, and linguistically homogeneous border. In other words, they reinforced an understanding of non-English languages as an "outside" element, as resources reflecting someone's allegiance to cultures or political institutions foreign to the United States.

Moreover, Holt and Chu repeatedly echoed the conference's theme, "a call to action," as a way to table debate about the ideal aims of language education. Chu, for example, did admit that it is unfortunate so many Americans are English monolinguals and relatively culturally illiterate. That being said, he argued, such a problem should not concern language policy stakeholders at the present moment. Chu maintained that America's monolingualism and cultural illiteracy is "a fact of life" that conference participants must accept for now ("Influence" 7). As a nation, Chu argued, we don't need more talk about ideals—"we need action" that shapes our nation's "raw materials" into the language competence "necessary for our survival in today's world" (7–8). Ultimately, both Holt and Chu tried to compel conference participants to work with them to craft a national language policy that would promote a specific kind of multilingualism, namely, one that could be deployed in the name of national security.

DOD officials and congressional leaders also presented a historical narrative to bolster their argument that the U.S. military can and should lead this process of defining, evaluating, and meeting the nation's language needs. Several presenters at the 2004 National Language Conference referred to the terrorist attacks of 11 September 2001 as this era's "Sputnik moment." By using this phrase, they invoked the U.S. government's response to the Soviet Union's perceived technological and military superiority after its December 1957 launch of the *Sputnik I* satellite (Chu, "Influence"; Holt; Lazio). Indeed, DOD officials and many other conference participants expressed the need for a contemporary policy on par with the U.S. National Defense Education Act (NDEA) of 1958, which provided substantial funds for science, mathematics, and foreign language education as a means to regain technological and strategic superiority over the Soviets.[7] In short, these presenters used the NDEA example to suggest that the federal government must once again lead the way in the nationwide effort to develop the educational infrastructure required to address the nation's pressing security needs.

Like all histories inserted into policy arguments, however, stories about the "Sputnik moment" present a selective interpretation of events that reinforces a particular belief system (Fischer 102). Representative Holt, Undersecretary Chu, and others used the story of the NDEA to invoke images of a massive, coordinated, and focused national response to building language resources, implying a direct connection between the U.S. government's funding of foreign language education and the nation's ability to "win" the Cold War. In reality, the NDEA provided significant funding to support a temporary surge in foreign language education, but it did not lead to a sustained effort to build the nation's language resources. As John S. Diekhoff reported in 1965, federal funds came with the imperative for foreign language programs to target the nation's immediate language needs. As a result, Diekhoff argued, scholars often were not as able as they had hoped to direct energy and money toward developing a stronger foundation of research exploring language, culture, and foreign language pedagogy (130).[8] In other words, the impetus to shore up national defense forced many educators to emphasize increasing the quantity of students graduating with foreign language degrees as opposed to improving the research-based quality of course offerings (128). Equally as important, when legislators were no longer convinced of a pressing need for foreign language education, the programs and institutes shrunk in size and scope (Presidential Commission 9).[9]

Chu, Holt, and others used the NDEA narrative, then, to affirm the DOD's claim that it should lead efforts to develop a national language policy.[10] In so doing, however, they limited debate about this particular language policy problem. Writing in 1965, Diekhoff critiqued how the NDEA forced foreign language scholars to direct attention toward "organizational, administrative, or financial problems of language education" and away from significant questions about the nature of language education and policy, such as ethical concerns about how accepting federal funds does or does not fit into "the framework of a larger, defensible philosophy of education" (16–17). Chu applied the same pressures that the NDEA did with his opening remarks at the 2004 National Language Conference, arguing that stakeholders must take a "pragmatic view" to the language policy debate ("Influence" 7). The nation, Chu warned, needs less debate, more action. Chu believed that just as federal leaders had done in 1958, the DOD had precisely and persuasively defined the *military's* language needs as the *nation's* pressing language need. In short, the "Sputnik moment" narrative was used to stifle debate about language policy and language practice, such as conversations about what the ideal aims of foreign language education should be, which languages should be taught by which schools, or how to cultivate a new American attitude that values multilingualism. Instead, the NDEA narrative projected an image that all stakeholders are committed to government-led action that would direct the nation's language resources to meet the military's language needs.

The DOD reinforced this perception of consensus about its leadership role and its language policy vision when in February 2005 it published *A Call to Action for National Foreign Language Capabilities*. This white paper emerged from working groups at the National Language Conference and, following the *Defense Language Transformation Roadmap*, serves as the second central document outlining the emerging post–9/11 national language policy. While the *Roadmap* focuses inward and addresses the DOD's own language attitudes and management practices, the *Call to Action* white paper looks outward, aiming to prompt congressional leaders to craft legislation that addresses the military and intelligence communities' language-related concerns. *A Call to Action* proposes a seven-part strategy for coordinating the nation's efforts to identify, manage, and expand its language resources. Foremost among the elements of this plan is the creation of a National Foreign Language Coordination Council, chaired by a National Language Authority, that would be responsible for "developing and overseeing the implementation of a national foreign language strategy across all sectors," from commercial, educational, and nonprofit organizations to local, state, and federal governments (3). Not surprisingly, a definition of *the military's* language needs as *the nation's* language needs dominates the white paper's analysis and recommendations. While its white paper does mention that the United States has a responsibility to ensure educational, professional, and civic opportunities for the nation's heritage communities (2), the DOD maintains that it is in the nation's best interest for the military and intelligence communities to lay immediate claim to "the limited language resources that exist right now" (12).

Upon its publication in 2005, the DOD's *Call to Action* sparked federal activity aimed at formalizing and implementing this national security language policy, and much of this legislation stands to—or has already begun to—affect language arts education in the United States. Not surprisingly, former president George W. Bush and congressional leaders consistently defined the nation's language needs in terms of national security concerns. President Bush's National Security Language Initiative (NSLI), unveiled on 5 January 2006, put $140.6 million over two years toward improving language education to secure the nation. The NSLI built on several existing federal programs, but this new funding was meant to encourage schools to refocus their educational efforts on military-defined "critical-need" languages such as Arabic, Chinese, Farsi, and Hindi and to develop continuous programs, kindergarten through university, for students of these languages.

Several undergraduate- and graduate-level activities were funded through the NSLI, and the U.S. Department of Education highlighted several of these programs in its August 2008 report *Enhancing Foreign Language Proficiency in the United States: Preliminary Results of the National Security Language Initiative*. For example, the U.S. Department of State used NSLI funds to make 330 Fulbright Critical Language Enhancement Awards, which provided Fulbright scholars the opportunity to take intensive coursework on a critical-need language for up to six months before their regular Fulbright grant began (12). The State Department also supported intensive language institutes overseas for undergraduate and graduate students in Arabic, Chinese, Indic, Korean,

Persian, Russian, and Turkic languages; well over a thousand scholarships were awarded during the program's first three years (2006–8), sending students to thirty-three institutes in thirteen different countries (11). And the State Department also received NSLI funding to bolster the Benjamin A. Gilman Scholarship Program, which enables financially disadvantaged American undergraduates to pursue one-year study abroad opportunities in nontraditional destinations; between 2006 and 2008, the State Department awarded more than six hundred Gilman Scholarships, along with Critical-Need Language Supplements that supported additional language study for seventy-five of those Gilman Scholarship students (12). Overall, the Education Department found many signs to indicate the NSLI's early success, including positive program assessments, "enthusiastic feedback and transformative personal stories of student and teacher participants," and bipartisan support in Congress (3).

Several congressional representatives also used the DOD's *Call to Action* to guide their own efforts to draft new and updated legislation that addressed the nation's critical language needs. Representative Holt introduced the National Security Language Act, which would have worked "to strengthen the national security" through expanding educational programs that combine science and technology instruction with foreign language study. After this bill, H.R. 678, never emerged from committee review during the 110th Congress (2007–8), Holt in the 111th Congress (2009–10) sponsored H.R. 4065, the Foreign Language Education Partnership Program Act. This legislation would provide incentives for schools to create partnership programs in foreign languages, with the aim of increasing the number of students who develop high-level proficiency in at least one foreign language. S.1010, the National Foreign Language Coordination Act of 2009, would formally establish the National Foreign Language Coordination Council called for in the DOD's *Call to Action* white paper; in May 2009 the bill, sponsored by Senator Daniel Akaka, was referred to the Senate Committee on Health, Education, Labor, and Pensions, but it had not risen from the committee level over one year later.[11] And finally, existing laws were also revised to better address the national security language crisis. In July 2008, for example, Congress reauthorized the Higher Education Act of 1965 for another five years. Congress inserted a broad, flexible definition of *critical foreign languages* to encompass all relevant sections of the law, thus allowing the Secretary of Education to prioritize programs that use this term when making funding decisions (NAFSA).

Examining Higher Education's Relationship with the U.S. Military

As the federal government worked to implement the national security language policy, it has sought advice from several major higher education associations, many of which have expressed support for this policy. Rather than addressing ethical concerns related to scholarship and teaching that explicitly supports military activities, however, their main concern has been logistical, focusing on administrative and financial problems of higher education. In other words, these associations focus on questions such as how federal funding can be spent most effectively to address the military's language needs. These organizations view the national security language policy—with the federal funding attached to it—as an opportunity for schools to redesign undergraduate and graduate education to prepare twenty-first-century students to respond to the political, economic, scientific, and social challenges facing the world. For example, the Association of American Universities (AAU) and the American Council of Education's Coalition for International Education (CIE) both applaud the government's efforts to expand foreign-language and study-abroad programs, but they also explain that for the desired ends to be reached, the federal government must increase its basic funding of science, mathematics, and foreign language research by 8–10 percent annually for the next seven years (AAU 17; CIE 1). The CIE, in fact, recommends that rather than appropriate NSLI funds to create new programs, Congress should redirect this money to bolster programs already established through both Title VI of the Higher Education Act, which specifically targets international education programs, and the Fulbright-Hays legislation, which provides material support for study abroad programs (2). The National Research Council of the National Academies similarly affirmed the necessity of NSLI funding but also called for the Department of Education to "consolidate oversight" of all these federally funded programs in language and international education "under an executive-level person who could also provide strategic direction, and consult and coordinate with other federal agencies" (6). The council declared that "universities must be ready partners willing to refine and direct their programs toward mutual goals" with the government (9). At the same time it called on federal officials to initiate more dialogue with higher education institutions to identify these mutual goals and determine the financial and administrative conditions needed to meet them (9).

As these examples suggest, major higher education associations support federal investment in university research and educational programs. They see the mission of universities and colleges in part to be using the research, teaching, and language skills of faculty and students to meet the nation's pressing needs, which in the present moment they take to be enhancing the nation's security. These associations focus on questions about what financial resources and administrative structures are needed to enable universities to achieve this goal. In attending to such concerns, these associations implicitly accept the military's definition of the nation's language needs. Moreover, they seemingly elide ethical concerns about what teachers and scholars' relationship vis-à-vis the U.S. military should be.

The American Anthropological Association (AAA), in fact, has been the only major academic organization to address these ethical concerns directly. The AAA's most notable statement has been the November 2007 report written by the AAA Commission on the Engagement of Anthropology with the U.S. Security and Intelligence Communities. This commission thoroughly investigated the types of work anthropologists were performing directly for military, defense, and intelligence communities, such as teaching cultural understanding to military units, doing organizational studies of the military, performing forensic analysis of military victims, and guiding the military to ensure its activities respect cultural preservation concerns. Ultimately, the AAA cautioned members about the risks of working with the military and intelligence communities because of the potential for such activities to place anthropologists in violation of the AAA Code of Ethics, particularly its admonitions to "do no harm" to subjects, to provide informed consent to research subjects, and to be transparent with research methods and findings (24). Higher education associations such as the AAU, CIE, and National Research Council, of course, perform a vital role as they engage congressional debates about crafting educational policy and allocating taxpayers' dollars in ways that best enable schools to meet federal legislation's aims. The AAA, however, has made an equally significant contribution to the conversation about educational policy and practice with reference to the federal government, as it helps its members to think about the nature of research, teaching, and public engagement in the globalizing, twenty-first-century world.

Indeed, by welcoming federal money and a specific, security-centered definition of the public interest, higher education associations such as the AAU and CIE accept the obligations for many students to use their language skills in service of the nation's military and intelligence needs. For example, David L. Boren Scholarships and Fellowships, which are part of the National Security Education Program, fund undergraduate (up to $20,000 for one school year) and graduate students (up to $30,000 for two full years) to travel to countries critical to U.S. national security interests and to study the languages written and spoken there through classroom, research, and personal experiences. In exchange, award recipients must commit to at least one year of U.S. government service after completing their programs of study (National Security Education Program). This type of language education legislation suggests that it is most important for the nation to support those students who will put critical language skills to immediate use overseas for the U.S. military, intelligence, and diplomatic communities.

As congressional legislation and related statements from higher education associations suggest, contemporary political and military leaders have directed the citizenry's attention, in Holt's words, to the "national deficiency in the languages and cultures of critical areas around the world" (1). By defining the military's language problems as *the* pressing language problem facing the entire nation, government and military leaders have declared their support for a national language policy that would make schools important spaces for securing the nation against terrorist threats. But defining the nation's language problems in terms of foreign military threats, whether in 1958 or 2012, directs attention away from other pressing language problems affecting the day-to-day experiences of people living within U.S. borders. Moreover, government efforts to frame this policy problem ignore a significant debate inside modern language studies about the aims and means of language education in the twenty-first century, a debate that suggests alternative ways to define the nation's language needs and build an educational infrastructure that can produce graduates with the advanced language skills to meet them.

Scouting the Theoretical Foundations of the National Security Language Policy

Because the national security language policy promotes learning multiple languages, it seems to align with the CCCC's similar calls in its 1974 Students Right resolution and 1988 National Language Policy. Indeed, the national security language policy, as it encourages more U.S. citizens to develop multilingual skills, provides an important counterbalance to English-only legislation of the sort that Senator James Inhofe introduced in the name of national security and political unity during the 2006 congressional debates on immigration reform (Inhofe Amendment). Senator Inhofe's English Language Amendment, which was approved by a 63–34 Senate vote, targeted immigrants in particular, demanding that they learn English in the belief that it will keep them from "importing dangerous, deadly philosophies that go against our American ideals" ("Inhofe Statement"). More recently, Senator Inhofe and Representative Steve King introduced the English Language Unity Act to the 110th Congress, which would have required the federal government to establish a uniform language requirement for naturalization so that all new citizens could, in King's words, "fully learn about American culture and what makes America truly unique" ("King Introduces"). While President Bush and other federal officials might have shared the same belief that all people living in the United States needed to learn English, they also sought to encourage—and to fund programs that would enable—more U.S. citizens to learn multiple languages.

At the same time, however, this emerging national language policy problematically promotes multilingualism as a strategic military weapon. The national language policy's primary focus on security-related concerns seems to be set, but scholars of English and foreign languages can still shape how this policy takes effect in their home institutions and communities. Before describing how to influence local implementation of the policy, however, this section first critiques the Defense Department's vision of what the national language policy should aim to achieve and how schools can help to bring about these ends, and it then builds on this analysis to outline several ideas that should inform an alternative to the national security language policy.

The government's emerging policy focuses almost exclusively on the military, intelligence, and business communities' "critical" language needs for activities outside U.S. borders and for dealing with "foreign" elements (i.e., terrorists) inside the United States. In so doing, it reinforces a belief that English is *the* language for public use in American civic life while non-English languages are "foreign" and only needed for reading and speaking "overseas." In this way, the national security language policy reinscribes a belief in an English-only U.S. public sphere, eliding the fact that this country is a multilingual society. It promotes English language literacy as a core skill that all students must develop to participate in civic and professional life in the United States, while it promotes foreign-language literacy as a skill that students will use overseas or to communicate with or infiltrate "foreigners." What the CCCC National Language Policy in particular prompts us to see is how the emerging national security language policy all but ignores the people who use non-English languages for professional, personal, or cultural reasons in their daily lives within U.S. borders, including over 47 million people who speak a language other than English at home (Shin 2). The DOD's perspective on speakers of languages other than English evades any debate about how a national language policy should account for them in defining the country's language needs, except when emphasizing the need to recruit them into government service for the United States' "foreign" concerns.

In the way that it reinscribes the notion of the United States as an English-only nation and ignores other language communities within U.S. society, the national security language policy mirrors the NDEA of 1958. Chu described the NDEA as a model for addressing a national language crisis, but a closer examination reveals how this earlier policy reinforced the marginalization of U.S. linguistic minorities. Bruce Gardner, then a foreign language education specialist for the U.S. Office of Education, observed in 1965 that the NDEA followed a long-standing educational and cultural policy whereby "in American school rooms it was quite respectable to study and try to learn a foreign language, but that the child who already knew one before he entered school was somehow at a disadvantage" (19). Gardner accused the NDEA of promoting an "anomalous national language policy," the result of which was "at best to ignore, at worst to stamp out, the native competence while at the same time undertaking the miracle of creating something like it in our monolinguals" (19). He explained that while governments and school districts made multi-million-dollar expenditures to create or bolster education programs in common and neglected languages, they directed no NDEA funds toward developing or maintaining the native language competence of the 11 percent of Americans (at the time, 19 million people overall, 5 million of whom were children) whose native languages were not English. By ignoring many students' abilities in their first languages, the NDEA as a national language education policy ignored both the social and cultural needs of people living in linguistic-minority communities as well as the untapped language abilities that could be developed to advanced levels and directed toward addressing local communities' and the nation's language needs.

With respect to the nation's language minority communities, the post–September 11 language policy threatens to take the country down the same road that the post-Sputnik one did. Indeed, as they defined the nation's language crisis in terms of "foreign" languages and the military's language needs, President Bush, DOD officials, and congressional leaders dissuaded schools and colleges from developing programs to serve and build on the existing linguistic resources within the communities where they are located. Mary Louise Pratt provides an example to illustrate this point in her 2004 essay "Building a New Public Idea about Language":

> Within its own borders the United States needs professionals and service people of all kinds who can operate in locally spoken languages. A few months ago, for example, two southern California primary school teachers told me of their frustration when a flagship Japanese program was set up in their school district, while an acute need for Tagalog-speaking nurses, doctors, lawyers, teachers, social workers, even tax preparers went unmet. There was no pipeline to track local Tagalog speakers into these professions and enable them to develop their Tagalog. (114)

Pratt's comments suggest that a national language policy conceived solely on international, militaristic concerns may keep the citizenry safe from enemies but will also ignore problems facing linguistic minority communities within U.S. borders. The national security language policy aims to improve domestic well-being in a single way: securing U.S. citizens from terrorist threats. Equally as important, it continues to marginalize those people who are too often situated outside the public imaginary in most debates about who we are as a community and what policy solutions we need to address our problems.

When proponents of the national security language policy do discuss heritage-language students, they only focus on those people who speak one of the military's critical languages and, more importantly, they assume these language skills would best be used to aid military and national security efforts. Specifically, President Bush and DOD leaders talked about languages being military tools. U.S. Colonel Michael R. Simone of the Defense Language Institute stated this view most bluntly at the 2004 National Language Conference when he declared, "Language is our weapon." Simone's assertion suggests that U.S. political and military leaders see foreign languages as tools used to ascertain and translate information, as tools used to help kill terrorists.

As it advocates increasing the number of people who can contribute language skills to help the U.S. military, the national security language policy relies on what Judith Rodby calls a universalist understanding of languages (31). According to this perspective, languages are currency, and their value is fixed according to narrowly defined prescriptions for use. This understanding leads to a hierarchy of value among languages that is based solely on instrumentalist concerns, as with the DOD's designation of Arabic, Farsi, Pashto, and Mandarin, among others, as "critical need" languages that it wants to invest in and press into immediate service. For example, people who can speak, read, and listen to Arabic have become increasingly valuable to the U.S. military and intelligence communities because they possess the most efficient means for getting information from Arabic-speaking terrorist suspects or potential informants on Islamic fundamentalist terrorist groups. As the previous section illustrated, however, determinations of "value" reflect the particular interests of the groups able to define this term. The military has successfully defined its language needs as the nation's language needs. In so doing, it reinforces the belief that the federal government should invest in programs teaching these critical need languages because it will bring the most immediate returns in terms of improving national security and economic well-being. Languages from which the nation stands to extract the most value, then, will receive government funds for training and staffing. Language programs needed to address more localized political or cultural concerns—say, for instance, the need for more government officials, social workers, and teachers in Lewiston, Maine, who possess professional competence in the Somali language (Finnegan)—attract fewer government resources not only because of the tendency to ignore non-English language concerns within U.S. borders but also because the economic or political return on such investment appears to be significantly less.

In addition to proposing investment only in those languages the nation can put to use in its war against terrorism, the national security language policy also reinforces the common belief that there are discrete, clearly defined contexts and purposes for using different languages (Lu, "Essay" 26). The policy in this way fails to value people, particularly heritage language speakers, who choose to use their languages in ways that accomplish something other than addressing the nation's critical security needs. As Min-Zhan Lu notes, individual language users "potentially hav[e] social and personal reasons to be interested in and concerned with" ways of using languages that disrupt dominant ideas about how, where, when, and why to use them (37). For example, a linguistic minority student's marginalization within the cultural imaginary of U.S. political life might influence whether or not she feels compelled to use her heritage language to help the nation advance its militaristic or economic interests. Another student might have learned to use the language in ways that connect him closely to a local community such that he wants to learn how to use the language to serve this community in a professional capacity. The national security language policy, unlike the CCCC National Language Policy, fails to consider goals for a multilingual education that do not directly relate to military or national security concerns, such as uniting diverse American communities and broadening people's understanding of what it means to be human.

Political scientist Deborah Schildkraut has called for paying closer attention to how an individual's conception of American identity can shape his or her ideas about language policies and practices. In particular, Schildkraut found in a focus group study that the ethnocultural tradition of American identity—that is, belief in "America as a nation of white Protestants" (6)—continues to influence many immigrants' and ethnic minorities' everyday experiences and, consequently, to affect how they "navigate their relationship with American politics and society" (204). For example, one of the participants in Schildkraut's study stated, "I was born here, but I don't feel that America includes me at all. I live here, but that's it" (204). Such an articulation of identity should remind scholars, politicians, and community leaders that a national language policy must account for people who do not "self-identify as members" of the U.S. political community (204). English-only language policies see this identification resulting from cultural and national allegiances connected to languages other than English, so they attempt to reinvent linguistic minorities as obedient political subjects by having them speak in English only. The national security language policy proposes a multilingual populace but nevertheless demands that linguistic minorities self-identify as members of the U.S. civic body in specific ways, namely, using "foreign" languages to advance the nation's security and economic missions. An alternative vision for the national language policy must attempt to bridge gaps that exist between the presumed "national" interest and the personal, professional, and civic possibilities that linguistic minorities imagine for themselves.

By reinforcing a belief in precisely defined contexts and purposes for language use, Colonel Simone, President Bush, and others ground the national security language policy in a problematic assumption about what languages are and how they shape people who use them. Simone defines languages as military "weapons," and former president Bush envisions U.S. State Department officials learning a foreign language and gaining knowledge about a culture only to translate and deliver a preformed policy message to allied or oppositional countries. These utilitarian views on language reinforce what Lu calls a "commodity approach" toward language learning and use ("Essay" 25). This perspective on linguistic and cultural learning, Lu argues, has focused educators' and policy makers' attention on identifying what language "tools" one needs while ignoring how an individual's languages choices have "real consequences for [his or her] well-being" (25). As Lu contends, this utilitarian perspective on language learning and language use problematically reassures people "that we can simply 'ease in and out' of disparate social domains, languages, englishes, discourses, prototypical selfhoods, relations with others and the world in the same way one picks up and puts down a tool (or slips into and out of a dress) without any 'real' effects on one's Authentic Selfhood" (43). Government officials do not acknowledge how language learning could reshape "one's actual, imagined, and possible self and life" (28) and, along with it, one's conception of the U.S. government's responsibilities in the world. Former president Bush, for example, talks about how learning to use a foreign language lets another speaker of that language "know that I'm interested in not only how you talk but how you live." His view on how and why foreign languages get used in international diplomacy and military activities, however, rests on an assumption that effective language use in cross-language and cross-cultural contexts entails being what Gemma Corradi Fiumara calls "masters of discourse" rather than "apprentices of listening" (qtd. in Ratcliffe 25). Bush and DOD leaders believe that acquiring a foreign language "tool" necessarily gives one the platform to deliver the United States' political message to people in other countries around the world, a message that echoes President Bush's declaration after the 11 September terrorist attacks: "Every nation, in every region, now has a decision to make. Either you are with us, or you are with the terrorists" (Bush, "Address"). Bush and other federal officials concerned solely with language as a military tool do not allow for the possibility that foreign language learning can open greater opportunities for listening to speakers of other languages; understanding how they view themselves and others; and through such listening, possibly reshaping one's conception of self, the nation, or the world. The CCCC Students' Right resolution and National Language Policy, on the other hand, emphasize learning second and third languages not merely to deliver one's message more effectively but rather to learn from others and to consider how their perspectives might prompt a new understanding of global activities and the relationships forged through them.

Composing an Alternative to the National Security Language Policy

While foreign language scholars have already coalesced in response to the national security language policy debate, rhetoric and composition scholars committed to promoting multilingualism also have a stake in this policy debate because of the potential for government funding to alter the infrastructure for and influence the responsibilities of U.S. language arts education. The CCCC Students' Right resolution and National Language Policy can help scholars not only to critique the emerging policy's assumptions about language but also to imagine an alternative language policy that advances a more pluralistic understanding of the nation's language needs. This policy would define the United States as a linguistically diverse nation, one with the need for a greater number of professionals as well as average citizens with the ability to speak multiple languages for not only overseas work but also a wide range of domestic activities.

The DOD's language policy implicitly suggests that the United States only needs enough multilingual people to address its national security needs, so a policy alternative should frame the national need in a way that emphasizes second-language learning for all Americans. Ideally, the policy would describe multilingualism as a skill that all citizens can and should possess as a means to foster dialogue, rather than relying on faith that English can and should be the only language linking the nation's people. Such work would extend the Students' Right policy's claim that "a nation proud of its diverse heritage and its cultural and racial variety will preserve its heritage of dialects" (Committee on CCCC Language Statement 3). This act of preserving would not simply be a matter of passively permitting people to use "other" languages. Rather, it would entail actively promoting language diversity, increasing the number of people who can speak different languages and expanding the range of public and professional contexts in which people can use these languages. This policy would promote greater cross-language relations within the U.S. as a means to foster democratic participation and reinvigorate American ideals of freedom, equality, and opportunity. This alternative language policy would talk of multilingualism in terms of strengthening the nation through plurilingual democratic debate, not just identifying and eliminating terrorist threats.

Along similar lines, an alternative to the national security language policy would emphasize the need to encourage students to develop advanced literacies in a variety of languages—not just those that meet the military's critical need—and for a range of personal, civic, and professional reasons—not just to help secure the nation. This policy should encourage students to work in and across different languages as a means to discover new ways to "include all citizens of all language communities in the positive development of our daily activities" (CCCC, "National Language Policy" 5). Toward these ends, this policy would advance alternative aims for language arts education, namely, enabling students to acquire the linguistic and rhetorical skills that would allow them to participate in public and professional life in any way they found to be meaningful, whether that involved serving local communities' medical needs, working in national security, exploring one's familial or communal histories, or contributing to public policy debates about the United States' critical language needs.

Any alternative to the national security language policy must also trouble the "commodity approach" toward language acquisition and disrupt the "language as tool" metaphor it advances. As the Students' Right resolution reminds us, using different languages and dialects is a way to "find [our] own identity and style" (Committee on CCCC Language Statement 2). A national language policy should define effective language use in a way that involves critical engagement with the cultural and linguistic contexts that influence how one can and wants to use the language within his or her personal, professional, and civic lives. It should acknowledge that acquiring and using another language, while not *determining* one's sense of political, cultural, and social identity, nevertheless creates possibilities for one to negotiate these identities in new ways and to reshape his or her relations to other cultures.

Finally, an alternative to the emerging national security language policy should also explicitly promote heritage language education that develops students' language skills to advanced levels. Language scholars must emphasize the fact that the nation's existing language resources can best be developed to these advanced levels through formal educational channels. Scholars would challenge the common belief that schools need not emphasize heritage language education because students can learn and maintain these languages simply by using them with their families and friends. As chapter 2 discussed, Ana Celia Zentella's 1997 study *Growing Up Bilingual: Puerto Rican Children in New York* revealed that sociocultural conditions shaping family and communal language use do not always encourage students to develop command of a heritage language, particularly in terms of reading and writing competencies (285). This analysis reinforces the CCCC National Language Policy's call for the majority culture to support educational opportunities for all Americans to learn a second or third language.

Ultimately, framing a national language policy in terms of military or even economic strength proves to be pragmatic because it brings greater governmental support for language education, but a more sustainable policy alternative is needed. Tying foreign language programs and funding to national security concerns means that public and governmental support for specific programs could likely abate once the security threat has passed. Moreover, the present focus on meeting the nation's most immediately pressing language needs suggests that attention and resources could be moved quickly from one target language to another rather than being committed to building a substantive educational infrastructure for particular languages. An alternative to the national security language policy would emphasize a more comprehensive, even domestically oriented, approach to language learning that builds on the language resources that already exist in the community, works to build the professional competence and civic literacy in those languages for the local student populations, and forges stronger bonds between schools and their surrounding communities.

Inventing Local Responses to the National Security Language Policy

MLA leaders Rosemary G. Feal, Mary Louise Pratt, and Domna C. Stanton, as well as other foreign-language scholars such as Heidi Byrnes and Leo van Lier, have been trying to intervene in the post–9/11 policy-making process. Their engagement with the national security language policy debate is motivated in part by a desire to ensure that the federal government's support for foreign language education is sustained, encompasses all levels of schooling, and promotes the learning of languages more generally rather than DOD "investment languages" more narrowly.

While foreign-language scholars have identified this national security language policy as a central disciplinary concern, many rhetoric and composition scholars have yet to explore this issue. Because the shaping and implementation of this policy is still in progress, their participation in these debates is vital. The policy will likely determine the languages and modes of communication (i.e., reading, listening, speaking, writing) that many schools decide to teach and also influence the attitudes and worldviews cultivated through language arts education. Given the discipline's emerging interest in transnational and translingual composition, rhetoric and composition scholars need to join these conversations about what the nation's language needs are and how a national language policy can support the creation of a language-competent society to meet them.[12]

Geneva Smitherman, who helped to draft both the Students' Right resolution and National Language Policy, explains that the CCCC's language policies provide scholars with the "intellectual basis and rhetorical frameworks" for participating in such debates about language policy and crafting public arguments about the political, cultural, and social value of linguistic diversity ("CCCC's Role" 373). With its National Language Policy, for example, the CCCC calls on compositionists to advocate for multilingual language learning because it can not only enable the United States to "participate more effectively in worldwide activities" but also "unify diverse American communities" and "enlarge our view of what is human" (5). This chapter's previous section uses the National Language Policy and the Students' Right resolution as prompts for outlining an alternative to a national language policy grounded on military and security concerns. Composition scholars and teachers similarly can draw on these rhetorical frameworks as they participate in the language policy debate by composing arguments for op-ed pages, government officials, and congressional panels.

This section, however, calls on compositionists to engage in not only these more common forms of public advocacy but also micro-level action to shape how the national language policy gets implemented locally. This argument is informed by lessons learned from studying the Language Curriculum Research Group and the CCCC Language Policy Committee, namely, that a language policy debate is never just about crafting a persuasive policy statement. Scholars need to initiate several different activities and sustain these efforts over a long period of time to heighten public understanding of policy alternatives and, equally important, to engrain such policy alternatives into the daily workings of a discipline, institution, or community. Specifically, composition scholars can read the CCCC National Language Policy and Students' Right resolution as heuristics to inform their work in public advocacy, teaching, interdisciplinary curriculum development, and institutional policy writing.

Operationalizing the Students' Right resolution and National Language Policy statement at the local level can be a means to influence how the emerging national security language policy shapes literacy education and writing instruction. Ultimately, these disciplinary language policies prompt scholars and teachers to work within the present policy debate to broaden the definition of the nation's language needs so that it represents a more diverse set of cultural, economic, political, and social interests in U.S. public life.

Providing Public Leadership in the National Security Language Policy Debate

The CCCC National Language Policy commits composition scholars to working within the professional and public realms to promote the learning of multiple languages by all Americans. One way the Language Policy Committee tried to fill the "language leadership vacuum" was through communicating with legislators about the dangers of English-only laws, joining with other advocacy groups to defend minorities' civil rights relating to language, and creating a brochure that outlined the National Language Policy and provided suggestions for how fellow composition scholars and other interested citizens could work to foster multilingualism in their communities. Similarly, composition scholars should find ways to provide leadership in the contemporary debate over the national security language crisis, for the policy can be seen as a means for students and citizens to develop the ability to communicate in a wide range of situations, both domestic and abroad, both professional and civic, both in English and other languages. This policy debate presents an opportunity to create not a more extensive foreign language education infrastructure in the United States but rather a multilingual language arts curriculum that develops students' abilities in English as well as a second or third language. In short, composition scholars who engage this national security language policy debate will be working to reshape the discipline in ways that reflect the visions outlined in the Students' Right resolution and National Language Policy.

Several foreign language scholars have already been active in a variety of forums to provide leadership and expertise in this present policy debate. Rosemary Feal, executive director of the MLA, was invited to the DOD-sponsored National Language Conference. In her presentation at the conference, Feal surveyed the existing infrastructure for language education in colleges and universities and presented strategies for improving and expanding these programs ("Higher"). Feal has also used the "Editor's Column" in the *MLA Newsletter* to share her analysis of the national security "language crisis" ("Scaring"; "Language"), and she appeared as a guest on National Public Radio's *Talk of the Nation* program in 2005 to discuss factors that shape Americans' decisions to learn or not learn a second language (Brecht, Feal, and Long). During their respective tenures as MLA president, meanwhile, Mary Louise Pratt (in 2003) and Domna Stanton (in 2005) each published an article in *Profession* to raise awareness of this policy debate and to propose strategies for the MLA's response to it. Moreover, Stanton noted that since Pratt's tenure as MLA president in 2003, the MLA "[has] been engaged in dialogue with government officials concerned with the role of language in national security" (77). Specifically, Pratt met with Pentagon officials to suggest alternatives to national security as the primary motivation for improving foreign language learning in the United States, and she has participated in the federal government's Interagency Language Roundtable, which is an unfunded organization that brings together representatives from several government agencies, academic organizations, and other nongovernmental organizations to coordinate and share information on federal-level foreign language activities. More recently, Pratt chaired the MLA Ad Hoc Committee on Foreign Languages, which published its report "Foreign Languages and Higher Education: New Structures for a Changed World," in *Profession 2007*. Meanwhile, Leo van Lier, editor of the *Modern Language Journal* (*MLJ*), and Heidi Byrnes, associate editor in charge of *MLJ*'s "Perspectives" column, organized panels at the national conferences of the MLA, the American Council on the Teaching of Foreign Languages, the Northeast Conference on the Teaching of Foreign Languages, and the American Association for Applied Linguistics, as well as a separate invited conference in 2007–8 focused on imagining what a permanent federal-level structure for foreign-language education policy making might look like, one that would "assure the development of encompassing, coherent, and long-term policies and practices" ("MLJ"). These panel discussions informed a December 2008 special issue of "Perspectives" (92.4) on the topic "From Representation at the Federal/National Level to Creating a Foreign Language Education Framework." All of this work by Feal, Pratt, Stanton, van Lier, and Byrnes shows foreign-language scholars making a concerted effort to establish a visible presence in the policy-making process, translate their knowledge and expertise into substantive recommendations, and persuade federal officials to heed them.

These activities—participating in roundtables and radio talk shows, presenting at conferences, writing editorials for both professional and public forums—illustrate more traditional forms of public advocacy that scholars can pursue, but Feal also led a more unique approach to position the MLA in a public leadership role in this debate about the nation's language needs. Specifically, Feal commissioned and publicized the MLA Language Map, a tool that allows people to gain a tangible sense of the linguistic composition of their communities. The on-line map, which is accessible through the MLA website, draws on 2000 U.S. Census data gathered in response to the question "Does this person speak a language other than English at home?" ("MLA Language Map"). People who consult the MLA Language Map can learn about the number of speakers of specific languages who reside in a particular state, county, city, town, or zip code. Ultimately, this data can prompt people to think about the nation's language needs in ways tethered to local linguistic communities' resources rather than to the military's activities overseas.

The MLA Language Map emerged from Pratt's and Feal's initial engagement in the post–9/11 language policy debate, and its consumption by various constituencies helps us to visualize what it means for academics to join with community members in addressing matters of public concern. A 2004 article in the *MLA Newsletter* explains that visitors to the on-line map "from outside the language and literature community have reported uses for the language map that its designers did not originally imagine" ("MLA Language Map" 21):

> A representative of a federal agency told us of using the map in research for a project on disability benefits for citizens who are not native speakers of English, and a state public health agency used the map in developing an HIV/AIDS education project. A regional disaster-preparedness planner has used the map to determine the need for translators for medical facilities, and an international firm has used the site to make decisions in a marketing campaign. (21)

Tracing how the MLA Language Map has circulated and been used in various social contexts reveals that academic work on and around language policies can and does have effects outside the academic community. This example speaks to the potential of scholarly projects that can be shared with the wider public and that link to activities addressing community problems. In the present policy debate, such projects would be ones that support efforts to define the nation's or a community's language needs and create communicative and educational solutions to meet them.

Federal officials, legislators, and the wider public most likely see why foreign language scholars should have a voice in the national security language policy debate, but teachers of English must disrupt the common conception that they work in linguistically homogenous classrooms and are concerned solely with teaching students to write effectively in English only (Matsuda, "Myth"). Composition scholars can speak to the increasing linguistic diversity of English language arts classrooms and their efforts to develop pedagogical responses that help ESL and other multilingual students build on the rhetorical resources they bring to the composition classroom. Composition scholars can also speak to the limits of being able to work in one language only in contemporary U.S. society and the larger world, and they can draw on the Students' Right resolution and National Language Policy as they articulate the discipline's mission of helping students learn how to use language to shape their identities and styles and preparing them to communicate effectively across culturally and linguistically diverse contexts.

As chapter 2 shows, compositionists such as Geneva Smitherman have worked tirelessly on the advocacy front to create better opportunities for students from the linguistic margins, and more generally the CCCC and NCTE have made significant efforts to put English language arts education on legislators' list of concerns. These scholars obviously are well aware that literacy educators have only so much time with federal officials and congressional representatives, and they are justified in keeping their messages focused when communicating with legislators. Nevertheless, English-language arts scholars must avoid looking at the contemporary debate about the national security language policy as a zero-sum game in which foreign language scholars get resources and English language scholars get none. Instead, compositionists must find creative ways to coalesce with foreign language scholars and advocate for policies that promote and fund multilingual language arts education to develop students' abilities in reading, speaking, listening, and writing in a foreign language as well as in English. As the MLA Language Map example shows, however, composition scholars should not envision scenarios where they alone set the terms of debate and exert their knowledge and expertise onto national language policy discussions. Instead, composition scholars can develop research-based projects that prompt public discussion about the nation's language resources and language needs, such as exhibits for local historical societies that explore past language controversies in the area, ethnographies of local linguistic minority communities, or rhetorical and material analyses of policies and management practices affecting language use in local communities.

Prompting Student Reflection on the Nation's Language Needs

As one learns from studying the CCCC Language Policy Committee, engaging a national language policy debate requires sustained effort over a long time period and coordination with other stakeholders. A more immediately accessible space in which to address the policy debate can be the rhetoric and writing classroom. Teachers can promote students' active learning about how national language policy debates play out in the lived experiences of people in their communities. Primary research projects can give students opportunities to explore the language diversity of their communities, and students can identify implicit or explicit local language policies and analyze how these policies shape public and private language use. Such projects can enable students to understand the material effects of language policies and consider how to define the nation's and their community's language needs.

For example, students in an advanced composition course can conduct primary research in which they explore the region's linguistic diversity and then examine language policy issues that affect local heritage language communities. The MLA Language Map described above can help students to gain a tangible sense of the linguistic composition of their communities. The map's data can prompt students to think about the nation's language needs in ways tethered to local resources rather than only to military activities. To extend their analysis in this way, students can use this data to pursue community-based research projects in which they identify ways to address such alternative definitions of the community's language needs. For example, students could conduct interviews to learn about how local government agencies do or might use census data in deciding what resources, if any, to make available for linguistic minority populations. Other students might use interviews to explore how this data informs nonprofit organizations' missions and activities or examine how local broadcasters do or do not consider language diversity when determining how to fulfill their obligation, as mandated by the Federal Communications Commission, to broadcast programs that serve a "public interest." Students could also build on these interviews by conducting secondary research to begin identifying the social, economic, and political costs to the community for making these types of resources and services available and, equally important, the potential costs facing communities when such resources are not made available. These various lines of inquiry could serve as the basis for a feasibility report or proposal for new hiring practices, new publications, new technologies, or new educational programs that better serve the community's or the nation's language needs and that promote opportunities for the voices of non-English speakers to be heard in debates about what a national language policy should aim to achieve.

To help students recognize how and why language minorities are often ignored in public policy debates, teachers must also guide student reflection on the politics of language and access raised by these research projects exploring local language policies and linguistic minority communities. In Lu's words, scholars pursuing research on transnational and translingual topics, such as examinations of how language policies affect linguistic minorities, must address this critical methodological question: what role does language play in mediating one's research? ("Knowledge" 533). This concern should prompt students to consider how they use language as a research tool to create knowledge about a particular linguistic minority community. For example, if students are able to work only in English, they would need to consider how that monolingual approach to research influences the types of topics they are able to explore, the range of perspectives they are able to gather through traditional print or interview-based research, and, by extension, the ways they define community problems and propose recommendations to address them. In short, these projects should prompt students to think about how language itself influences whose experiences and worldviews shape definitions of the nation's language needs, definitions that in turn influence language policy. Following Lu's suggestion, then, research and writing projects that engage students in the national language policy debate would focus students' attention not only on how implicit and explicit language policies affect the political, economic, and social conditions of linguistic minorities but also how language itself—and the policy of unidirectional English monolingualism that has long shaped writing instruction in U.S. schools (Horner and Trimbur 594)—affects how we come to build knowledge, teach, and enact civic life in relation to these communities.

These types of reflective research projects provide a way into discussing the national security language policy debate because they prompt questions concerning how we as a community or as a nation define our critical language needs. Through these class explorations, teachers can pose questions about the terms on which various groups in society are able to participate in public debates about our language problems, and they can encourage students to reflect on whether they imagine the local public to be monolingual or multilingual when they write about "community" issues. These projects can also help students to strategize and debate how the university should or should not connect to these language communities. Through such discussions, students not only critically engage the current language policy debate. They also begin to reflect on the university's mission and consider how educational institutions might build a greater public commitment to language learning. Much like the Language Curriculum Research Group did, language arts scholars can work to affirm students' and citizens' rights to their own language by making the community's linguistic diversity and local language policies the subject of study in the writing classroom. These types of reflective research projects attune students to the linguistic realities of their communities and serve as one small step toward realizing a guiding principle of the Students' Right resolution—"[a] nation proud of its diverse heritage and its cultural and racial variety will preserve its heritage of dialects [and languages]" (Committee on CCCC Language Statement 3).

Designing a Multilingual Rhetorical Education

When the federal government declared a national "language crisis," the MLA Executive Committee appointed an Ad Hoc Committee on Foreign Languages to create an agenda for MLA members' research, pedagogy, and political advocacy that would present "persuasive alternatives to security-driven approaches" to foreign language education (MLA Ad Hoc Committee, "Transforming" 288). The MLA created this committee in part to critique the security-centered vision of foreign language education, but it also hoped to identify ways to improve college-level foreign language education. MLA leaders seem to agree with French language scholar Gilles Bousquet, who warns, "if traditional foreign language curriculum and governance do not evolve" to begin fulfilling the nation's language needs, "[government] leaders will look elsewhere for language education" (305). In short, foreign language scholars understand the need to graduate more students with advanced competencies, but their reasons for doing so involve improving communication and understanding in a globalizing world rather than deploying languages as military tools to identify and neutralize enemies.

Rhetoric and composition scholars should see tremendous opportunity in foreign language studies' new disciplinary agenda, as the Ad

Hoc Committee calls for interdisciplinary research and pedagogical collaboration as one strategy for evolving foreign language education in ways that better meet the nation's diverse language needs. Indeed, the Ad Hoc Committee's 2007 report, "Foreign Languages and Higher Education: New Structures for a Changed World," echoes the same pedagogical goals that the CCCC articulated in the 1988 National Language Policy and that have become increasingly important to rhetoric and composition scholars in a globalizing, multilingual world. Just as the CCCC sees widespread multilingualism as a means to enable all people to participate in U.S. public life, the MLA wants to change foreign language learning such that students gain greater awareness of how power and cultural worldviews affect communication across lines of linguistic difference. Interdisciplinary collaboration with colleagues in foreign languages, then, would begin the important work of creating a multilingual writing pedagogy that prepares students to communicate across a range of dialects and languages in their personal, professional, and civic lives. In advancing an alternative to the national security language policy, interdisciplinary collaboration between foreign language and rhetoric and composition scholars and teachers could lead to local, institutional-level efforts to revitalize language learning for the sake of a broad range of humanistic values.

Whereas pedagogical emphasis has long been given to the lower-level foreign language courses taken by most college students, the MLA Ad Hoc Committee calls for making foreign language study more relevant in this present moment of "language crisis." Its plan entails redesigning the upper division of the foreign language major to attract a greater number of students and more effectively develop their advanced language competencies. Too many upper-division courses, the committee argues, focus solely on the practices of reading and interpreting literary texts as a means of cultural and aesthetic appreciation ("Foreign Languages" 236). The committee speculates that more college students would pursue foreign language learning if "multiple paths to the major" were available, that is, if more classes encouraged students to connect foreign language study to their academic and professional aspirations in the natural and applied sciences, engineering, health and social sciences, or other disciplines (238). Just as important, the committee argues, a move away from a literature-centered curriculum would more "explicitly advance [students'] language competency" ("Transforming" 290). Given the present need to revitalize foreign language education, the Ad Hoc Committee calls for redesigning the major in ways that give students opportunities to read, analyze, and compose a variety of public texts and to gain metalevel knowledge about the particular language they are studying.[13] This agenda for curricular redesign can be one way to strengthen foreign language educators' claims that their departments can meet the nation's language needs—albeit a more varied, less security-driven definition of these language needs. Emphasizing a wider variety of textual genres and focusing more explicitly on developing students' advanced language competencies would show, in Bousquet's words, that the foreign language curriculum is evolving and staying relevant in the context of the social, political, and economic demands of an increasingly interconnected world.

As it emphasizes developing students' advanced language competencies rather than focusing solely on their ability to analyze literature, the Ad Hoc Committee makes an important professional and political statement about the ideal aims of foreign language education. Specifically, the committee calls for developing students' "translingual and transcultural competence," or "the ability to operate between languages" ("Foreign Languages" 237). The committee sets this pedagogical goal in opposition to the more conventional notion that students should strive to become like "native speakers." The committee wants foreign language educators to discourage students from thinking they can move among a new linguistic and cultural community in the same way that a native-born speaker would. Given this concern, the committee calls for teaching that develops students' ability to negotiate communication across lines of linguistic difference. In short, translingual competence entails both necessary linguistic skills as well as the capacity "to reflect on the world and themselves through the lens of another language and culture" (237). This reflective capacity, the committee explains, requires one to "learn to comprehend speakers of the target language as members of foreign societies and to grasp themselves as Americans—that is, as members of a society that is foreign to others" (237). The Ad Hoc Committee's vision for "translingual and transcultural competence," then, would lead to redesigned foreign language curricula and pedagogies that teach students to see foreign language use not as a simple matter of adhering to grammatical rules but rather as a rhetorical literacy that involves making, in Byrnes's words, "culturally and situationally conscious" choices among the linguistic resources available to them in any particular context ("Locating" 5). A translingually and transculturally competent student would also make such choices through "broaden[ed] and deepen[ed] frames of reference" (6) such that they acknowledge differences in meaning and worldview among themselves and members of the target language community.

Compositionists should see an overlap in research interests and pedagogical goals here. For example, scholars such as Horner, Lu, Royster, and Trimbur similarly aim to design a reflective language pedagogy that develops students' abilities to communicate in multiple languages across a range of contexts. As Lu contends, language arts pedagogy should develop students' competencies in multiple languages while at the same time challenging the commodity approach to language, disrupting students' and military officials' notion that one "can simply 'ease in and out' of disparate social domains, languages, . . . [and] relations with others" ("Essay" 43). This shared vision for language arts education is especially significant given the MLA Ad Hoc Committee's call to develop students' translingual and transcultural competence through interdisciplinary, team-taught courses. These courses, the committee explains, would link English-language courses and credit-bearing, target-language discussion modules that together explore topics such as language acquisition theory, various popular and professional texts from the linguistic community being studied, and the dominant cultural narratives shaped by these texts ("Foreign Languages" 239). Echoing Lu's concerns, the committee argues that this interdisciplinary curriculum should teach students to see language not as a "vessel" for delivering an already formed set of ideas and values that constitute a "culture." Instead students should come to see language as a meaning-making system that through its use helps people to produce the culture.

Rhetoric and composition scholars can make two important contributions to this interdisciplinary effort to develop students' translingual and transcultural competence. First, scholars in rhetoric and composition can teach courses that deepen students' historical and theoretical knowledge of various cultures' rhetorical traditions. For example, Standardized Mandarin writing and discussion modules could be linked with courses focused on Chinese rhetorical traditions, drawing on research by scholars such as Vernon Jensen, Mary Garrett, XiaoMing Li, Yameng Liu, and Xiaoye You, among others, as well as Asian American rhetorics of the sort explored by LuMing Mao and Morris Young.[14] One part of these courses, conducted primarily in English, would increase students' knowledge of the rhetorical concepts and cultural and political contexts of Chinese and Chinese American communities, while the Mandarin discussion sections would give students opportunities to examine and practice the rhetorical and linguistic conventions of the culture's public texts. To borrow a term from David Fleming, these courses would help students learn what it means to "become rhetorical" within particular linguistic and cultural communities (105). In keeping with the ethics infused in the MLA's concept of "translingual competence," however, this idea of "becoming rhetorical" means more than simply learning how to create texts that follow all of the grammatical, syntactical, and lexical rules for a language. Instead, students would deepen their understanding of what it means to enact citizenship within linguistically diverse global and local contexts. Here students would consider how different cultural and linguistic worldviews of audiences and speakers constrain as well as open up opportunities and available resources for rhetorical negotiation and meaning-making.

Another body of research that rhetoric and composition can contribute to this interdisciplinary pedagogy of translingual and transcultural competence is the increasing number of studies exploring the rhetorical knowledges and skills of multilingual writers. As they argue about strategies for teaching students how to develop linguistic competence in a second language and for helping teachers to assess student performance, foreign language scholars also are trying to better understand "advanced language competence" from a variety of linguistic and educational psychology perspectives.[15] A growing number of scholars in linguistics and composition studies share similar research and pedagogical agendas, and their scholarship has identified knowledge and skills that constitute advanced competence in multiple languages. Canagarajah, for one, has traced multilingual writers' composing processes in multiple languages across a range of contexts and for varied audiences and purposes. This research methodology helps him contribute to language scholars' definition of translingual competence. Canagarajah defines this competence not simply in terms of one's aptitude for "construct[ing] a rule-governed text" in a target language but rather as an ability to perform "rhetorical negotiation for achieving social meanings and functions" ("Toward" 602). This attention to rhetorical negotiation adds specificity and theoretical depth to the MLA Ad Hoc Committee's concern for students to reflect on the linguistic and cultural contexts in which they use languages. In other words, successful multilingual writers must understand how different cultural and linguistic worldviews of audiences and speakers constrain opportunities and available resources for rhetorical negotiation and meaning-making. Foreign language scholars should look to research findings such as Canagarajah's as they work to define linguistic and rhetorical dimensions of "translingual and transcultural competence."

In short, the movement in interdisciplinary language pedagogy must be two-way. Rhetoric and composition scholars should look to foreign language scholarship as they continue to explore ways of teaching students how to negotiate written and oral communication in a globalizing, multilingual world. At the same time, foreign language scholars can and should make use of rhetorical scholars' analysis of different cultures' rhetorical traditions as well as composition scholars' examinations of second-language writers, particularly research that focuses on their multilingual composing strategies, as they look to deepen their understanding of what skills and knowledge constitute "advanced-ness" and to design research-based curricula and pedagogies that develop it in students.

English-language scholars who work to build such interdisciplinary language pedagogy must be aware of criticism that this collaboration would simply reinforce foreign language departments' existing culture-over-language hierarchy. Byrnes, for one, argues that "interdisciplinary work will downplay the role of language and language acquisition, precisely because this is not the major interest of colleagues in history or art or philosophy or political science, or gender or film studies, who might contribute to this kind of interdisciplinary enterprise" (qtd. in Wasley; see also Byrnes, "Transforming"). German scholar Peter Pfeiffer similarly warns that interdisciplinary collaboration could negatively affect not only language pedagogy but also foreign language scholars' own research. He claims that too much work remains for scholars to identify and characterize advanced language abilities and to invent pedagogies that develop students' advanced competencies. This work, he argues, must necessarily precede any expenditure of effort to create an interdisciplinary pedagogy (297).

The concerns of Byrnes, Pfeiffer, and other foreign language scholars are important to keep in mind, especially their belief that scholars from other disciplines are not first and foremost committed to developing students' linguistic competencies. English-language scholars, however, particularly those working in applied linguistics and rhetoric and composition, do share this focus on advanced language learning. Just as foreign language scholars are devoting more attention to advanced literacies and upper-division language courses, many compositionists are designing vertical curricula that give students opportunities to acquire both advanced linguistic competencies in English and "a deep understanding of rhetorical situatedness" (Miles et al. 508). Given their commitment to teaching students both to produce texts and to gain metalevel knowledge of a language, rhetoric and composition scholars can be important collaborators for foreign language scholars working to develop students' advanced literacies across linguistic and cultural contexts.

To create a curriculum that engages yet also redirects the security-driven national language policy, composition studies must expand its vision of rhetorical education and writing pedagogy to involve foreign language study. In a moment when the U.S. government is looking toward and, in many instances, funding foreign language programs and expecting results in the form of professional-level language competencies, a team-taught, multilingual approach to rhetorical education could help students to develop the linguistic and rhetorical skills necessary to communicate across multiple language and cultural groups. As the examples of the Language Curriculum Research Group and the CCCC Language Policy Committee demonstrate and as Pfeiffer warns, developing the pedagogical dimension of an alternative language policy will take a significant amount of time and resources, not to mention creativity and reflective analysis. Nevertheless, a rhetorically based language pedagogy can be a way, in the spirit of the Students' Right resolution, to counter a purely utilitarian, "commodity" approach to language study. Ideally, this teaching should heighten students' awareness of how language use shapes people's experiences in the world. Moreover, this multilingual approach to rhetorical education can be a way to revitalize the CCCC National Language Policy and its vision of teaching students to work across languages as a means to more deeply understand other communities' cultural knowledge and worldviews.

Reworking Departmental Language Policies

Whether or not the discipline of English studies can make significant contributions to emerging research on translingual competencies—and, by extension, debates about defining and implementing the national security language policy—depends in large part on English-language scholars' ability and willingness to develop their own advanced skills in a second language. As Canagarajah notes, "researchers themselves have to be multilingual" in order to conduct empirical research examining the rhetorical performance of multilingual writers ("Toward a Writing Pedagogy" 591). Unfortunately, multilingual language skills are not often seen as being fundamental to English scholars' teaching and research, a fact illustrated by the relative lack of weight given to the foreign language requirement in many graduate programs. As Doug Seward of the MLA's Office of English Programs maintains, this requirement has lost its significance within English studies because of "the utilitarian devaluation of any skill, such as knowing a foreign language, that does not yield quickly tangible research benefits" (qtd. in Feal, "Language" 6). The view that foreign language skills don't yield "quickly tangible research benefits" stems from an implicit assumption that languages exist in discrete, separate spheres and that the politics of language use and writing instruction can be studied through the lens of one language alone. Seward reminds us, though, that English is "a world language" and, as such, "bumps elbows and noggins with all manner of other languages and literatures and, in the worst cases, tramples them underfoot" (6). Monolingualism for English language scholars, Seward concludes, "means ignorance of context and of one's limits" (6).

This warning should prompt rhetoric and composition scholars and teachers to attend to their respective department's language policies. For example, both the language requirement and coursework at the graduate level should become places for addressing this ignorance, as they shape new scholars' definitions of the discipline. Through their coursework, both in "traditional" composition studies courses and in courses that fulfill foreign language requirements, graduate students come to understand significant research questions for the discipline to answer, relevant research subjects and texts to examine, and appropriate research methods to employ. Graduate faculty can help students to identify projects through which they can use their required foreign language learning as a research tool. For example, students in a rhetoric and composition studies seminar could conduct research on ethnic presses, Internet message boards, or other forums for "public writing" in which writers use non-English languages, World Englishes, or multiple languages to negotiate the demands of their everyday lives. Even when taking required literature courses, composition graduate students could pursue transnational projects that explore how the politics and economics of translation influence the circulation of texts and ideas both into and out of communities where English is a dominant language. Student decisions about what languages to study in order to fulfill their requirement can and should be guided by these types of research endeavors. Faculty should also promote multilingual language competence as a pedagogical tool, as well, such that graduate students see value in deepening their understanding of multilingual students' literacy practices and developing communication skills necessary to guide students' rhetorical development in second languages.

Rhetoric and composition scholars can also revise their program's or department's language policies so that students demonstrate their linguistic competence within the context of their own teaching or research, such as theorizing about multilingual writing from students or translating non-English writing in primary or secondary sources related to their research projects. Departments could promote this type of work in large part by revising local institutional policies to prioritize greater financial and logistical support for graduate students and faculty to study second and third languages. While acknowledging the value of Seward's concern for scholars to study foreign languages for nonutilitarian reasons, a more extensive yet practically applicable language requirement can help emerging scholars to see foreign language competency as a valuable addition to their repertoire of research methods. As Bruce Horner, Samantha NeCamp, and Christiane Donahue have shown, learning and using a foreign language can help scholars to add depth and breadth to their analysis of textual practices and the national and global contexts in which they take place. Equally important, multilingual competence can usefully inform rhetoric and composition scholars' contributions to national language policy debates, particularly those concerning the ends and means of language arts education in moments of military conflict and global economic crisis.

Revising Institutional Values and Practices through Policy Writing

The preceding discussion of graduate language requirements relies on a belief that composition scholars can respond to the present language policy debate through micro-level policy writing, weaving the CCCC's values concerning languages and language study into the documents that shape everyday activities in their colleges and universities. To engage the current language policy debate in this way, scholars and teachers can draw on institutional critique. This action-oriented methodology analyzes the rhetorical nature of institutions, examining how texts give shape to institutions as they inform the daily practices of individuals within them. Institutional critique, as developed by James Porter, Patricia Sullivan, Stuart Blythe, Jeffrey Grabill, and Libby Milles, can be a useful tool for scholars in their efforts to promote language diversity because, rather than taking institutions to be impenetrable monoliths, it acknowledges that their guiding missions and daily activities can be incrementally redirected toward different ends.[16] Micro-level policy writing informed by institutional critique can be a means for language scholars to create substantive, sustained change that challenges the implementation of an educational infrastructure designed solely to meet the military's needs. This rhetorical approach aims to redefine the university and its surrounding community as linguistically heterogeneous and to connect the institution's teaching, research, and service activities to the local community's diverse language resources and needs.

In short, employing institutional critique involves pinpointing "places where writing can be deployed to promote change" (Porter et al. 631). Scholars identify policy texts that give their local institution its rhetorical and material shape and that govern the daily activities of its members. A necessary first step, of course, is to clearly understand a school's established policy-making structure, as the extent to which shared governance among faculty, administrators, and trustees marks the policy-making process varies significantly across the range of academic institutions in which scholars work. Here language scholars and teachers must identify what Adelphi University president Robert Scott, speaking at the 2004 National Language Conference, called colleges' and universities' "points of leverage" (5), texts such as the mission statement, strategic plan, annual academic program reviews, staffing decisions, funds for faculty and curriculum development, annual awards, and other forms of recognition for meritorious service. These texts serve as points of leverage in that they can be written or revised in ways to make commitment to local language diversity a core element driving the schools' research, teaching, and service activities.

A few examples here can illustrate how one might use institutional critique to strengthen a school's commitment to linguistic diversity in the name of not only a more efficient military but also a more robust democracy. As we have seen, the NSLI encourages schools to develop programs that address the military's critical-need languages, without regard to the specific language minority groups that might live in the communities or regions around the schools. Scholars employing institutional critique to address this concern would first identify policy texts that articulate the school's mission to "the public" or "the community." A university's strategic plan and trustees' public agenda are two examples of texts that shape institutional activities in a top-down fashion. Among their many rhetorical functions, these texts, particularly at land-grant and metropolitan institutions, articulate how the school will fulfill its responsibility to serve the public interest. Scholars can work to intervene in the policy-making structure of their respective institutions to redefine "the community" or "the public" in ways that reflect its linguistic heterogeneity. Such a textual maneuver could prompt conversation, for example, about whether to request NSLI funding to implement programs in Mandarin Chinese or Arabic or to pursue other funding sources to create programs that develop professionals who can serve the local population through bilingualism in English and Vietnamese. Moreover, to appeal to the range of values held by faculty, administrators, and trustees involved in the policy-making process, faculty would define these local linguistic minority communities in terms of not only their unmet social and political needs but also the resources that exist within them that can be developed to promote new forms of economic, cultural, and intellectual development. As Pratt maintains,

> These communities should also be sources of scholars, diplomats, international professionals of all kinds. Why shouldn't Sacramento, with some 75,000 Russian speakers, be the crucible of the next generation of Slavicists? Why shouldn't the 100,000 Vietnamese speakers in Texas make that state the place for a bilingual research nucleus in Vietnamese studies? Why shouldn't Dearborn, Michigan, with some 50,000 native speakers of Arabic, be a crucible for a new pool of Middle East scholars and diplomats? (116)

Institutional critique could be used to redirect schools' attention toward such local language resources. Scholars would work to identify policy texts within their own universities and colleges that, through either top-down or bottom-up writing and revision, could heighten administrators' and faculty members' commitment to valuing such local language resources. This policy revision can be one way to fulfill linguist Joshua Fishman's vision of bringing linguistic minorities "into the educational 'main tent,' where our national well-being is given its most serious attention and most ample support" ("300-Plus Years" 95). Institutional critique, in other words, can be employed so that more resources are directed toward anchoring educational programs on local language resources and building greater public support, within both campus and local communities, for second-language learning.

Changes in institutional culture can also happen from the bottom up, of course, and composition scholars and teachers who employ institutional critique should use rhetorical strategies for prioritizing departmental programs and faculty activities that build on the community's linguistic resources to develop the school's intellectual strengths. For example, scholars might compose arguments within their faculty development grant applications or their annual faculty evaluation narratives to legitimize multilingualism as an important skill for academics to possess.

Depending on one's departmental and institutional contexts, these arguments might range from the intellectual benefits of expanding one's cultural and linguistic frameworks for research to the opportunities for creating teaching and service activities that connect faculty to the local communities within which they live and work. The goal here would be to use these texts to circulate, through formal institutional channels, arguments about the interests and concerns not just of the U.S. military but also of local linguistic minority communities, whose existence is often not acknowledged when universities talk about the "public" they serve.

Advocacy for linguistically diverse communities should entail incrementally changing the values that guide daily practices within U.S. schools. During this present moment when former president George W. Bush's NSLI has funneled over $140.6 million into foreign language education, rhetoric and composition scholars can strategically leverage the rhetorical resources available within their school's policy-making networks to shape public ideas about the need for linguistic diversity and the civic values of serving, unifying, and building on the strengths and resources of local communities.

Asserting Composition's Relevance in Policy Debates about Multilingualism

Labeling this policy debate a "national security language crisis" highlights an important aspect of language policy debates in general, namely, that language problems do not simply exist "out there" but instead get defined by groups with specific interests and with specific relationships to the material and social conditions being defined. A "language crisis" exists only when it is named as such, and this defining move brings with it a particular set of beliefs about what causes the problem, how severe the problem is, and what should be done to address it. As policy theorist Frank Fischer explains, defining a policy problem constructs "target populations," creating identities for groups as contributors to or victims of the problem and deeming particular groups to be worthy or unworthy of policy investment (66–67). The group defining the policy problem also makes arguments about its origins and does so in a way that narrows the range of actions to be considered as solutions to the problem. In short, defining a language policy problem one way instead of another at the outset of a public debate constructs a rhetorical framework that shapes what types of policy proposals are most likely to result and who those proposals are likely and unlikely to benefit.

By identifying a "national security language crisis," the DOD defines the nation's language needs in terms of the U.S. military's shortage of language resources. This definition clears the way for policy solutions that tailor the education infrastructure to address the military's language shortfalls while also allowing the military to lay immediate claim to "the limited language resources that exist [in the United States] right now" (U.S. Dept. of Defense, *Call* 12). As Deborah Brandt warns in her 2004 essay "Drafting U.S. Literacy," however, "when literacy links up with competition, with the need to win the war," "this competition . . . justifies . . . the production of just-in-time literacy" (499)—that is, literacy aimed at meeting the military's and corporations' inexhaustible and ever-changing demand for skills to support security and economic activities they deem important right now. The national security language policy applies pressure to language arts education in this way. While the language policy does criticize how the U.S. military has previously failed to develop and manage its own language resources, it also suggests that schools are failing Americans because they have not built "instructional capacity" in DOD "investment languages" (Chu, "Meeting" 6). This particular argument about the policy problem's origins depicts schools and teachers as being inattentive to the nation's language needs and, without the military's policy leadership, unable to efficiently develop programs of foreign language study. To address this concern, the military's national language policy proposes to fund schools' efforts to build foreign language programs that align with the U.S. military's critical language needs. In so doing, the DOD and other federal officials implicitly define teachers and students as passive recipients of this language policy, as resources to be manipulated toward the ends of meeting the military's immediate language needs.

Inevitably, the national security language policy sets up moving targets of language- and literacy-learning goals that schools could be constantly trying to adjust to and meet. Indeed, one DOD directive calls for an annual policy review to identify "emerging language requirements" (U.S. Dept. of Defense, Directive 5160.41E, 5). Given the "global" and asymmetrical nature of the United States' War on Terrorism, these language requirements will likely expand, contract, and shift more rapidly than during the Cold War era, when U.S. colleges and universities could over time build an educational infrastructure to meet the language needs posed by a relatively stable core of "foreign enemies." As Feal argues, connecting educational goals to emerging security crises rather than focusing on building a foreign language education infrastructure itself only ensures the United States "will never be prepared for the next language crisis because we don't know where it is, when it is or what it will be" (qtd. in "Reforming"). Ultimately, the military's ever-evolving set of language needs, combined with the federal government's expressed commitment to short-term spending to solve only the nation's most pressing security-related language needs, sets up schools, teachers, and students to be considered failures in the public eye. As Brandt notes, "there will always be a shortage of the newest, latest skills and there will always be a surplus of older, obsolete skills" (500).

Equally important for language arts scholars, this definition of the language crisis directs public attention toward the military's desire for foreign languages to fight terrorists overseas and away from the presence of linguistic minorities who speak these and other "foreign" languages within the United States. The point here is not that the United States should ignore language education that could support national security, international diplomacy, and global economics. Instead, what must happen presently is for language arts scholars to define the nation's language needs more broadly so that the policy objective is building a language education infrastructure able to anticipate and address a variety of domestic and international concerns. Although military and other government officials might depict teachers as passive recipients of this language policy, rhetoric and composition scholars and teachers do have the ability to shape this policy by continually offering new visions of the language practices that can develop from it.

A national language policy must make the nation's language minorities more visible rather than reinforcing a concept of non-English languages as "foreign" to the United States and useful only in overseas spaces. Defining the nation's linguistic identity in this way can direct funding to educational programs in which teachers and students work with and build on the language and cultural resources in their communities. This definition deems these language communities as worthy of investment, as key contributors to the long-term development of a language education infrastructure. An alternative to the national security language policy must promote a new attitude toward non-English speakers, one that values highlighting the intellectual and cultural resources within the country that can benefit local communities as well as the larger society. As Pratt suggests, "In higher education, involvement with local language communities is a good way to develop a public commitment to language education" (116). This alternative national language policy, then, would promote research and teaching centers that can build bridges between colleges and universities and area communities that are home to significant concentrations of language minorities. Ultimately, this policy would aim to produce not students who wield language as weapons for infiltrating and defeating enemies but rather students who use multiple languages in their civic and professional lives with an awareness of how language use itself shapes worldviews and influences transcultural communication.

The ideals articulated in both the Students' Right resolution and its National Language Policy should prompt composition scholars to engage this language policy debate, given its focus on issues of educational funding, language learning, citizenship, and communication. Equally important, positioning this national language policy debate on composition studies' disciplinary map can be an important step toward challenging the discipline's implicit assumption that it should deal with English language concerns only. During his chair's address at the 2005 CCCC convention, Doug Hesse called on scholars and teachers of English to engage public conversations concerning literacy education and writing assessment, contributing their "knowledge of what writing is and what it can be, the whole of it, in every sphere" as well as "the never-done knowledge of how writing develops, within a person or a populace" (355). This knowledge about writing could help rhetoric, composition, literacy, and literature scholars to position themselves more centrally within this national security language policy debate. As Jaime Mejía, Renee Moreno, and Paul Velazquez noted in their 2006 CCCC panel, however, multilingual concerns too often remain invisible inside the field's efforts at knowledge creation. Rhetoric and composition scholars must continue to problematize—and in so doing, strengthen—the discipline's theories about writing and communication by considering the linguistic realities of people who move between languages or use only one non-English language in their daily lives. Compositionists and literacy theorists working to promote linguistic diversity, then, must undertake not only both large- and small-scale language policy work but also, following the lead of the Language Curriculum Research Group and CCCC Language Policy Committee, the attending practices that can inform how these policies get implemented in day-to-day life. In particular, scholars should pursue research, teaching, and service projects through which they can discover how language minorities use writing, why they use writing, and what they want to be able to do with writing.

Composition scholars must come to terms with the monolingual perspectives that shape much of the work done in the name of "progressive" research on and teaching of writing in the United States. Hesse claims that "those who teach writing must affirm that we, in fact, own it" (338). To provide significant leadership in this public debate over a national language policy that promotes multilingualism, compositionists must come to terms with the great linguistic diversity of writing in the United States and in the world that they do *not* own because of the material and symbolic constraints within the discipline that have focused their attention on writing in English only. By researching multilingual and multidialectical writing in the public realm, composition scholars could bring to the field a greater sense of what language diversity looks like in local communities. Indeed, they would begin to discover how a national language policy could better account for the language needs of Americans who would learn a second or third language in order to "write themselves into the world" (351) or to dialogue across national and cultural differences rather than simply to meet the military's ever-intensifying demands on teachers, students, and schools.

CONCLUSION
REDEFINING LANGUAGE POLICY'S ROLE IN COMPOSITION STUDIES

AMONG THE MATERIALS IN THE NCTE ARCHIVES IN URBANA, ILLINOIS, are orientation packets given to new members of CCCC committees in the mid-1990s. When these new committee members opened their packets, the first materials they saw were three CCCC policy statements: the 1974 Students' Right to Their Own Language resolution and background document; the 1989 Statement of Principles and Standards for the Postsecondary Teaching of Writing, known more commonly as the Wyoming Resolution; and the 1988 National Language Policy.[1] These three documents were meant not only to give new CCCC committee members an overview of the policies and procedures that governed their committee's activities but also to convey a sense of the organizational identity that new committee members now represented. The positioning of these three CCCC policy statements, then, is significant. These orientation packets encouraged the new committee members to see the Students' Right resolution, the Wyoming Resolution, and the National Language Policy as core documents that shape the identity of the CCCC. Positioning the materials in this way conveyed a clear message: these policy statements provide a critical theoretical foundation for compositionists' work in classrooms, in colleges and universities, in the profession, in communities, and in the larger society.

Yet because these statements often stand alone, as they did in the CCCC orientation folders, one can see why scholars might be confused about their disciplinary significance. As Geneva Smitherman explains in "CCCC's Role in the Struggle for Language Rights," the field of composition studies holds conflicting ideas about the rhetorical work performed by language policies: "If it is true . . . that changing language attitudes is tantamount to changing a world view, then there may not be a lot that a policy from a professional organization can do about the myths and misconceptions about language that continue to plague the struggle for language rights" (370). Smitherman even goes so far as to concede the limitations of language policy statements. On one hand, she explains, the CCCC's language policies are "weapons which language rights warriors can wield against the opponents of linguistic democratization" (373), but on the other hand, "one cannot erase long-held attitudes and deeply-entrenched biases and stereotypes with the stroke of a pen—you know, go henceforth and sin linguistically no more" (370).

Both scholars and the lay public alike, then, have expressed confusion about what the purposes and the consequences of language policies such as the Students' Right to Their Own Language resolution, the CCCC National Language Policy, English Language Amendments and English-only laws, and the national security language policy might be. For example, compositionists both past and present have criticized the CCCC for presenting too few pedagogical suggestions to help them visualize what a Students' Right classroom can look like. English-only advocacy groups in Florida and Colorado leveraged similar confusion about the effects of language policy during their successful campaigns in 1988 to add an ELA to their respective state constitutions. As Mary Carol Combs contends, these ELAs likely passed by wide margins because many voters didn't understand their significance; "the text of the proposals," she writes, "seemed harmless to most voters" (148). And while public leaders such as U.S. Representative Rush Holt and DOD Undersecretary David Chu believe that the National Defense Education Act of 1958 stands as a shining example of how the government can successfully motivate and materially support foreign language education in the United States, others such as current CIA director Leon Panetta have concluded that this legislation did little to reshape the majority culture's attitude that foreign language learning is simply a form of academic enrichment (3). Here, then, are just three examples of conflicting ideas that compositionists, government officials, and the general public hold about language policies. Some people see language policies as inconsequential, while others expect language policies to bring sweeping changes and to resolve language problems facing the public.

In many ways, *Shaping Language Policy in the U.S.* does the work of these CCCC orientation packets: it situates language policies at the center of compositionists' pedagogical, professional, and civic work. Nevertheless, while this book seeks to clarify confusion about language policies and gain a clearer sense of what these texts are and what they can do, it does not let these language policies stand alone. Read by themselves, these documents seem only to be short, focused statements, but this study argues that language policies are much more complex than that. Each chapter in *Shaping Language Policy in the U.S.* situates a language policy statement within its particular historical moment, in conversation with other texts that language arts scholars produced, and alongside various activities they performed. This analysis reveals that language policies are meant to be generative. As these chapters have shown, the CCCC language policies are statements that provide guidance for professional and civic activities and prompt invention of new teaching practices. They are written with an expectation of response, an expectation that conversation will always continue about how best to implement their visions. But while the three previous chapters have each meditated on the significance of a specific policy statement within both its original and contemporary moments, this final chapter synthesizes their arguments and draws more general conclusions, mapping out seven important ideas composition scholars and literacy educators gain about what language policies are and what rhetorical work they can do.

1. Language policies should not be read as stand-alone documents.

The approach taken in *Shaping Language Policy in the U.S.* has been to contextualize all the language policies individually, investigating them within their original rhetorical situations in order to better understand them before making any attempt to articulate their relevance for present-day concerns. Examining the political, social, and cultural moments that prompted each language policy provides a more nuanced understanding of the vision for schools and society that a particular policy tried to advance and the rhetorical strategies its authors used for doing so. Such analysis also demonstrates to compositionists how crafting language policies in part involves identifying the specific roles in which scholars can best respond to pressing controversies. Chapters 1 and 2 make this point clear. The Students' Right policy speaks directly to compositionists in their role as teachers, providing them a text grounded in linguistic and rhetorical theories that, as the LCRG demonstrated, they could translate into pedagogical practice. The CCCC National Language Policy, on the other hand, defines compositionists as academics performing a civic role, providing public leadership that countered the English-only movement's arguments about the nation's identity.

This historical analysis should enrich scholars' understanding of the political and cultural currents that shape language policies and the specific goals that any particular language policy aims to achieve. While chapter 3 demonstrates that composition scholars can and should use the CCCC language policy statements to guide public advocacy, teaching, research, and policy-writing activities in response to the national security language initiative, the contextual nature of language policies also speaks to the value of drafting a new language policy statement that addresses the unique conditions of the present-day debate. The Students' Right resolution and the National Language Policy responded to teaching practices, legislation, and public and professional attitudes that effectively restricted language diversity, while the contemporary situation is one that has seen the federal government and corporations promote multilingualism, albeit a limited notion of multilingualism that deems only certain languages as necessary ones to learn and implicitly restricts where and for what purposes languages others than English should be put to use. In this present moment, composition scholars should coalesce with modern language scholars to develop a language policy that frames the goals for literacy education within this increasingly complex political, economic, and cultural situation and also outlines ethical concerns that composition scholars, students, and university officials should attend to when engaging with the federal government over how to address the nation's language needs. Like the Students' Right policy and the National Language Policy, this new language policy would be a valuable text for composition scholars, who could use it as a prompt to invent teaching practices, research projects, institutional policy-writing strategies, and community service activities that promote all Americans' learning and using multiple languages for a variety of purposes in their personal, professional, and civic lives.

2. Language policies are an important part of composition's disciplinary history.

Histories of composition studies by scholars such as John Brereton, James Berlin, Robert Connors, Lester Faigley, Sharon Crowley, Joseph Harris, Susan Miller, and Stephen North focus our attention on student writing, teaching practices, and instructional materials as well as books and journal articles outlining the philosophies on writing and pedagogy that inform them. In focusing attention on such texts, these historians accentuate the field's theoretical and pedagogical traditions as a means to strengthen the discipline's position within the academy.

Shaping Language Policy in the U.S. argues that by placing language policies at the center of composition's historiographic investigations, one sees composition scholars redefining their professional and civic identities and reimagining the writing classroom's relationship to the wider social world. Indeed, the libraries of the Ford Foundation and the NCTE offer what Susan Wells describes as one of the gifts of archives: "the possibility of reconfiguring our discipline" (60). In countless pages of correspondence, meeting minutes, and policy drafts, one sees compositionists debating what the field should be. One finds in the archives compositionists' competing ideas about what teachers' responsibilities to students are. One finds in these materials scholars debating how the field should respond to misguided arguments about the public value of Spanish or African American language varieties.

Indeed, archival materials related to language policies in composition can help scholars to fill in the fine details of the disciplinary history that Smitherman first began to tell of the field's "language rights warriors" ("CCCC's Role" 373). As scholars recover and reconstruct these stories, the entire field sees *what* compositionists created when they wrote language policies. More importantly, the entire field learns *why* they wrote them: to bridge scholar-teachers' theoretical understanding of language and writing instruction with their political and social goals of promoting civic participation and equal opportunity. In this way, a historical, archival-based study of the CCCC's language policies, such as this one, advances the project that Stephen Parks describes of "plac[ing] composition, as a field, against the shifting political and social terrain" (4). At a moment when rhetoric and composition scholars have good reason to communicate to the public their theories about language learning and literacy education, they need to see the important parts that language policy texts and their attendant activities play in the discipline's history. These histories of scholars negotiating cultural, political, and social contexts in order to do language policy work can help present-day compositionists to invent productive strategies for engaging language policy debates.

3. Language policies and the variety of texts they generate bring into view an expanded definition of "academic writing."

Shaping Language Policy in the U.S. defines language arts scholars' professional practice in a way that accounts for a wide range of material and discursive practices, including the LCRG's grant writing, conference presentations, and teacher-training workshops as well as their colleagues' written evaluations of their textbook manuscript; the LPC's extensive survey of NCTE and CCCC members; and MLA leaders' work in designing and publicizing the MLA Language Map, dialoguing with federal officials about the nation's language needs, and generating reports that chart new directions for the foreign language curriculum. Significantly, then, this book situates these journal articles, conference presentations, textbook manuscripts, and pedagogical practices—the materials at the heart of many histories of composition studies—alongside drafts of language policy statements, CCCC committee meeting minutes, grant applications for curricular redesigns, and public service activities.

The synthesis of these archival materials helps to redefine academic writing in broader terms than the usual subjects of teaching materials, journal articles, and books. Rather than seeing academic work present only in these "fixed forms" of writing, *Shaping Language Policy in the U.S.* accounts for "all the discourse, formal and informal, written and spoken by academics in both their official and unofficial capacities, in a variety of contexts" (Horner, *Terms* 105, 114). By considering all of this work, this book underscores what Bruce Horner calls a materialist definition of academic discourse, one that situates academic writing within the social contexts in which it is produced and examines the distribution and consumption of academic texts in relation to all texts within the lay community. This definition promotes an understanding of academic writing as part of the social context, engaged with it rather than removed from it.

Shaping Language Policy in the U.S. contends that language policy texts and language policy writing are important parts of composition's disciplinary practice, and it underscores the need for this materialist conception of academic writing both by highlighting the cultural, political, and social contexts within which scholars write language policies and by illuminating the various activities that composition scholars perform and the various texts they draft in order to create, circulate, and build on these language policy statements. Accounting for this constellation of everyday documents and discursive activities underscores the need to expand the criteria for judging a policy's efficacy and effectiveness. Equally as important, looking at academic writing from a materialist perspective can prompt composition scholars to read language policies in ways that help them to invent a range of strategies for engaging contemporary debates about language policy, linguistic diversity, and literacy education.

4. *Language policies position compositionists as public intellectuals who can provide leadership in public debates on linguistic diversity.*

Shaping Language Policy in the U.S. presents a robust description of academic work, as it uses a variety of traditional and nontraditional textual materials to tell the story of how compositionists have used language policies to engage professional and public debates about linguistic diversity. As composition scholars have composed these public, supposedly "nonacademic" documents, they have redefined themselves as public intellectuals. Chapter 2, for example, details how Geneva Smitherman and her fellow LPC members first identified and then filled a "language leadership vacuum" by drafting letters to legislators and school administrators and corresponding with other language rights activists and the organizers of the English Plus Information Clearinghouse. Chapter 3, meanwhile, highlights a variety of discursive practices employed by modern language scholars to provide leadership in the debate about our nation's post–9/11 "language crisis." Mary Louise Pratt published "Building a New Public Idea about Language" in *Profession 2003* to propose a rhetorical strategy for engaging this debate, but then she went public with her ideas, meeting with Pentagon officials and the federal government's Interagency Language Roundtable to suggest alternatives to security-related motivations for improving foreign language learning in the United States. Rosemary Feal, meanwhile, used several of her quarterly *MLA Newsletter* columns to highlight the relevance of this national language policy debate to the association's work; she then presented at the National Language Conference on the state of foreign language education in U.S. colleges and universities, and she commissioned and publicized the MLA Language Map. Finally, in her position as associate editor of *Modern Language Journal*, Heidi Byrnes has tried to coordinate her field's public advocacy efforts, as she organized panels at several conferences and edited a special issue of *MLJ*'s "Perspectives" that collectively "envision[ed] forms of institutional representation for the foreign language field at the national or federal level" (Byrnes, "Perspectives: From Representation" 615).

Analyzing the various discursive activities that the LCRG, the LPC, and leading modern language scholars performed can deepen one's understanding of what it means to use language policy as a platform from which to speak as "public intellectuals." Former *CCC* editor Joseph Harris urges compositionists to transform their understanding of "public intellectual." This conception, Harris lamented, is one that unfortunately had "devolve[d] into that of the maven or the pundit" who wages battles on MSNBC's *Hardball* or the *New York Times'* op-ed pages ("Public Scholarship" 151). Following media critic Jay Rosen, Harris argues instead for a different form of "public scholarship," one in which academics "join *with* (rather than simply speak *to*) other members of our communities in addressing matters of common concern" (151). Rosen presents three characteristics marking "public scholarship":

> First, the scholar's work is made to be shared with others outside the professional domain of academic inquiry; second, the quest to know originates in some problem or challenge that could usefully be called "public" business; third, the others with whom one is inquiring are not limited to experts, policy professionals, academics, or government officials seeking technical advice, but may include all manner of people. (qtd. in Harris, "Public Scholarship" 151)

The studies of language policy in this book may help readers to visualize how composition scholars can become public intellectuals by producing work that can be used outside the profession. Most notably, MLA leaders created the organization's Language Map, which was then used by federal and local agencies to make decisions on social service and educational programs, emergency management plans, and marketing campaigns. Such work reveals how scholars can become public intellectuals who "join with" rather than "speak to" other community members in addressing matters of public concern. Scholars in the LCRG, LPC, and the MLA present visions of academics as public intellectuals who can and do shape their work in ways that contribute to larger communal efforts to address the nation's language and literacy needs.

5. Language policies prompt scholars to redesign professional and institutional policies.

Each chapter of *Shaping Language Policy in the U.S.* highlights strategies for engaging public and professional debates about linguistic diversity through activities in the classroom and in the public sphere. But as chapter 3 argues, composition scholars also need to build on the broader policy statements provided by the CCCC to reshape a middle space, that of the institution, as a means to revise local policies so they reflect the theoretically informed visions for communities and classrooms that these language policies provide. Following the institutional critique model, scholars would work to insert values at the heart of the Students'

Right resolution and the National Language Policy into the key policy texts of their local institutions. This micro-level policy writing would help to refocus the institutional values that guide day-to-day practices, giving greater weight to research, teaching, and service activities that respond to and build on the language diversity in local communities, the larger nation, and the globalizing world.

This form of local policy writing is an essential part of language policy work because, as James Porter and his colleagues argue in their 2000 "Institutional Critique" article, the discipline's policy documents provide only macro-level critique and, as a result, "are by themselves not effective strategies for institutional change." "Institutions," they contend, "can too easily ignore global arguments for local reasons" (616). For example, a dean could explain to a Writing Program Administrator (WPA) that while she agrees in principle with the values outlined in the CCCC National Language Policy, she cannot support its use as a means for redesigning the writing program because the university is situated within a linguistically homogeneous area. Indeed, as Christine Tardy contends, creating substantive change in an institution's classroom practice first requires getting the writing program faculty involved, "work[ing] with administrators to articulate, reflect on, and where appropriate, transform their local practices" (635). In such situations, compositionists can respond by pursuing a strategy of micro-level policy writing that entails first identifying key documents outlining the college or university's diversity initiatives and then enacting strategies to revise these documents so they define diversity not only in terms of ethnicity, nationality, and gender but also in terms of language. Such revised policy texts could give WPAs greater leverage for material support of curricular, professional development, or community service initiatives that promote linguistic diversity. Indeed, the micro-level policy work needed to support language policy texts would bring greater attention to linguistic diversity that does indeed exist in the communities that universities purportedly serve; identify language diversity as a core element of diversity alongside ethnic, gendered, and international diversity; and promote multilingual skills as an important aspect of a humanities education and a civically engaged person.

6. Language policies should be assessed from a long-term perspective.
While it certainly is vital to investigate the immediate rhetorical situation within which a language policy emerged, one also needs to adopt a long-term view, tracing the work that accompanied the policy over

an extended period of time. The analysis in chapter 2 is a case in point. Analyzing the National Language Policy and the LPC's work *only* in relation to the English-only movement of the late 1980s suggests that the policy spoke solely to public debates about immigration, multiculturalism, bilingual social services, and the link between the English language and national identity. A long-term perspective on the LPC's work, however, reveals that the group did not ignore the pedagogical relevance of the National Language Policy. Instead, once it reconvened, the committee took pains to conduct an extensive survey of language arts scholars' ideas about language diversity so that the LPC could design more focused and effective strategies for teacher-training and classroom practice that could work toward realizing the National Language Policy's vision for a multilingual public sphere.

Seeing these long-term influences of the National Language Policy should remind scholars not to focus solely on immediate reactions to language policies because, as is the case with the Students' Right resolution, the National Language Policy, and the national security language policy, language policies can be theoretically rich texts. Consequently, attempts to respond to them can be multilayered, taking significant time to develop. Moreover, using a long-term lens to examine work by the LCRG, LPC, and MLA accentuates the fact that the language policy statement is just one tool in language arts scholars' collection of strategies for intervening in public debates about language diversity. Moreover, when this strategy does get used and a language policy is drafted, several other activities must necessarily accompany it in order to ensure that the policy circulates to necessary audiences and that it gets implemented into the day-to-day practices of colleges and universities.

7. Language policies are pedagogical heuristics.

Given that the purpose of the CCCC's language policies in particular is to provide clarity in public debates on language practices and the goals of literacy education, compositionists should not read them expecting to find a host of activities to use the next time they step into the classroom. Instead, compositionists should read these polices in ways that the LCRG and LPC members did, that is, as a means for sparking pedagogical reflection and invention.

The LPC's 2003 collection *Language Diversity in the Classroom* serves as just one example of composition scholars' recent efforts to read the CCCC's language policies in just this way. These scholars invent concrete pedagogical strategies grounded on the Students Right resolution and

National Language Policy, creating classroom practices that value diverse languages and dialects. In addition to this volume, scholars such as Keith Gilyard and Elaine Richardson; Valerie Felita Kinloch; and Kim Brian Lovejoy, Steve Fox, and Katherine V. Wills, among others, have presented discussion guidelines, in-class activities, assignment prompts, and assessment techniques for teaching composition in ways that affirm students' right to their own language. Gilyard and Richardson, for example, draw on theoretical principles at the heart of the Students' Right resolution to design and test a curriculum that helps scholars understand, in concrete terms, "to what extent African American speech styles can be instrumental to the development of critical academic writing" (39). Kinloch, meanwhile, describes how she uses the Students' Right resolution "to engender multilingual, multicultural, multigenerational perspectives, grounded in critical and creative pedagogies, in the composition class" (103). These contemporary pedagogical studies complement the archival and historical analysis of the CCCC language policies that *Shaping Language Policy in the U.S.* presents. Kinloch contends that these pedagogical inventions can help other compositionists to see how the CCCC language policies speak to concerns of not just the past but also the present (87). Moreover, this scholarship extends our disciplinary conversations about how to create the types of learning conditions outlined in these policies, ones that enable all students to develop as confident, skilled writers.

For language policies to serve as valuable heuristics, however, compositionists also must probe the theories that give them their shape. The Students' Right resolution and the National Language Policy, of course, synthesized an extensive amount of research on language variation and its implications for literacy education.[2] Teacher-training programs need to give new writing instructors opportunities to begin learning about the rhetorical and linguistic features of the dialects and languages that are part of their students' cultural backgrounds. As Arnetha Ball and Ted Lardner explain, "Teachers who lack any familiarity with the cultural-rhetorical resources their [African American Vernacular English]–speaking students bring with them to the classroom are at a distinct disadvantage when it comes to skillfully responding to their students' writing" (49). The presence of multilingual students, speakers of World Englishes, and ESL students in college classrooms only underscores the need for teachers to learn about the rhetorical and linguistic strategies these language learners employ. Training programs, then, should not only introduce future teachers to language policies but also the scholarship that informs them.

Ball and Lardner, echoing the LCRG members, nevertheless have warned that presenting writing teachers with linguistics research, studies of students' rhetorical practices, language policies, and teaching strategies will not in and of themselves transform teachers' thinking about the value of language diversity in writing courses. Ball and Lardner therefore propose a construct of teacher knowledge that considers the "unspoken dimensions of teaching, for example, its felt reality, and trace[s] them to their sources" (65). More specifically, they call for us to attend "not just to what teachers know about linguistically and culturally diverse students but what teachers believe about their ability to teach students from various cultural and linguistic backgrounds" (65). Ball and Lardner, along with scholars such as Rashidah Jaami' Muhammad; Gail Okawa; Nancy Shelton; and Laurie Katz, Jerrie Cobb Scott, and Xenia Hadjioannou, caution us to see that teachers' beliefs about language differences are deeply rooted. These "unspoken dimensions" influence how teachers read and make use of language policies. For these reasons, compositionists need to create opportunities in teacher-training programs for participants to reflect on the sources and the manifestation of their attitudes toward nonstandardized language varieties and to construct positive frameworks for identifying and encouraging students to build on the language resources they bring to the composition classroom.

While keeping in mind that teachers' affective dimensions influence their readings of language polices, *Shaping Language Policy in the U.S.* provides examples of compositionists reading these texts in ways that help them to develop pedagogical projects that affirm students' linguistic backgrounds. One effective way that compositionists such as the LCRG members have encouraged students to make productive links between their academic subjects and their cultural backgrounds has been to put language variation itself at the center of class investigations, designing projects that give students the chance to be language researchers who explore the linguistic diversity of surrounding communities and examine policy issues that affect local heritage language communities.

Reading language policies as heuristics, then, can help compositionists to create teaching practices such as these that promote students' active learning about how language debates play out in the lived experiences of people in their communities. Since these primary research projects ask students to examine local language policies and promote writing as a means for participating in the cultural and political lives of their communities, they also build on the university's mission to prepare students for both their professional and civic lives. Even more, students come to understand the significance of language policies while also gaining the facility and adeptness to engage language debates. Ultimately, by creating the conditions for students themselves to critically engage current language policy debates, compositionists can reinvigorate the spirit of the three language policies at the heart of *Shaping Language Policy in the U.S.* Indeed, while chapters 1 and 2 show how the Students' Right resolution and the National Language Policy emerged from and were parts of a coordinated effort to shape language policy debates in their particular historical moments, chapter 3 shows how these language policies also prompt present-day action to redirect the goals and practices of contemporary languages arts education and, in turn, build on the diversity of the communities in which scholars live and work.

Reading Language Policies to Realize New Professional Possibilities

As the introduction to this book set out, *Shaping Language Policy in the U.S.* addresses the confusion among composition scholars and the broader public about what language policies are and what purpose they serve, and the conclusion in particular highlights seven different ways to understand their significance. In doing so, this combination of historical and contemporary analysis ultimately responds to Shirley Wilson Logan's call in her 2003 CCCC Chair's Address to "revisit and reread" the organization's language policy statements to identify and revitalize those principles within the policies that have "salience at this moment in history" (333). Concrete actions within the discursive spaces of our classrooms and local institutions are necessary in order to begin using language policy documents such as the Students' Right resolution or the National Language Policy as frameworks for reshaping civic life in the United States. These policy statements helped compositionists to invent arguments and activities for engaging past debates about linguistic diversity, but scholars similarly need to analyze contemporary language debates affecting both English and non-English languages, such as those concerning the national security language policy, the English Language Unity Act, and high-stakes literacy testing. As compositionists pursue this work, they should also consider joining with language scholars in the MLA and other organizations in order to craft a language policy that counters the DOD's national language security policy and also addresses what John Baugh and Aaron Welburn call the "hidden linguistic legacies" of national educational initiatives such as the No Child Left Behind Act.

Compositionists need to work on all fronts to realize the values written into the Students' Right resolution and National Language Policy. Teachers need to develop pedagogical practices that affirm students' diverse languages. Scholars need to draft language policies that articulate the field's theories about language and literacy education to a broader constituency. And they need to revise institutional policies in order to create the material conditions necessary to support these progressive language projects. By strategically employing all the available means of persuasion, compositionists can begin to build a public idea about the need for language competencies grounded on the civic value of promoting greater social inclusion for all of America's diverse language communities.

NOTES
WORKS CITED AND CONSULTED
INDEX

NOTES

Introduction: Situating Language Policy within Composition's Past, Present, and Future

1. I use the term *Standardized English* instead of *Standard English* throughout this book, following Romy Clark and Roz Ivanič, who do so in order "to emphasise that [the dialect's] privileged position is the result of an ideologically shaped process, not an objective fact" (211).

2. For a broader survey of legal scholars' contributions to U.S. language policy studies, see Edward M. Chen, "Statement on the Civil Liberties Implications of Official English Legislation before the United States Committee on Governmental Affairs, December 6, 1995," González and Melis (Vol. 2) 30–62; Randy H. Lee and David F. Marshall, "'Shooting Themselves in the Foot': Consequences of English Only Supporters 'Going to Law,'" González and Melis (Vol. 2) 171–93; Martha Jimenez, "The Educational Rights of Language-Minority Children," Crawford, *Language Loyalties* 243–51; and Joseph Leibowicz, "The Proposed English Language Amendment: Sword or Shield?" *Yale Law and Policy Review* 3 (1985): 519–50. Also worth noting is Arnold H. Leibowitz's "English Literacy: Legal Sanction for Discrimination," *Notre Dame Lawyer* 45.7 (1969): 7–67. Leibowitz submitted this article for inclusion in the public record of the 11 May 1988 U.S. Senate Subcommittee hearings on English Language Amendments, thereby making it of interest to scholars interested in studying how academics have intervened in public and political debates on language policy.

3. For examples of language revitalization projects in Native American communities, see the essays by Ann Batchelder (1–8); Brian Bielenberg (132–51); Michael Fillerup (21–34); and Mary Ann Goodluck, Louise Lockard, and Darlene Yazzie (9–20) in *Learn in Beauty: Indigenous Education for a New Century*, ed. Jon Reyhner, Joseph Martin, Louise Lockard, and W. Sakiestewa Gilbert (Flagstaff: Northern Arizona UP, 2000). For a brief historical analysis of the forces that have affected the use of Native American

languages in the United States, see Andrew Dalby, *Language in Danger: The Loss of Linguistic Diversity and the Threat to Our Future* (New York: Columbia UP, 2003): 149–66.

4. A recent example of the U.S. government's explicit and implicit policies toward indigenous languages illustrates the political and economic pressures against which language revitalization projects must work. The federal government outlined a plan for protecting indigenous languages with the Native American Languages Acts of 1990 and 1992. The legislation stated, "It is the policy of the United States to preserve, protect, and promote the rights and freedom of Native Americans . . . to use, practice, and develop Native American languages" (*Cong. Rec.* 11 Oct. 1990: 15024–30). This legislation authorized spending for a grant program to work toward these ends. The federal government's support remained purely symbolic, however, until the Clinton administration awarded $1 million in 1994 to launch 18 language revitalization projects nationwide. The federal government's initial unwillingness to fund this program, of course, speaks to the need for scholars to do more than simply study overt language policy texts in their efforts to describe U.S. language policy.

1. The Language Curriculum Research Group: Translating the Students' Right to Their Own Language Resolution into Pedagogical Practice

1. The LCRG stated in its initial Ford Foundation grant proposal that its curriculum materials were meant to help both black and Puerto Rican students whose writing reflected influences of the Black English Vernacular dialect (Reed, Baxter, and Lowenthal 1). The reading materials in the textbook manuscript, however, come almost exclusively from African American writers, the lone exception being Pedro Pietri's "Unemployed," a poem from his 1973 collection *Puerto Rican Obituary*. To reflect this emphasis on writings by African Americans and about African American culture, this chapter discontinues use of the phrase "African American and Puerto Rican students" at this point. That said, the chapter's conclusion discusses the implications of both the LCRG and this book's own elisions in this regard. Victor Villanueva, who reviewed an earlier essay-length version of this chapter for *CCC*, drew attention to this omission of Puerto Rican students, and described the consequences for the discipline's understanding of the educational and linguistic politics of the Students' Right era.

2. I use the designation *Black English Vernacular* in this chapter in order to reflect the terminology used by many sociolinguists and compositionists during the period under discussion. In its teacher's manual, in fact, the

LCRG emphasized the significance of terminological distinctions about the language of African Americans. The project staff explained, for example, that the word *vernacular* in the term *Black English Vernacular* signaled that not all blacks spoke the dialect (44). The researchers also encouraged teachers to let students invent their own label for the language, since *Black English Vernacular, Black English, Inner-City Dialect,* and *Nonstandard Negro English* were all created by nonblacks, a fact that often "was sufficient to create suspicion among Blacks about the terms and what they represented" (44).

Each of the terms in this designation has been subject to analysis and criticism since the 1970s. Scholars have critiqued uses of the words *Black* (Baugh 86), *English* (Smith 50–58), and *Vernacular* (Phillipson 40) to describe African American language practices on the grounds that they stigmatize the language, its speakers, and the culture from which they have emerged. For similar reasons, Smitherman began to use the term *language* instead of *dialect* in the mid-1970s in part to avoid the pejorative connotations almost always attached to the term. More significantly, however, she explains that "as I got deeper into the study of my Mother Tongue, it became starkly clear that the speech of Africans in America is so fundamentally different, in so many ways, from the speech of European Americans that it seems to get right up in yo face and *demand* that you address it as a 'language'" (*Talkin that Talk* 14). Given the rich analysis concerning these designations, this chapter follows the contemporary practice of many present-day scholars by using the term *African American Language* when not directly referencing the texts and ideas of the LCRG and its contemporaries.

3. The LCRG also received funding from the following sources: the City University of New York Research Foundation's Faculty Research Award Program ($15,000); the Brooklyn College Search for Education, Excellence, and Knowledge Program's release-time funds ($15,000); the New York State Higher Education Opportunity Program ($5,000); and the New York Board of Higher Education ($25,539). All told, the LCRG received over $311,000 in funding from 1969 to 1974.

4. Among the LCRG's contemporaries who did reference the group's work, if only briefly, are Mina Shaughnessy, who provides a footnote mentioning the group's work on cross-dialect interference (157, n14), and Robbins Burling, who presents excerpts from a controversy about the LCRG project that erupted in the pages of the *Crisis* in 1971 (109–10). Present-day discussions of the LCRG can be found in Keith Gilyard's "African American Contributions to Composition Studies," in which he surveys this same 1971 controversy (637–38), and Elaine Richardson's *African American Literacies,*

in which she describes the theoretical foundations of the LCRG's textbook manuscript (14–15).

5. CUNY's City College inaugurated the SEEK program in the fall 1965 semester. Originally titled the "Pre-Baccalaureate Program," it offered remedial coursework, academic counseling, and stipends to 109 black and Puerto Rican students during this first year. The program was renamed the SEEK program one year later and expanded to include CUNY as well as the state of New York's college and university system. For a detailed account of Shaughnessy's role in shaping the SEEK program and creating a central place within it for writing instruction, see Maher 91–123.

6. Sylvia Lowenthal, with an M.S. in speech pathology and audiology, and Carol Reed, who held an M.A. in German language and literature, both participated in the Linguistic Society of America's 1969 summer institute, where their course of study included descriptive linguistics and second-language learning. Milton Baxter, meanwhile, was working toward a Ph.D. in linguistics at New York University, consulting in the Black English Linguistics Department at Brooklyn College, and entering a new teaching position at the Borough of Manhattan Community College.

7. In 1970, Reed worked part-time with Stewart at Columbia University's Teachers College, teaching about BEV to inner-city teachers enrolled in his "Introduction to American Negro Dialects" course. For a description of early pedagogical approaches to what he labeled a "quasi-foreign language situation," see Stewart.

8. Cohen and Redrick, both of whom held master's degrees in linguistics, joined the LCRG in 1970. One year later, Moore became both a member and the coordinator of the LCRG. Unlike the other researchers, Moore trained in the education field, earning a master's degree in education from Columbia University's Teachers College, where he focused on the philosophy of education and curriculum building.

9. When the LCRG used the term *Standard English* throughout it materials, it referred almost exclusively to the standardized *written* code of English. Linguists at the time, however, were developing terminology to differentiate the spoken and written standards of English: *Standard American English* (SAE) and *Edited American English* (EAE), respectively. This distinction was meant to counter the type of argument made by E. D. Hirsch in *The Philosophy of Composition*, namely, that if one learned to speak Standard English, he or she would necessarily be able to write it (39). Although the CCCC 1974 Students' Right background document reflects the then-emerging SAE-EAE distinction, this chapter uses the abbreviation

SE to reflect the LCRG's practice throughout its materials for referring to written Standard English.

10. The zero copula and the invariant *be* have been two of the most frequently studied aspects of African American Language. The term *copula* refers to the linguistic units *is* and *are* that couple, or join, a sentence's subject and its predicate; *zero copula*, then, refers to sentences created without this joining unit, as with the absent *is* in the sentence "He at home now." The invariant *be*, meanwhile, describes habitual action or activities performed regularly, as illustrated in this sentence from the LCRG teacher's manual: "When Nixon *be* saying that he is going to help Blacks, he really don't mean it" (48). As John Russell Rickford and Russell John Rickford note, even though quantitative sociolinguistics analyses of the zero copula and the invariant *be* demonstrate that African American Language is systematic, many people viewing the language from outside the culture fail to recognize that numerous rules govern its use, leading to uninformed conclusions that African American Language is ungrammatical or its speakers are lazy and uneducated (109). For a succinct overview of grammatical rules governing African American Language, see Rickford and Rickford, Chapter 7. For an example of the argument that BEV speakers cannot develop complex forms of abstract thinking, see Farrell. For a linguist's critique of this "difference as deficit" type of theory reinforced by Farrell, see Baugh.

11. Hypercorrection occurs when a writer applies grammatical rules to irregular words for which these rules don't apply. For example, the common rule for SE pluralization calls for adding an *-s* to a noun. Hypercorrection might occur when a writer uses *-s* to mark plural nouns in cases where words do so by internal vowel changes instead; hypercorrection, then, would explain the pluralization of *woman* as *womans*. The LCRG had concluded from its extensive research on student writing that hypercorrection reflected the forms students most often wrote in, rather than fully BEV dialect writing ("Teacher's Manual" 196–97). As a result, several student essays in the textbook manuscript showed hypercorrection, and students were to revise these essays according to SE grammatical conventions.

12. While the LCRG was developing its ESD curriculum, several linguists had begun to argue that learning to write Standard English was not analogous to learning a second dialect. For example, Carol Chomsky and Irene Moscowitz each showed that one's ability to write Standard English correlates more closely with one's reading ability, not his or her spoken dialect (Hartwell 104). As Patrick Hartwell explains, this research connecting reading to writing would eventually erode support for bidialectalist

and Standard English as a Second Dialect pedagogies, based as they were on the claim that students' spoken dialects "interfered" with their writing (104–5).

13. Smitherman defines *toasts* as epic-poem tributes to a hero who displays fearlessness, defiance, and open rebellion to white power (*Talkin and Testifyin* 157).

14. For one extended example of a pedagogy grounded on Eurocentric approaches to African American writers' rhetorical styles, see Fleischauer.

15. The original source of this quotation is Shaughnessy, "Basic Writing." Citing this quotation indirectly acknowledges its central importance to Horner's analysis of how attention to grammar and mechanics came to dominate the field of basic writing.

16. An example of such elision within composition scholarship can be seen in Marian E. Musgrave's 1971 *CCC* essay "Failing Minority Students." In this article, Musgrave presents an important critique of how first-year composition courses "seldom meet the needs of minority group students, and in fact often destroy these students" (24), adding, "I am talking as much about Indians, Puerto-Ricans, Eskimos, Cubans, Mexican-Americans, poor whites, and Cajun French as I am about Blacks" (24). As she unpacks biased assumptions about "black dialects," however, Musgrave notes in passing, "for 'black' read Appalachian, Spanish-American, etc." (26), but she never articulates the similarities and differences in the biases faced by students from these linguistic communities.

2. The CCCC National Language Policy: Reframing the Rhetoric of an English-Only United States

1. According to the 1981 report *U.S. Immigration Policy and the National Interest*, the average number of immigrants to the United States each year between 1931 and 1970 varied between 52,000 and 332,000 (Select Commission 230–31). By 1988, the U.S. Immigration and Naturalization Service (INS) estimated that the number of immigrants admitted to the United States had grown to 570,000 in 1985 and over 600,000 annually from 1986 to 1988 (Rivera-Batiz 1).

2. Dinesh D'Souza likewise argued during this period that multicultural education encouraged students, particularly historically marginalized students, to identify more strongly with these marginalized communities than with the larger nation (xiii–xiv). From D'Souza's perspective, the fragmented multicultural curriculum was more concerned with uncritical inclusion of repressed voices than with intellectual rigor. As a result, he argued, schools

failed to provide students with the freedom to develop the habits of critical thought that democracy required.

3. Lou Zaeske founded the Bryant, Texas–based American Ethnic Coalition in 1986, ten years after he first saw both English and Spanish together on a voting ballot. Zaeske, whose parents were both bilingual (his father spoke English and German and his mother English and Czech), explained that he formed the nonpartisan, nonprofit organization to combat the country's "pandering . . . to one ethnic group when there are many other ethnic groups in this country" (qtd. in Keever 1C). Zaeska described the coalition's concerns in this way: "The official English issue is but one tentacle of the octopus that is causing us problems. The other tentacles are the move from same-day, on-site voter registration; the move to count all foreigners in the state in the 1990 census for reapportioning; and the immigration problem" (qtd. in Keever 1C). This statement suggests that for the American Ethnic Coalition, the language crisis reflected a much larger problem that needed to be corrected, namely, that many minorities were more concerned with accruing power and influence for their ethnic communities than with advancing the nation's common interest.

4. Chávez, along with John Tanton and Walter Cronkite, resigned from U.S. English's Board of Directors in October 1988. These resignations occurred after the release of Tanton's private 10 October 1986 memo to WITAN, a discussion group focused on the need for immigration restrictions. In this memo, Tanton links the issues of English-only, immigration restriction, and population control, asking, "In this society, will the present majority peaceably hand over its political power to a group that is simply more fertile?" (qtd. in Crawford, "What's behind Official English?" 172). James Crawford reads this memo as evidence that the real interests of the English-only movement have more to do with racism and xenophobia than with language itself. Crawford bolsters his argument by pointing out that until 1992, U.S. English was part of a large tax-exempt lobbying project called U.S., Inc., which also funded the Center for Immigration Studies, Californians for Population Stabilization, Americans for Border Control, and the Federation for American Immigration Reform. At the time of her resignation, Chávez claimed that she had known nothing about the links between U.S. English and these organizations concerned with restricting Latino immigration to the United States (172).

5. As other scholars have demonstrated, when Hayakawa claimed that bilingual education "often results in no English being taught at all" (19), he grossly misrepresented the research findings on bilingual education that

were available at the time. For representative examples of this research critiquing Hayakawa's claim, see Fillmore; Hakuta; and Krashen and Biber.

6. The LPC's 19 October 1987 report to the CCCC Executive Committee provides a glimpse of the issues that were on the table during the committee's initial meetings. The group prepared for its first working session by reading a variety of materials on the issues of language diversity in general and English-only policies in particular. These readings included journalistic updates on the status and strategies of the English-only movement, particularly its 1986 victory in California; resolutions and policy statements opposing English-only that had been adopted by other professional organizations; English-plus policy documents then being developed by the Language Advocacy Coalition of the Joint National Committee for Languages; and scholarly articles that addressed linguistic diversity and language policy issues from sociological, psychological, and legal perspectives. On the first evening of its working weekend, the LPC members also viewed and discussed "American Tongues," a fifty-minute video on American dialects. (CCCC Language Policy Committee, "Interim Report #1" 2–4)

7. The CCCC National Language Policy also reflects the major tenets of an English-plus policy then being promoted by the National Immigration Forum and the Joint National Committee for Languages. Underpinning this English-plus policy was the belief that "the national interest can best be served when all persons of our society have access to effective opportunities to acquire strong English proficiency *plus* mastery of a second or multiple languages" (English Plus Information Clearinghouse).

8. The Language Policy Committee's three-hour panel, "The English-Only Movement: Background and Current Status," featured two hours of presentations followed by a one-hour discussion period. Below is a list of the panel participants and the titles of their presentations:

1. Jeffrey Youdelman, "Background—The English-Only Movement"
2. Elizabeth Auleta, "The Threat of English-Only: What Does It Mean?"
3. Guadalupe Valdés, "English-Only: What It Can and Can't Do"
4. Elizabeth Baldwin, "Ironies and Realities of the English-Only Movement"
5. Elizabeth McPherson, "What Can *We* Do?"
6. Geneva Smitherman, "A National Language Policy: The Solution"
7. Ana Celia Zentella, "Social, Linguistic, and Cultural Bases for the National Language Policy"

8. James Stalker, "Implications of the Policy for the Profession"
9. Thomas Kochman, "Issues and Questions"

9. The LPC proposed the following outline for a National Language Policy background statement:
   I. English Plus—English Only: Similarities and Differences
      a. Background of the English Only Movement
      b. Background of the English Plus Movement
      c. Social and Cultural Implications of English Only
      d. Social and Cultural Implications of English Plus
      e. Towards a National Language Policy
   II. Historical parallels in U.S. History
   III. Learning from Other Nations: Cultural Diversity and Political Unity
   IV. What Knowledge about Language, Culture and Society Do Professionals Need?
      a. Language variation and change
      b. Language and teaching-learning
      c. Language and cognition
   V. Implications of English Plus
      a. Testing and evaluation
      b. Classroom teaching
      c. Teacher as citizen (Smitherman, Memo to CCCC Officers Committee, 3 Feb. 1989, 3)

10. Other professional organizations that supported English-plus policies and joined the English Plus Information Clearinghouse included the Modern Language Association, the American Council of Teachers of Foreign Languages, the Center for Applied Linguistics, the American Psychological Association, and the National Council of Black Studies. Advocacy groups working toward the same ends were, among others, the National Council of Churches of Christ, the National Council of La Raza, the American Jewish Committee, the National Puerto Rican Coalition, the American Civil Liberties Union, the Haitian American Anti-Defamation League, and the Organization of Chinese Americans.

11. The following CCCC members were named to the reconstituted LPC in 1995: Geneva Smitherman, Ana Celia Zentella, Liz Hamp-Lyons, James Harris Jr., Richard Lloyd-Jones, Kim Brian Lovejoy, Elizabeth McTiernan, Gail Okawa, and Victor Villanueva Jr. (Smitherman, "CCCC Committee Report Form"). By 2000, when the LPC published its *Language Knowledge*

and Awareness Survey, Hamp-Lyons and Harris had left the committee while Victoria Cliett, Rashidah Jaami' Muhammad, Elaine Richardson, and C. Jan Swearingen had joined.

12. For example, a report in the 1 July 1983 *New York Times* revealed that a majority of Americans could not say what side the U.S. government was backing in the wars in Honduras, El Salvador, and Nicaragua (Clymer 1).

13. To understand how U.S. activities can inform Latino immigrants' "more ambivalent, certainly more critical" attitude toward the United States (J. González 191), consider the decision-making process of the U.S. Immigration and Nationalization Service (INS) in cases affecting asylum seekers from Central America during the 1980s. As journalist Juan González reports, between 1983 and 1990, the INS granted 2.6 percent of political asylum requests from Salvadorans, 1.8 percent from Guatemalans, and 2.0 percent from Hondurans, but 25.2 percent of requests from Nicaraguans, whose Sandinista government the Contra guerillas were trying to overthrow with not-so-covert help from the Reagan administration (131).

14. In this same letter, the LPC reworked the "imprisonment" metaphor central to the English-only movement's rhetorical strategies. Larry Pratt, former president of English First, drew on this metaphor in his organization's fund-raising letter as a means to tap into many Americans' concerns about the economy in the late 1980s: "Tragically, many immigrants these days refuse to learn English! They never become productive members of American society. They remain stuck in a linguistic and economic ghetto, many living off welfare and costing working Americans millions of tax dollars every year" (L. Pratt). The LPC argued instead in its letter to superintendents and political leaders that English-only policies would "ghettoize language minorities" and create a barrier to immigrants learning English (CCCC Language Policy Committee, Letter from CCCC Chair).

15. Additional research on the "costs of monolingualism" supported the National Language Policy's argument that heritage language maintenance needed public support in order to succeed. In particular, research on language instruction in the home revealed that parents and children needed to make significant investments in order to develop and sustain competencies in heritage languages such as Spanish. Education scholars Catherine E. Snow and Kenji Hakuta speculated in 1989 that "the psychological energy needed to keep using both languages or to risk losing proficiency in one" has been a significant factor contributing to the demographic trends toward English monolingualism in heritage-language families and communities (387). They also emphasized the mental and emotional demands bilinguals experienced in their everyday lives given that every single language choice

they made affected their relationships with others, their self-images, and their personal identities (387–88).

16. "Nuestro Himno" features Puerto Rican singers Carlos Ponce and Olga Tanon and hip-hop artists such as Wyclef Jean and Pitbull singing lyrics based on the original theme of the English-language "Star-Spangled Banner." At certain points, however, the song switches to English lyrics and directs sharp criticism at U.S. immigration policy, particularly in lines such as "let's not start a war with all these hard workers / they can't help where they were born" (qtd. in Wides-Muñoz A5). Pitbull suggests that "the American dream is in that record ['Nuestro Himno']: struggle, freedom, opportunity, everything they are trying to shut down on us" (qtd. in Wides-Muñoz A5). As Senator Alexander's response suggests, however, such appeals to America's democratic ideals fell on deaf ears.

3. The Defense Department's National Security Language Policy: Composing Local Responses to the United States' Critical Language Needs

1. The assertion that General Amit's warning has motivated the federal government's language policy makers is based on the widespread use of this quotation in several texts that circulated within the planning process, including Clifford Porter's *Asymmetrical Warfare, Transformation, and Foreign Language Capability* (4) and Major Deborah Ellis's *Integrating Language and Culture* (3). Both Porter's and Ellis's documents supported DOD planning that eventually led to its 2006 *Defense Language Transformation Roadmap*, which outlines a strategy for the U.S. military to build a foundation of language and cultural expertise. Meanwhile, Rick Lazio, chief executive officer of the Financial Services Forum, concluded his talk at the 2004 National Language Conference with Amit's warning, adding that until the United States learns terrorists' languages, it cannot defeat them and "can't sell them soda either" (5). Presentations at the conference collectively shaped the DOD's February 2005 white paper *A Call to Action for National Foreign Language Capabilities*, which circulated to members of Congress and informed several pieces of language-related legislation, particularly the National Language Coordination Act of 2005 (S.1089) introduced by Senator Daniel Akaka (D-Hawaii).

2. The Defense Language Institute (DLI), located at the Presidio of Monterrey, California, serves as the DOD's primary means of teaching languages of strategic importance to the U.S. military. The DLI's Foreign Language Center (DLIFLC) is the DOD's foreign language school, and the DLI's English Language Center (DLIELC), located at Lackland Air Force Base in

San Antonio, Texas, manages the U.S. military's ESL Program as well as English-language instruction for international military and civilian personnel, particularly for NATO member countries. Since October 2001, the DLIFLC has had the authority to grant Associate of Arts in Foreign Language degrees to qualified graduates of its language programs.

3. This section quotes from both the final version of the DOD's *Defense Language Transformation Roadmap*, published in January 2005, and an earlier June 2004 draft. It draws on the earlier draft at certain points because it contains more extensive description and analysis of the DOD's language capabilities, whereas the final version only makes recommendations for future action.

4. For the MLA survey Chu cites here, see Welles. Chu likely heard MLA executive director Rosemary G. Feal's presentation at the June 2004 National Language Conference, during which she discussed these survey results at great length ("Higher Education").

5. This attention to language skills as war-fighting tools aligns with emerging DOD policy about how to wage war in the twenty-first century. Specifically, many department officials argue that analytical precision and speed need to become the U.S. military's new sources of power because terrorists' asymmetrical warfare has offset the United States' technological superiority. Pentagon officials first outlined this new vision for military policy in the document *Joint Vision 2020*. DOD officials stated in this text that the U.S. military needs to focus on achieving "decision superiority" within any security environment, a superiority defined as "better decisions arrived at and implemented faster than an opponent can react" (U.S. Dept. of Defense, Joint Chiefs of Staff 20). To achieve "decision superiority," the U.S. military needs to gather accurate, timely, and relevant information. More importantly, the military needs personnel with the analytical skills to convert "superior information" to "superior knowledge," particularly in terms of examining information within its multicultural context and identifying the implications of this information on U.S. combatant commanders' planning and execution of military operations (20).

6. The University of Maryland's Center for Advanced Study of Language was founded in spring 2003 to pursue interdisciplinary research projects that address the U.S. intelligence community's post–9/11 need "to mobilize language capability in areas of the world that were unfamiliar and not well studied" (University of Maryland, "About CASL"; University of Maryland, "Language").

7. With NDEA language funding, Language and Area Studies centers were created to train specialists in less commonly taught languages such as Arabic, Chinese, Hindustani, Japanese, Portuguese, and Russian; fellowship programs were developed to enable promising undergraduate and graduate students to pursue studies in these "critical" languages; and language institutes were started to train secondary school foreign language teachers in topics such as culture, descriptive and comparative linguistics, oral and written expression, and teaching methods (Sufrin 7–8).

8. As John S. Diekhoff argues in a 1965 report, the Language Institutes program ideally would have been founded on a substantial research base exploring effective teaching methods, research that was steadily being conducted by the increasing number of scholars trained at the Language and Area Centers. Instead, Diekhoff explains, the impetus to shore up national defense forced educators to emphasize increasing the quantity of Language Institute course offerings rather than improving their research-based quality (128).

9. Between the late 1960s and the late 1970s, federal spending on university-based foreign affairs research declined by 58 percent, from $20.3 million to $8.5 million. By 1979, the number of foreign language and area studies fellowships funded by the federal government had dwindled to 828, down from 2,557 a decade earlier (President's Commission 9).

10. Chu used a second, closely related historical narrative in his opening remarks to legitimate the DOD's claims to lead this language policy effort. Through this narrative, he portrayed the U.S. military as a reliable instigator of progressive social change. Specifically, Chu presented several examples in which the DOD has identified critical social problems and then initiated effective policy solutions to resolve them, as with the 1946 National School Lunch Act aimed at "safeguard[ing] the health and well-being of the Nation's children" and the Defense Advanced Research Projects Agency, or DARPA, which "played a formative role in the development of the Internet" ("Influence" 4–5). Chu argued that because of these previous contributions to American society, "it is appropriate that the Department of Defense also sponsor efforts in language and cultural studies as matters of vital concern to the nation's future" (5). Of course, the DOD should not be denied a role in the national language policy debate. At the same time, this narrative problematically advances an argument that the DOD, given its role in convening the National Language Conference, should also be the sole definer of the nation's language needs and the sole recipient of the resources a language policy develops.

11. For an insightful critique of S. 451 (formerly S. 1089), the National Foreign Language Coordination Act, see Erard.

12. Evidence of rhetoric and composition studies' emerging interest in transnational and translingual writing exists in the form of journal special issues (*Cross-Language Relations in Composition*, ed. Bruce Horner, spec. issue of *College English* 68 [July 2006]; and *Working English in Rhetoric and Composition: Global-Local Contexts, Commitments, Consequences*, ed. Bruce Horner, with Min-Zhan Lu, Samantha NeCamp, Brice Nordquist, and Vanessa Kraemer Sohan, spec. issue of *JAC* 29.1–2 [2009]); books (Theresa Lillis and Mary Jane Curry's *Academic Writing in a Global Context: The Politics and Practices of Publishing in English*; and Horner, Lu, and Matsuda's 2010 *Cross-Language Relations in Composition*); conference themes ("Working English in Rhetoric and Composition: Global-Local Contexts, Commitments, Consequences," 2010 Thomas B. Watson Conference at the University of Louisville; and "Rhetoric and Writing across Language Boundaries," 2011 Penn State Conference on Rhetoric and Composition); and CCCC committees and special interest groups (the CCCC Committee on the Globalization of Postsecondary Writing Instruction and Research, charged with presenting an initial set of findings and recommendations to the CCCC Executive Committee by February 2012, and the CCCC Transnational Composition Special Interest Group, which first appeared at the 2009 convention). Another significant sign of how this area of interest has grown can be seen in the critiques that have emerged of the discipline's assumptions about and approaches to studying transnational and translingual writing, such as the 2008 CCCC panel entitled "Internationalizing Composition: A Reality Check," which featured presentations by Lu, Matsuda, Chris Anson, Xiaoye You, and Deborah Holdstein. See also Donahue.

13. For a discussion of one foreign language department's efforts to redesign the curriculum in ways that focus on a variety of cultural texts rather than solely on literature, see Bollag.

14. The following texts are among those that have deepened scholars' historical and theoretical understanding of Chinese rhetorical practices: Mary Garrett, "Classical Chinese Conceptions of Argumentation and Persuasion," *Argumentation and Advocacy* 29 (Winter 1993): 105–15, and "Pathos Reconsidered from the Perspective of Classical Chinese Rhetorical Theories," *Quarterly Journal of Speech* 29 (1993): 19–39; Vernon J. Jensen, "Values and Practices in Asian Argumentation," *Argumentation and Advocacy* 28 (Spring 1992): 153–66; George A. Kennedy, *Comparative Rhetoric: An Historical and Cross-Cultural Introduction* (New York: Oxford UP, 1996); Xiao-Ming Li, *"Good Writing" in Cross-Cultural Context* (Albany: State

U of New York P, 1996); Yameng Liu, "To Capture the Essence of Chinese Rhetoric: An Anatomy of a Paradigm in Comparative Rhetoric," *Rhetoric Review* 14.2 (1996): 318–35; Xing Lu, *Rhetoric in Ancient China, Fifth to Third Century B.C.E.: A Comparison with Classical Greek Rhetoric* (Columbia: U of South Carolina P, 1998); LuMing Mao, "What's in a Name?: That Which Is Called 'Rhetoric' Would in the Analects Mean 'Participatory Discourse,'" *De Consolatione Philologiae*, ed. Anna Grotans, Heinrich Beck, and Anton Schwob (Gopingen: Verlag, 2000): 507–22; and Xiaoye You, *Writing in the Devil's Tongue: A History of English Composition in China* (Carbondale: Southern Illinois UP, 2010). For insight on how Asian American rhetorics have been and are being made in spaces where European and Asian rhetorical practices come together, see Mao; and the essays in Mao and Young.

15. For examples of recent foreign language research exploring "advanced language competence," see Byrnes, *Advanced Language Learning*.

16. Porter, Sullivan, Blythe, Grabill, and Miles's formulation of "institutional critique" involves localized, micro-level analysis of specific institutions. They distinguish their critique of localized institutions from analysis of macro-level "Institutions" (e.g., the state or the university) and "Disciplines" (e.g., English studies). This distinction can be seen most clearly in the following passage: "This [micro-level] view focuses on institutional actions or policies of places such as Lafayette Adult Reading Academy, the Lafayette Public Schools, and the Purdue University campus server (as opposed to Community Literacy, K-12 education, and the Internet)" (621). Porter and his colleagues contend that this level of analysis can be an effective way to empower compositionists to see how change of macro-level institutions can be possible. They state, "We believe, to be direct about it, that local institutions (and local manifestations of national or international ones) are important locations for written activity, and furthermore, we believe that constructing institutions as local and discursive spaces makes them more visible and dynamic and therefore more changeable" (621).

Conclusion: Redefining Language Policy's Role in Composition Studies

1. The CCCC's 1989 "Statement of Principles and Standards for the Postsecondary Teaching of Writing" responded to colleges' and universities' increasing use of nontenured full-time and part-time faculty to teach first-year writing courses. Sharon Crowley, one of the coauthors of the "Statement of Principles and Standards," summarized the policy's core argument in this way: "All college writing teachers who present the appropriate qualifications and who are hired under appropriate circumstances are entitled to

the same academic benefits enjoyed by any other college teacher, including and especially academic freedom" (237). For the full text of this policy, see *CCC* 40 (1989): 329–36. For a discussion of the invention, drafting, and revision of this policy, see Linda Robertson, Sharon Crowley, and Frank Lentricchia, "The Wyoming Conference Resolution Opposing Unfair Salaries and Working Conditions for Post-Secondary Teachers of Writing," *College English* 49 (1987): 274–80; and Linda Robertson and James Slevin, "The Status of Composition Faculty: Resolving Reforms," *Rhetoric Review* 5 (187): 190–94. For analyses and discussions of strategies for implementing the policy, see Shirley K. Rose and Susan Wyche-Smith, "One Hundred Ways to Make the Wyoming Resolution a Reality," *CCC* 41 (1990): 318–24; John Trimbur and Barbara Cambridge, "The Wyoming Conference Resolution: A Beginning," *WPA: Writing Program Administration* 12 (1988): 13–17; and James C. McDonald and Eileen E. Schell, "The Spirit and Influence of the Wyoming Resolution: Looking Back to Look Forward," *College English* 73.4 (2011): 360–78.

2. The Students' Right background statement gives readers a tangible sense of such synthesis. It includes an annotated bibliography of 129 entries that would allow readers to understand the theoretical foundations of the CCCC resolution.

WORKS CITED AND CONSULTED

Aguilera, Dorothy, and Margaret D. LeCompte. "Restore My Language and Treat Me Justly: Indigenous Students' Rights to Their Tribal Languages." Scott, Straker, and Katz, *Affirming* 68–84. Print.

American Anthropological Association Commission on the Engagement of Anthropology with the U.S. Security and Intelligence Communities. Final Report. 4 Nov. 2007. Web. 16 July 2009.

American Council on Education/Coalition for International Education. Memo to Members of the House Subcommittee on Labor, Health and Human Services, and Education Appropriations. 18 Apr. 2006. Web. 16 July 2009.

Aronowitz, Stanley, and Henry A. Giroux. *Education Still under Siege.* 2nd ed. Westport: Bergin & Garvey, 1993. Print.

Association of American Universities. *National Defense Education and Innovation Initiative: Meeting America's Economic and Security Challenges in the 21st Century.* Washington, DC: Association of American Universities, 2006. Web. 20 July 2009.

Avidon, Elaine. Letter to Carol Reed. 26 Apr. 1972. TS. PA70–444. Ford Foundation Archives, New York.

Baca, Damián. *Mestiz@ Scripts, Digital Migrations, and the Territories of Writing.* New York: Palgrave, 2008. Print.

Bailey, Beryl L. "Report to the Ford Foundation on Project Initiated by the Language Curriculum Research Group." June 1972. TS. PA70–444. Ford Foundation Archives, New York.

Ball, Arnetha, and Ted Lardner. *African American Literacies Unleashed: Vernacular English and the Composition Classroom.* Carbondale: Southern Illinois UP, 2005. Print.

Ball, Arnetha, and Rashidah Jaami' Muhammad. "Language Diversity in Teacher Education and in the Classroom." Smitherman and Villanueva, *Language Diversity* 76–88. Print.

Baron, Dennis. *The English-Only Question: An Official Language for Americans?* New Haven: Yale UP, 1990. Print.

———. "The Legal Status of English in Illinois: Case Study of a Multilingual State." Daniels, *Not Only English* 13–26. Print.

Baugh, John. *Out of the Mouths of Slaves: African American Language and Educational Malpractice*. Austin: U of Texas P, 1999. Print.

Baum, Joan. "An Exhortation for Teachers of English in Open-Admissions Programs." *CCC* 25 (1974): 292–97. Print.

Baxter, Milton. "Educating Teachers about Educating the Oppressed." *College English* 37 (1976): 677–81. Print.

———. Letter to Marjorie Martus. 6 Oct. 1976. TS. PA70–444. Ford Foundation Archives.

Berlin, James. *Rhetoric and Reality: Writing Instruction in American Colleges, 1900–1985*. Carbondale: Southern Illinois UP, 1987. Print.

———. *Rhetorics, Poetics, and Cultures: Refiguring College English Studies*. Urbana: NCTE, 1996. Print.

———. *Writing Instruction in Nineteenth-Century American Colleges*. Carbondale: Southern Illinois UP, 1984. Print.

Berlinger, Manette. Letter to Carol Reed. 11 May 1972. TS. PA70–444. Ford Foundation Archives.

Bloom, Lynn Z. "The Essay Canon." *College English* 61.4 (1999): 401–30. Print.

Bollag, Burton. "Foreign Language Departments Bring Everyday Texts to Teaching." *Chronicle of Higher Education* 9 Nov. 2007, Faculty sec.: 1.

Bousquet, Gilles. "A Model for Interdisciplinary Collaboration." *MLJ* 92.2 (2008): 304–6.

Brandt, Deborah. "Drafting U.S. Literacy." *College English* 66 (2004): 485–502. Print.

———. "Losing Literacy." *Research in the Teaching of English* 39 (2005): 305–10. Print.

Brecht, Richard, Rosemary Feal, and Michael Long. "Americans and Learning a Second Language." Interview with Neal Conan. *Talk of the Nation*. Natl. Public Radio. Washington, DC. 11 Oct. 2005. Radio.

Brodinsky, Ben. "Back to the Basics: The Movement and Its Meaning." *Phi Delta Kappan* 58 (1977): 522–26. Print.

Bruch, Patrick, and Richard Marback. "Critical Hope, 'Students' Right,' and the Work of Composition Studies." Introduction. Bruch and Marback, *Hope* vii–xvii.

———, eds. *The Hope and the Legacy: The Past, Present and Future of "Students' Right to Their Own Language."* Cresskill: Hampton, 2005. Print.

---. "Race, Literacy, and the Value of Rights Rhetoric in Composition Studies." *CCC* 53 (2002): 651–74. Print.
Bruffee, Kenneth A. Letter to Carol Reed. 2 June 1972. TS. PA70-444. Ford Foundation Archives.
Burling, Robbins. *English in Black and White*. New York: Holt, 1973. Print.
Bush, George W. University Presidents' Summit on International Education. U.S. Dept. of State, Washington, DC. 5 Jan. 2006. Address.
Byrnes, Heidi, ed. *Advanced Language Learning: The Contribution of Halliday and Vygotsky*. New York: Continuum, 2006. Print.
---"Locating the Advanced Learner in Theory, Research, and Educational Practice." *Educating for Advanced Foreign Language Capacities: Constructs, Curriculum, Instruction, Assessment*. Ed. Heidi Byrnes, Heather Weger-Guntharp, and Katherine A. Sprang. Washington, DC: Georgetown UP, 2006. 1–14. Print.
---. "Perspectives: From Representation at the Federal/National Level to Creating a Foreign Language Education Framework." *MLJ* 92.4 (2008): 614–20. Print.
---. "Perspectives: Transforming College and University Foreign Language Departments." *MLJ* 92.2 (2008): 284–87. Print.
Canagarajah, A. Suresh. "The Place of World Englishes in Composition: Pluralization Continued." *CCC* 57.4 (2006): 586–619. Print.
---. "Toward a Writing Pedagogy of Shuttling between Languages: Learning from Multilingual Writers." *Cross-Language Relations in Composition*. Spec. issue of *College English* 68.6 (2006): 589–604. Print.
Carter, Jimmy. "Energy and the National Goals: A Crisis of Confidence." American Rhetoric Online Speech Bank. 15 July 1979. Web. 4 Feb. 2010.
CCCC. Annual Business Meeting minutes. 21 March 1987. NCTE Archives, Urbana, IL.
---. "The National Language Policy." 1988. Web. 27 Oct. 2004.
---. "Statement on Ebonics." *CCC* 50 (1999): 524.
CCCC Language Policy Committee. "CCCC Committee Report Form: Language Policy Committee." 5 March 1995. CCCC Executive Committee Meeting Minutes, Agenda Item 9.F.2. 22 March 1995. TS. NCTE Archives, Urbana, IL.
---. "Interim Report #1." 19 Oct. 1987. TS. NCTE Archives, Urbana, IL.
---. *Language Knowledge and Awareness Survey*. Urbana: NCTE Research Foundation, 2000. Web. 1 Dec. 2003.

———. Letter from CCCC Chair to Superintendents, Educational Policymakers, Legislators, and Selected Others. 1988. TS. NCTE Archives, Urbana, IL.

———. "Outline/Draft: Brochure on National Language Policy for College Composition Teachers." Appended to CCCC Language Policy Committee, "Language Policy Committee Preliminary Report." Memo to Jane Peterson. 23 March 1990. TS. NCTE Archives, Urbana, IL.

———. Program Proposal for Invited Roundtable at 1988 CCCC Convention. Appended to CCCC Language Policy Committee. "Interim Report #1." 19 Oct. 1987. TS. NCTE Archives, Urbana, IL.

———. "Proposal for Language Knowledge and Awareness Survey to be Conducted by the CCCC Language Policy Committee." 1994. TS. NCTE Archives, Urbana, IL.

———. "Revised Draft: Background Document." Appended to Smitherman, Geneva. "Request for Funding for Language Policy Committee." Memo to CCCC Officers Committee. 3 Feb. 1989. TS. NCTE Archives, Urbana, IL.

CCCC Officers Committee. Meeting minutes. 21 Mar. 1987. TS. NCTE Archives, Urbana, IL.

———. Meeting minutes. 22 Nov. 1987. TS. NCTE Archives, Urbana, IL.

———. Meeting minutes. 15 March 1994. TS. NCTE Archives, Urbana, IL.

Chávez, Linda. *Out of the Barrio: Toward a New Politics of Hispanic Assimilation*. New York: Basic, 1991. Print.

Chu, David S. C. Foreword. "A Call to Action for National Foreign Language Capabilities." U.S. Dept. of Defense. 1 Feb. 2005. Web. 16 Aug. 2005.

———. "The Influence of Security on National Agendas: A Look at History and Our Current Needs." National Language Conference: A Call to Action. Adelphi, MD. 22 June 2004. Address.

———. "Meeting the Need for World Languages." States Institute on International Education in the Schools. Washington, DC. 16 Nov. 2004. Address.

Clark, Romy, and Roz Ivanič. *The Politics of Writing*. London: Routledge, 1997. Print.

Cliett, Victoria. "The Expanding Frontier of World Englishes: A New Perspective for Teachers of English." Smitherman and Villanueva, *Language Diversity* 67–75.

Clymer, Adam. "Polls Find Americans Don't Know Positions in Central America." *New York Times* City final ed., 1 July 1983: 1. Print.

Coleman, Charles F. "Our Students Write with Accents—Oral Paradigms for ESD Students." *CCC* 48 (1997): 486–500. Print.
Colquit, Jesse L. "The Student's Right to His Own Language: A Viable Model or Empty Rhetoric?" *Communication Quarterly* 25.4 (1977): 17–20. Print.
Combs, Mary Carol. "Public Perceptions of Official English/English Only: Framing the Debate in Arizona." Huebner and Davis 131–54.
Committee for Economic Development. Research and Policy Committee. *Education for Global Leadership: The Importance of International Studies and Foreign Language Education for U.S. Economic and National Security.* Washington, DC: CED, 2006. Web. 15 May 2010.
Committee on CCCC Language Statement. *Students' Right to Their Own Language.* Spec. issue of *CCC* 25.3 (1974): 1–32. Print.
Committee to Review the Title VI and Fulbright-Hays International Education Programs. *International Education and Foreign Languages: Keys to Securing America's Future.* Ed. Mary Ellen O'Connell and Janet L. Norwood. Washington, DC: National Academies Press, 2007. Print.
Connal, Louise Rodríguez. "Transcultural Rhetorics for Cultural Survival." González and Melis (Vol. 1) 318–32.
Connors, Robert J. *Composition-Rhetoric: Backgrounds, Theory, and Pedagogy.* Pittsburgh: U of Pittsburgh P, 1997. Print.
Cope, Bill, and Mary Kalantzis, eds. *Multiliteracies: Literacy Learning and the Design of Social Futures.* London: Routledge, 2000. Print.
Council of Europe. *Common European Framework of Reference for Languages: Learning, Teaching, Assessment.* Cambridge: Cambridge UP, 2001.
Crawford, James. Editor's Introduction. Crawford, *Language Loyalties* 1–8.
———, ed. *Language Loyalties: A Source Book on the Official English Controversy.* Chicago: U of Chicago P, 1992. Print.
———. "What's behind Official English?" Crawford, *Language Loyalties* 171–77.
Crowley, Sharon. *Composition in the University: Historical and Polemical Essays.* Pittsburgh: U of Pittsburgh P, 1998. Print.
Daniels, Harvey A., ed. *Not Only English: Affirming America's Multilingual Heritage.* Urbana: NCTE, 1990.
———. Preface. Daniels, *Not Only English* vii–ix.
Davis, Kathryn A. "The Sociopolitical Dynamics of Indigenous Language Maintenance and Loss: A Framework for Language Policy and Planning." Huebner and Davis 67–97.

Davis, Vivian I. "Paranoia in Language Politics." Daniels, *Not Only English* 71–76.

Dean, Terry. "Multicultural Classrooms, Monocultural Teachers." *CCC* 40 (1989): 23–37. Print.

Dick, Galena Sells. "I Maintained a Strong Belief in My Language and Culture: A Navajo Language Autobiography." *Intl. Journal of the Sociology of Language* 132 (1998): 23–25. Print.

Diekhoff, John S. *NDEA and Modern Foreign Languages*. New York: MLA, 1965. Print.

Dixon, L. Quentin. "The Bilingual Education Policy in Singapore: Implications for Second Language Acquisition." *ISB4: Proceedings of the 4th International Symposium on Bilingualism*. Ed. James Cohen, Kara T. McAlister, Kellie Rolstad, and Jeff MacSwan. Somerville, MA: Cascadilla P, 2005. 625–35. Print.

Donahue, Christiane. "'Internationalization' and Composition Studies: Reorienting the Discourse." *CCC* 61.2 (2009): 212–43. Print.

D'Souza, Dinesh. *Illiberal Education: The Politics of Race and Sex on Campus*. New York: Vintage, 1992. Print.

Dudley-Marling, Curt, and Carole Edelsky. "No Escape from Time and Place." Introduction. *The Fate of Progressive Language Policies and Practices*. Ed. Curt Dudley-Marling and Carole Edelsky. Urbana: NCTE, 2001. vii-xx. Print.

Éditeur Officiel du Québec. "Charter of the French Language." 1977. Revised 14 Feb. 2011. Canadian Legal Information Institute. Web. 29 July 2011.

Elbow, Peter. "Vernacular Englishes in the Writing Classroom? Probing the Culture of Literacy." *AltDis: Alternative Discourses and the Academy*. Ed. Christopher Schroeder, Helen Fox, and Patricia Bizzell. Portsmouth: Heinemann, 2002. 126–38. Print.

Ellis, Deborah. *Integrating Language and Culture*. Fort Leavenworth, KS: U.S. Army School of Advanced Military Studies, 26 May 2005. Print.

Enoch, Jessica. *Refiguring Rhetorical Education: Women Teaching African American, Native American, and Chicano/a Students, 1865–1911*. Carbondale: Southern Illinois UP, 2008. Print.

English Language Unity Act of 2009. 111th Cong., 1st sess. H.R. 997. 11 Feb. 2009. Print.

English Plus Information Clearinghouse. "Statement of Purpose." *EPIC Events* 1.1 (1988): 2. Print.

Erard, Michael. "Tongue Tied." *New Republic* 24 (Oct. 2005): 14.

Espinosa-Aguilar, Amanda. "Analyzing the Rhetoric of the English Only Movement." González and Melis (Vol. 2) 268–88.

Farrell, Thomas J. "IQ and Standard English." *Coherence and Cohesion: What Are They and How Are They Achieved?* Spec. issue of *CCC* 34 (1983): 470–84. Print.

Feal, Rosemary G. "Higher Education and Languages: An Overview of Resources, Progress, and Potential." National Language Conference: A Call to Action. Adelphi, MD. 23 June 2004. Address.

———. "Language Requirements and the English PhD: 'A Gesture of Interest.'" *MLA Newsletter* 38.1 (2006): 5–6. Print.

———. "Responding to 'Foreign Languages and Higher Education: New Structures for a Changed World." *MLA Newsletter* 39.3 (2007): 5–7. Print.

———. "Scaring (Up) 'Foreign' Language Speakers: One Hundred Years of Multitude." *MLA Newsletter* 36.4 (2004): 4–5. Print.

Fillmore, Lily Wong. "Against Our Best Interest: The Attempt to Sabotage Bilingual Education." Crawford, *Language Loyalties* 367–76. Print.

Finnegan, William. "Letter from Maine: New in Town, the Somalis of Lewiston." *New Yorker* 11 Dec. 2006, 46. Print.

Fischer, Frank. *Reframing Public Policy: Discursive Politics and Deliberative Practices.* Oxford: Oxford UP, 2003. Print.

Fishman, Joshua A. "The Displaced Anxieties of Anglo-Americans." Crawford, *Language Loyalties* 165–70.

———. *Language and Ethnicity in Minority Sociolinguistic Perspective.* Philadelphia: Multilingual Matters, 1989. Print.

———. "300-Plus Years of Heritage Language Education in the United States." *Heritage Languages in America: Preserving a National Resource.* Ed. Joy K. Peyton, Donald A. Ranard, and Scott McGinnis. Washington, DC: Center for Applied Linguistics, 2001. 81–97. Print.

Fleischauer, John F. "James Baldwin's Style: A Prospectus for the Classroom." *CCC* 26 (1975): 141–48. Print.

Fleming, David. "Becoming Rhetorical: An Education in the Topics." *The Realms of Rhetoric: The Prospects for Rhetoric Education.* Ed. Joseph Petraglia and Deepika Bahri. Albany: State U of New York P, 2003. 93–116. Print.

Foreign Language Education Partnership Program Act. 111th Cong., 1st sess. H.R. 4065. 7 Nov. 2009. Print.

Gardner, A. Bruce. "Conserving Our Linguistic Resources." *PMLA* 80.2 (1965): 19–23. Print.

Gee, James Paul. *Social Linguistics and Literacies: Ideology in Discourses.* 2nd ed. London: Falmer, 1996. Print.

Gilyard, Keith. "African American Contributions to Composition Studies." *A Usable Past: CCC at 50*, Part 2. Spec. issue of *CCC* 50 (1999): 626–44. Print.

———. *Voices of the Self: A Study of Language Competence.* Detroit: Wayne State UP, 1991. Print.

Gilyard, Keith, and Elaine Richardson. "Students' Right to Possibility: Basic Writing and African American Rhetoric." *Insurrections: Approaches to Resistance in Composition Studies.* Ed. Andrea Greenbaum. Albany: State U of New York P, 2001. 37–51. Print.

Gold, David. *Rhetoric at the Margins: Revising the History of Writing Instruction in American Colleges, 1873–1947.* Carbondale: Southern Illinois UP, 2008. Print.

González, Juan. *Harvest of Empire: A History of Latinos in America.* New York: Penguin, 2000. Print.

González, Roseann Dueñas. "In the Aftermath of the ELA: Stripping Language Minorities of Their Rights." Daniels, *Not Only English* 49–60.

———. Introduction. González and Melis (Vol. 1) xxvii–xlvii.

González, Roseann Dueñas, and Ildikó Melis, eds. *Language Ideologies: Critical Perspectives on the Official English Movement.* Vol. 1: Education and the Social Implications of Official Language. Urbana: NCTE, 2000. Print.

———, eds. *Language Ideologies: Critical Perspectives on the Official English Movement.* Vol. 2: History, Theory, and Policy. Urbana: NCTE, 2001. Print.

Grognet, Allene Guss. Letter to Richard Lacey. 2 July 1974. TS. PA70–444. Ford Foundation Archives.

Hakuta, Kenji. *Mirror of Language: The Debate on Bilingualism.* New York: Basic, 1986. Print.

Hall, Edward T. *The Silent Language.* Garden City: Doubleday, 1959. Print.

Hall, Robert A. *Linguistics and Your Language.* Garden City: Anchor, 1960. Print.

Harris, Joseph. "Public Scholarship." *CCC* 50 (1998): 151–52. Print.

———. "'A Usable Past: CCC at 50." *A Usable Past: CCC at 50*, Part 1. Spec. issue of *CCC* 50 (1999): 343–47. Print.

Hartwell, Patrick. "Dialect Interference in Writing: A Critical View." *Research in the Teaching of English* 14 (1980): 101–18. Print.

Hayakawa, S. I. "One Nation . . . Indivisible?" 1985. *English: Our Official Language?* Ed. Bee Gallegos. New York: Wilson, 1994. 15–21. Print.
Heath, Shirley Brice. *Ways with Words: Language, Life, and Work in Communities and Classrooms.* New York: Cambridge UP, 1983. Print.
Hesse, Douglas D. "Who Owns Writing?" *CCC* 57 (2005): 335–57. Print.
Hill, Jane H. "The Racializing Function of Language Panics." González and Melis (Vol. 2) 245–67.
Hirsch, E. D., Jr. *Cultural Literacy: What Every American Needs to Know.* Boston: Houghton Mifflin, 1987. Print.
———. *The Philosophy of Composition.* Chicago: U. of Chicago P, 1977. Print.
Holt, Rush. "Is American Security Being Lost in Translation?" National Language Conference: A Call to Action. Adelphi, MD. 22 June 2004. Address.
Horner, Bruce. "Discoursing Basic Writing." *CCC* 47 (1996): 199–222. Print.
———"From 'English Only' to Cross-Language Relations in Composition." Introduction. Horner, Lu, and Matsuda 1–17.
———. "'Students' Right,' English Only, and Re-imagining the Politics of Language." *College English* 63 (2001): 741–58. Print.
———. *Terms of Work for Composition: A Materialist Critique.* Albany: State U of New York P, 2000. Print.
Horner, Bruce, Min-Zhan Lu, and Paul Kei Matsuda. *Cross-Language Relations in Composition.* Carbondale: Southern Illinois UP, 2010. Print.
Horner, Bruce, Samantha NeCamp, and Christiane Donahue. "Toward a Multilingual Composition Scholarship: From English Only to a Translingual Norm. *CCC* 63.2 (201): 269–300.
Horner, Bruce, and John Trimbur. "English Only and U.S. College Composition." *CCC* 53 (2002): 594–630. Print.
Horner, Bruce, Min-Zhan Lu, Jacqueline Jones Royster, and John Trimbur. "Language Difference in Writing: Toward a Translingual Approach." *College English* 73.3 (2011): 303–21. Print.
Howard, Rebecca Moore. "The Great Wall of African American Vernacular English in the American College Classroom." *JAC* 16 (1996): 265–83. Print.
Huebner, Thom. "Sociopolitical Perspectives on Language Policy, Politics, and Praxis." Huebner and Davis 1–16.
Huebner, Thom, and Kathryn A. Davis, eds. *Sociopolitical Perspectives on Language Policy and Planning in the USA.* Amsterdam: John Benjamins, 1999. Print.

Inhofe, James. "Inhofe Statement upon the Introduction of an Amendment Designating English as the National Language of the United States." Official Website of U.S. Senator James Inhofe. 16 May 2006. Web. 19 May 2006.

The Inhofe National Language Amendment. 109th Cong., 2nd sess. S.Amdt. 4064 of S.2611. 17 May 2006. Print.

Jang, Deena. "Improving Access to Health and Human Services Programs for Persons with Limited English Proficiency." National Language Conference: A Call to Action. Adelphi, MD. 22 June 2004. Address.

Jordan, Miriam. "Arizona Grades Teachers on Fluency." *Wall Street Journal*, 30 Apr. 2010, late ed.: A3. Print.

Judd, Elliot L. "English Only and ESL Instruction: Will It Make a Difference?" González and Melis (Vol. 1) 163–76.

———. "The Federal English Language Amendment: Prospects and Perils." Daniels, *Not Only English* 37–46.

Judy, Stephen. "'The Students' Right to Their Own Language: A Dialogue." *English Journal* 67.9 (1978): 6–8. Print.

Kates, Susan. *Activist Rhetorics and American Higher Education, 1885–1937.* Carbondale: Southern Illinois UP, 2001. Print.

Keever, Jack. "Crusade for 'Official English' Hits Hispanic Language Barrier." *Houston Chronicle* 11 December 1988: 7. Print.

Kells, Michelle Hall. "Understanding the Rhetorical Value of *Tejano* Code-switching." Kells, Balester, and Villanueva 24–39.

Kells, Michelle Hall, Valerie Balester, and Victor Villanueva, eds. *Latino/a Discourses: On Language, Identity, and Literacy Education.* Portsmouth: Boynton/Cook, 2004. Print.

Kelly, Ernece B. "Murder of the American Dream." *CCC* 19 (1968): 106–8. Print.

"King Introduces Bill to Make English Official Language." Official Website of U.S. Congressman Steve King. 18 Feb. 2009. Web. 15 May 2010.

Kinloch, Valerie Felita. "Revisiting the Promise of 'Students' Right to Their Own Language': Pedagogical Strategies." *CCC* 57 (2005): 83–113. Print.

Krashen, Stephen D. "Bilingual Education: The Debate Continues." González and Melis (Vol. 1) 137–60. Print.

Krashen, Stephen D., and Douglas Biber. *On Course: Bilingual Education's Success in California.* Sacramento: California Association for Bilingual Education, 1988. Print.

Labov, William. *Sociolinguistic Patterns*. Philadelphia: U of Pennsylvania P, 1972. Print.

Lacey, Richard A. Letter to the Language Curriculum Research Group. 18 July 1974. TS. PA70–444. Ford Foundation Archives, New York.

——. Memo to Marjorie Martus. 12 July 1974. TS. PA70–444. Ford Foundation Archives, New York.

——. Memo to Marjorie Martus. 29 July 1974. TS. PA70–444. Ford Foundation Archives, New York.

Language Curriculum Research Group. "Final Report to Ford Foundation." 15 July 1975. TS. PA70–444. Ford Foundation Archives, New York.

——. "LCRG-CUNY Teacher-Training Workshop Sign-up Sheet." n.d. TS. PA70–444. Ford Foundation Archives, New York.

——. "Students' Manual for Teaching Standard English Writing to Speakers Showing Black English Influences in Their Writing." 1972. TS. PA70–444. Ford Foundation Archives, New York.

——. "Teacher's Manual for Teaching Standard English Writing to Speakers Showing Black English Influences in Their Writing." 1973. TS. PA70–444. Ford Foundation Archives, New York.

Lasch, Christopher. *The Culture of Narcissism*. New York: Norton, 1979. Print.

Lazio, Rick. "Foundations Needed for a Strong American Position." National Language Conference: A Call to Action. Adelphi, MD. 23 June 2004. Address.

Leaverton, Lloyd, Olga Davis, and Mildred Gladney. *The Psycholinguistics Reading Series: A Bi-Dialectical Approach, Teacher's Manual*. Chicago: Chicago Board of Education, 1969. ERIC. Web. 1 May 2011.

Lillis, Theresa M., and Mary Jane Curry. *Academic Writing in a Global Context: The Politics and Practices of Publishing in English*. London: Routledge, 2010. Print.

Little, David. "The Common European Framework of Reference for Languages: Perspectives on the Making of Supranational Language Education Policy." *MLJ* 91.4 (2007): 645–53. Print.

Logan, Shirley Wilson. "Changing Missions, Shifting Positions, and Breaking Silences." *CCC* 55 (2003): 330–42. Print.

——. *Liberating Language: Sites of Rhetorical Education in Nineteenth-Century Black America*. Carbondale: Southern Illinois UP, 2008. Print.

Lovejoy, Kim Brian. "Practical Pedagogy for Composition." Smitherman and Villanueva, *Language Diversity* 89–108.

Lovejoy, Kim Brian, Steve Fox, and Katherine V. Wills. "From Language Experience to Classroom Practice: Affirming Linguistic Diversity in Writing Pedagogy." *Pedagogy: Critical Approaches to Teaching Literature, Language, Composition, and Culture* 9.2 (2009): 261–87. Print.

Lu, Min-Zhan. "Composing Postcolonial Studies." *Crossing Borderlands: Composition and Postcolonial Studies.* Ed. Andrea A. Lunsford and Lahoucine Ouzgane. Pittsburgh: U of Pittsburgh P, 2004. 9–32. Print.

———. "An Essay on the Work of Composition: Composing English against the Order of Fast Capitalism." *CCC* 56 (2004): 16–50. Print.

———. "Knowledge Making within Transnational Connectivities." Rev. of *Transnational America: Feminisms, Diasporas, Neoliberalisms*, by Inderpal Grewal. *Transnational Feminist Rhetorics.* Spec. issue of *College English* 70.5 (May 2008): 529–34. Print.

———. "Professing Multiculturalism: The Politics of Style in the Contact Zone." *CCC* 45 (1994): 442–58. Print.

Lu, Min-Zhan, and Bruce Horner. "Composing in a Global-Local Context." *College English* 72.2 (2009): 113–33. Print.

Maher, Jane. *Mina P. Shaughnessy: Her Life and Work.* Urbana: NCTE, 1997. Print.

Mao, LuMing. *Reading Chinese Fortune Cookie: The Making of Chinese American Rhetoric.* Logan: Utah State UP, 2006. Print.

Mao, LuMing, and Morris Young, eds. *Representations: Doing Asian American Rhetoric.* Logan: Utah State UP, 2008. Print.

Marback, Richard. "Ebonics: Theorizing in Public Our Attitudes toward Literacy." *CCC* 53 (2001): 11–32. Print.

Marshall, Margaret J. "Marking the Unmarked: Reading Student Diversity and Preparing Teachers." *CCC* 48 (1997): 231–48. Print.

Matsuda, Paul. "Composition Studies and ESL Writing: A Disciplinary Division of Labor." *A Usable Past: CCC at 50*, Part 2. Spec. issue of *CCC* 50 (1999): 699–721. Print.

———. "The Myth of Linguistic Homogeneity in U.S. College Composition." Horner, Lu, and Matsuda 81–96.

———. "The Politics of Knowledge Making across Borders: The Case of Writing Researchers in Taiwan." Penn State Conference on Rhetoric and Writing across Language Boundaries. University Park, PA. 12 July 2011. Address.

———. "Second-Language Writing in the Twentieth Century: A Situated Historical Perspective." *Exploring the Dynamics of Second Lan-*

guage Writing. Ed. Barbara Kroll. New York: Cambridge UP, 2003. 15–34. Print.

Meier, Terry. "Teaching Teachers about Black Communication." Perry and Delpit 117–25.

Mejía, Jaime. "Bridging Rhetoric and Composition Studies with Chicano and Chicana Studies: A Turn to Critical Pedagogy." Kells, Balester, and Villanueva 40–56.

Mejía, Jaime Armin, Renee Moreno, and Paul Velazquez. "Bringing Chicano/a Studies into the Center of Rhetoric and Composition Studies." Concurrent Panel. Conference on College Composition and Communication. Palmer House, Chicago. 23 Mar. 2006. Address.

Miles, Libby, Michael Pennell, Kim Hensley Owens, Jeremiah Dyehouse, Helen O'Grady, Nedra Reynolds, Robert Schwegler, and Linda Shamoon. "Thinking Vertically." *CCC* 59.3 (2008): 503–11. Print.

Miller, Susan. *Textual Carnivals: The Politics of Composition.* Carbondale: Southern Illinois UP, 1991. Print.

Milroy, Lesley. *Language and Social Networks.* 2nd ed. Oxford: Basil Blackwell, 1987. Print.

MLA Ad Hoc Committee on Foreign Languages. "Foreign Languages and Higher Education: New Structures for a Changed World." *Profession* (2007): 234–45. Print.

———. "Transforming College and University Foreign Language Departments." *MLJ* 92.2 (2008): 287–92. Print.

"The MLA Language Map." *MLA Newsletter* 36.3 (Fall 2004): 21. Print.

"MLJ Perspectives Panels: Representing Foreign Language Education." Professional Website of Georgetown University Faculty Member Heidi Byrnes. 7 Apr. 2008. Web. 31 Oct. 2008.

Mok, Sam. "Language Capabilities of the U.S. Workforce." National Language Conference: A Call to Action. Adelphi, MD. 23 June 2004. Address.

Monroe, Kelvin. "Writin da Funk Dealer: Songs of Reflections and Reflex/shuns." *College English* 67 (2004): 102–20. Print.

Moore, Samuel A. Letter to Marjorie Martus. 28 March 1972. TS. PA70-444. Ford Foundation Archives, New York.

Morse, J. Mitchell. "The Shuffling Speech of Slavery: Black English." *College English* 34 (1973): 834–43. Print.

Musgrave, Marian E. "Failing Minority Students: Class, Caste, and Racial Bias in American Colleges." *CCC* 22 (1971): 24–29. Print.

NAFSA: Association of International Educators. "Higher Education Reauthorization." n.d. Web. 1 July 2010.

Native American Language Act. *Cong. Rec.* 11 Oct. 1990. 15024–30. Print.

National Commission on Terrorist Attacks upon the United States. *The 9/11 Commission Report*. New York: Norton, 2004. Print.

National Foreign Language Coordination Act. 110th Cong., 1st sess. H.R. 747. 31 Jan. 2007. Print.

National Foreign Language Coordination Act of 2007. 110th Cong., 1st sess. S.451. 31 Jan. 2007. Print.

National Security Education Program. *National Security Education Program: Strengthening U.S. National Security through Critical Language and Culture Expertise*. Washington, DC: NSEP, 2007. Web. 15 May 2010.

National Security Language Act. 110th Cong., 1st sess. H.R. 678. 24 Jan. 2007. Print.

NCTE. "Resolution on English as the 'Official Language.'" 1986. Web. 27 Oct. 2004.

NCTE Executive Committee. Meeting Minutes. San Antonio, TX. 25 Nov. 1986. TS. NCTE Archives, Urbana, IL.

———. "NCTE Speaks Out on Arizona Department of Education Ruling on Teacher Speech." NCTE Homepage. 7 June 2010. Web. 8 June 2010.

New London Group. "A Pedagogy of Multiliteracies: Designing Social Futures." Cope and Kalantzis 9–37.

Nunberg, Geoffrey. "The Official English Movement: Reimagining America." Foreword. Crawford, *Language Loyalties* 479–94.

Oakland Unified School District Board of Education. "Resolution of the Board of Education Adopting the Report and Recommendations of the African-American Task Force." Dec. 1996. *Ebonics: The Urban Education Debate*. 2nd ed. Ed. J. David Ramirez, Terrence G. Wiley, Gerda de Klerk, Enid Lee, and Wayne E. Wright. Clevedon, UK: Multilingual Matters, 2005. 115–31. Print.

Okawa, Gail Y. "'Resurfacing Roots': Developing a Pedagogy of Language Awareness from Two Views." Smitherman and Villanueva, *Language Diversity* 109–33.

O'Neil, Wayne. "The Politics of Bidialectalism." *College English* 33 (1972): 433–38. Print.

Ortmeier-Hooper, Christina. "(Re)Positioning the CCCC Statement on Second Language Writing and Writers." Conference on College Composition and Communication. Atlanta, GA. 7 Apr. 2011. Address.

Pai, Mahealani. "Culture, Language, and Oral History and Their Relationship to the Land." Tokai University Conference on Literacy for Change: Community-Based Approaches. Tokai University, Honolulu, HI. 1997. Address.

Panetta, Leon E. "Foreign Language Education: If 'Scandalous' in the 20th Century, What Will It Be in the 21st Century?" Stanford Language Center, Palo Alto, CA. 7 May 1999. Address.

Parks, Stephen. *Class Politics: The Movement for the Students' Right to Their Own Language*. Urbana: NCTE, 2000. Print.

Pennell, Michael. "Implementing 'Students' Right to Their Own Language': Language Awareness in the First Year Composition Classroom." Bruch and Marback, *Hope* 227–44.

Perea, Juan F. "The New American Spanish War: How the Courts and the Legislatures Are Aiding the Suppression of Languages Other than English." González and Melis (Vol. 2) 121–39.

Perry, Theresa, and Lisa Delpit, eds. *The Real Ebonics Debate: Power, Language, and the Education of African American Children*. Boston: Beacon, 1998. Print.

Phillipson, Robert. *Linguistic Imperialism*. Oxford: Oxford UP, 1992. Print.

Piatt, Bill. *¿Only English?: Law and Language Policy in the United States*. Albuquerque: U of New Mexico P, 1990. Print.

Pixton, William. "A Contemporary Dilemma: The Question of Standard English." *CCC* 25 (1974): 247–53. Print.

Porter, Clifford F. *Asymmetrical Warfare, Transformation, and Foreign Language Capability*. Fort Leavenworth, KS: Combat Studies Institute, 2002. Print.

Porter, James E., Patricia Sullivan, Stuart Blythe, Jeffrey T. Grabill, and Libby Miles. "Institutional Critique: A Rhetorical Methodology for Change." *CCC* 51 (2000): 610–42. Print.

Pratt, Larry. English First Fund-raising Letter. n.d. TS. NCTE Archives, Urbana, IL.

Pratt, Mary Louise. "Building a New Public Idea about Language." *Profession* (2003): 110–19. Print.

Prendergast, Catherine. *Buying into English: Language and Investment in the New Capitalist World*. Pittsburgh: U of Pittsburgh P, 2008. Print.

President's Commission on Foreign Language and International Studies. *Strength through Wisdom: A Critique of U.S. Capability: A Report to the President*. Washington, DC: GPO, 1979. Print.

"Proposed Official English Amendments to the U.S. Constitution (1981–1989)." Crawford, *Language Loyalties* 112–13.

Ratcliffe, Krista. *Rhetorical Listening: Identification, Gender, Whiteness*. Carbondale: Southern Illinois UP, 2005. Print.

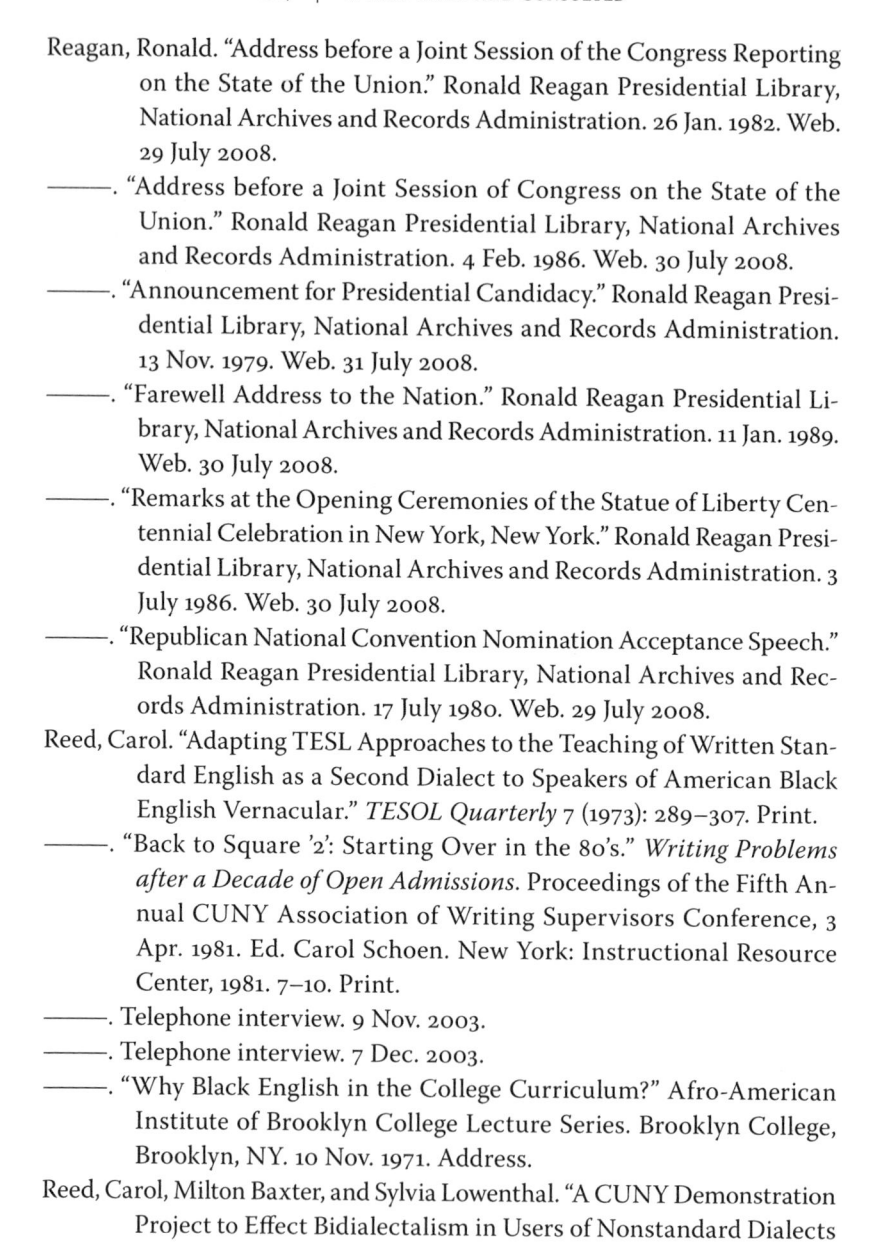

Reagan, Ronald. "Address before a Joint Session of the Congress Reporting on the State of the Union." Ronald Reagan Presidential Library, National Archives and Records Administration. 26 Jan. 1982. Web. 29 July 2008.

———. "Address before a Joint Session of Congress on the State of the Union." Ronald Reagan Presidential Library, National Archives and Records Administration. 4 Feb. 1986. Web. 30 July 2008.

———. "Announcement for Presidential Candidacy." Ronald Reagan Presidential Library, National Archives and Records Administration. 13 Nov. 1979. Web. 31 July 2008.

———. "Farewell Address to the Nation." Ronald Reagan Presidential Library, National Archives and Records Administration. 11 Jan. 1989. Web. 30 July 2008.

———. "Remarks at the Opening Ceremonies of the Statue of Liberty Centennial Celebration in New York, New York." Ronald Reagan Presidential Library, National Archives and Records Administration. 3 July 1986. Web. 30 July 2008.

———. "Republican National Convention Nomination Acceptance Speech." Ronald Reagan Presidential Library, National Archives and Records Administration. 17 July 1980. Web. 29 July 2008.

Reed, Carol. "Adapting TESL Approaches to the Teaching of Written Standard English as a Second Dialect to Speakers of American Black English Vernacular." *TESOL Quarterly* 7 (1973): 289–307. Print.

———. "Back to Square '2': Starting Over in the 80's." *Writing Problems after a Decade of Open Admissions.* Proceedings of the Fifth Annual CUNY Association of Writing Supervisors Conference, 3 Apr. 1981. Ed. Carol Schoen. New York: Instructional Resource Center, 1981. 7–10. Print.

———. Telephone interview. 9 Nov. 2003.

———. Telephone interview. 7 Dec. 2003.

———. "Why Black English in the College Curriculum?" Afro-American Institute of Brooklyn College Lecture Series. Brooklyn College, Brooklyn, NY. 10 Nov. 1971. Address.

Reed, Carol, Milton Baxter, and Sylvia Lowenthal. "A CUNY Demonstration Project to Effect Bidialectalism in Users of Nonstandard Dialects of English." Proposal to the Ford Foundation. 24 March 1970. TS. PA70-444. Ford Foundation Archives, New York.

"Reforming Study of Foreign Languages." *Blue and Gray* 28 Apr. 2008. Web. 3 June 2009.

Rich, Adrienne. "Teaching Language in Open Admissions." *On Lies, Secrets, and Silence*. New York: Norton, 1979. 51–68. Print.

Richardson, Elaine. *African American Literacies*. London: Routledge, 2003. Print.

———. "The Anti-Ebonics Movement: 'Standard' English Only." *Journal of English Linguistics* 26.2 (1998): 156–69. Print.

———. "Race, Class(es), Gender, and Age: The Making of Knowledge about Language Diversity." Smitherman and Villanueva, *Language Diversity* 40–66. Print.

Rickford, John, and Angela Rickford. "Dialect Readers Revisited." *Dialects and Education*. Spec. issue of *Linguistics and Education* 7.2 (1995): 107–28. Print.

Rickford, John Russell, and Russell John Rickford. *Spoken Soul: The Story of Black English*. New York: Wiley, 2000. Print.

Rivera-Batiz, Francisco L. Introduction. *U.S. Immigration Policy Reform in the 1980s: A Preliminary Assessment*. Ed. Francisco L. Rivera-Batiz, Selig L. Sechzer, and Ira N. Gang. New York: Praeger, 1991. 1–16. Print.

Rodby, Judith. *Appropriating Literacy: Reading and Writing in English as a Second Language*. Portsmouth: Boynton/Cook, 1992. Print.

Rodriguez, Richard. *Hunger of Memory: The Education of Richard Rodriguez*. New York: Bantam, 1982. Print.

Royster, Jacqueline Jones, and Jean C. Williams. "History in the Spaces Left: African American Presence and Narratives of Composition Studies." *A Usable Past: CCC at 50*, Part 2. Spec. issue of *CCC* 50 (1999): 563–84. Print.

Schildkraut, Deborah J. *Press "One" for English: Language Policy, Public Opinion, and American Identity*. Princeton: Princeton UP, 2005. Print.

Schneider, Stephen. "Freedom Schooling: Stokely Carmichael and Critical Rhetorical Education." *CCC* 58.1 (2006): 46–69. Print.

Science Applications International Corporation. *Foreign Area Officer Programs: Changing DOD's Culture, Defense Language Transformation Task 2*. McLean, VA: SAIC, 2004. Print.

Scott, Jerrie Cobb, Dolores Y. Straker, and Laure Katz, eds. *Affirming Students' Right to Their Own Language: Bridging Language Policies and Pedagogical Practices*. New York: Routledge and NCTE, 2009. Print.

———. Preface. Scott, Straker, and Katz, *Affirming* xvii–xxi.

Scott, Robert A. "Many Calls, Little Action: Global Illiteracy in the United States." National Language Conference: A Call to Action. Adelphi, MD. 23 June 2004. Address.

Sealy, Rose. Letter to Samuel Moore. 31 May 1972. TS. PA70–444. Ford Foundation Archives.

Select Commission on Immigration and Refugee Policy. *U.S. Immigration Policy and the National Interest.* Washington, DC: GPO, 1981. Print.

"Sen. Alexander to Introduce Senate Resolution on Singing National Anthem in English." Official Website of U.S. Senator Lamar Alexander. 28 Apr. 2006. Web. 19 May 2006.

Shaughnessy, Mina P. "Basic Writing and Open Admissions." Intradepartmental Memorandum to Theodore Gross, 10 Dec. 1970. City College Archives, City College of New York. Print.

———. *Errors and Expectations: A Guide for the Teacher of Basic Writing.* New York: Oxford UP, 1977. Print.

Sheils, Merrill. "Why Johnny Can't Write." *Newsweek* 8 Dec. 1975, 58–62+. Print.

Shin, Hyon B., with Rosalind Bruno. *Language Use and English-Speaking Ability: Census 2000 Brief.* Washington, DC: U.S. Dept. of Commerce, 2003. Print.

Shor, Ira. *Culture Wars: School and Society in the Conservative Restoration, 1969–1984.* Boston: Routledge, 1986. Print.

Simone, Michael R. "Language Is Our Weapon." National Language Conference: A Call to Action. Adelphi, MD. 22 June 2004. Address.

Simpkins, Gary A., Grace Holt, and Charlesetta Simpkins. *Bridge: A Cross-Cultural Reading Program.* Boston: Houghton-Mifflin, 1977. Print.

Simpkins, Gary A., and Charlesetta Simpkins. "Cross-Cultural Approach to Curriculum Development." *Black English and the Education of Black Children and Youth.* Proceedings of the National Invitational Symposium on the King Decision. Ed. Geneva Smitherman. Detroit: Center for Black Studies, Wayne State UP, 1981. 221–40. Print.

Skutnabb-Kangas, Tove. *Linguistic Genocide in Education—or Worldwide Diversity and Human Rights?* London: Routledge, 2000. Print.

Sledd, James. "Anglo-Conformity: Folk Remedy for Lost Hegemony." Daniels, *Not Only English* 87–95.

———. "Doublespeak: Dialectology in the Service of Big Brother." *College English* 33 (1972): 439–56. Print.

Smith, Ernie. "What Is Black English? What Is Ebonics?" Perry and Delpit 49–58.

Smitherman, Geneva. "CCCC and the 'Students' Right to Their Own Language.'" Smitherman, *Talkin That Talk* 375–99.

———. "CCCC's Role in the Struggle for Language Rights." *A Usable Past: CCC at 50*, Part 1. Spec. issue of *CCC* 50 (1999): 349–76. Print.

———. "'Lessons of the Blood': Toward a National Public Policy on Language." *College English* 49 (1987): 29–36. Print.

———. Letter to CCCC Executive Committee. 9 Mar. 1994. TS. NCTE Archives, Urbana, IL.

———. "The 'Mis-Education of the Negro'—and You Too." Daniels, *Not Only English* 109–20.

———. Personal interview. 26 March 2004.

———. *Talkin and Testifyin: The Language of Black America*. Detroit: Wayne State UP, 1977. Print.

———. *Talkin That Talk: Language, Culture, and Education in African America*. London: Routledge, 1999. Print.

Smitherman, Geneva, and Victor Villanueva. Introduction. Smitherman and Villanueva, *Language Diversity* 1–6.

———, eds. *Language Diversity in the Classroom: From Intention to Practice*. Carbondale: Southern Illinois UP, 2003. Print.

Snow, Catherine E., and Kenji Hakuta. "The Costs of Monolingualism." Crawford, *Language Loyalties* 384–94.

Soliday, Mary. *The Politics of Remediation: Institutional and Student Needs in Higher Education*. Pittsburgh: U of Pittsburgh P, 2002. Print.

Spolsky, Bernard. *Language Policy*. Cambridge: Cambridge UP, 2004. Print.

"State Official Language Statutes and Constitutional Amendments." Crawford, *Language Loyalties* 132–135.

Stewart, William A. "Foreign Language Teaching Methods in Quasi-Foreign Language Situations." *Teaching Standard English in the Inner City*. Ed. Ralph W. Fasold and Roger Shuy. Washington, DC: Center for Applied Linguistics, 1970. 1–19. Print.

Street, Brian V. *Social Literacies: Critical Approaches to Literacy in Development, Ethnography and Education*. London: Longman, 1995. Print.

"Student Course-Evaluation Questionnaire." 4 Mar. 1975. Appendix. Language Curriculum Research Group, "Final Report." PA70-444. Ford Foundation Archives, New York.

Sufrin, Sidney C. *Administering the National Defense Education Act*. Syracuse: Syracuse UP, 1963. Print.

Sundberg, Trudy J. "The Case against Bilingualism." *English Journal* 77.3 (1988): 16–17. Print.

———. "Response to Gonzalez, Schott, and Vasquez." *English Journal* 77.5 (1988): 85. Print.

Tardy, Christine M. "Enacting and Transforming Local Language Policies." *CCC* 62.4 (2011): 634–61. Print.

Trimbur, John. "Linguistic Memory and the Politics of U.S. English." *Cross-Language Relations in Composition*. Spec. issue of *College English* 68 (2006): 575–88.

———. "Literacy and the Discourse of Crisis." *The Politics of Writing Instruction: Postsecondary*. Ed. Richard Bullock and John Trimbur. Portsmouth: Boynton/Cook. 277–95. Print.

University of Maryland Center for Advanced Study of Language. "About CASL." 2007. Web. 27 May 2008.

———. "Language Research in Service to the Nation: Annual Report, FY 2007." 2007. Web. 27 May 2008.

U.S. Congress. House. Subcommittee on Civil and Constitutional Rights. *English Language Constitutional Amendments: Hearings on H.J. Res. 13, H.J. Res. 33, H.J. Res. 60, and H.J. Res. 83*. 100th Congress, 2nd session. 11 May 1988. Washington, DC: GPO, 1988. Print.

U.S. Dept. of Defense. *A Call to Action for National Foreign Language Capabilities*. 1 Feb 2005. Print.

———. *Defense Language Transformation Roadmap*. Draft. U.S. Dept. of Defense Transformation Website. 16 June 2004. Web. 15 Oct. 2004.

———. *Defense Language Transformation Roadmap*. U.S. Dept. of Defense Transformation Website. January 2005. Web. 1 June 2008.

———. Joint Chiefs of Staff. *Joint Vision 2020*. Washington, DC: GPO, 2000.

———. Office of the Undersecretary of Defense for Personnel and Readiness. *Defense Language Institute Foreign Language Center*. Transformation White Paper. 30 March 2004. Web. 16 Jan. 2005.

U.S. Dept. of Education. Office of Postsecondary Education. *Enhancing Foreign Language Proficiency in the United States: Preliminary Results of the National Security Language Initiative*. Washington, DC: GPO, Aug. 2008. Web. 15 May 2010.

U.S. Dept. of State. Office of the Spokesman. "Fact Sheet on National Security Language Initiative." 5 Jan. 2006. Web. 9 Jan. 2006.

U.S. English. "In Defense of Our Common Language." Crawford, *Language Loyalties* 143–47.

U.S. General Accounting Office. *Foreign Languages: Human Capital Approach Needed to Correct Staffing and Proficiency Shortfalls*. Washington, DC: GPO, 2002. Print.

Valdés, Guadalupe. *Learning and Not Learning English: Latino Students in American Schools*. New York: Teachers College P, 2001. Print.
van der Heide, Marijke. Remarks to panel on "Present and Future Needs for Language Skills in the Federal Sector." National Language Conference: A Call to Action. Adelphi, MD. 22 June 2004. Address.
Villa, Daniel. "*No nos dejaremos*: Writing in Spanish as an Act of Resistance." Kells, Balester, and Villanueva 85–95.
Villanueva, Victor. *Bootstraps: From an American Academic of Color*. Urbana: NCTE, 1993. Print.
———. "On English Only." Afterword. González and Melis (Volume 1) 333–42.
———. "The Voice of Voices in the Writer of Color." *Multiple Intelligences*. Spec. issue of *English Journal* 84.8 (1995): 68–69. Print.
———. "Whose Voice Is It Anyway? Rodriguez' Speech in Retrospect." *English Journal* 76.8 (1987): 17–21. Print.
Ward, F. Champion. "Request for Grant Action." 22 June 1970. TS. PA70-444. Ford Foundation Archives.
Wasley, Paula. "MLA Report on Foreign Language Education Continues to Provoke Debate." *Chronicle of Higher Education* 14 May 2008, Faculty sec.: 12. Print.
Watzke, John L. *Lasting Change in Foreign Language Education: A Historical Case for Change in National Policy*. Westport: Praeger, 2003.
Welles, Elizabeth B. "Foreign Language Enrollments in United States Institutions of Higher Education, Fall 2002." *ADFL Bulletin* 35.2–3 (2004): 7–26.
Wells, Susan. "Claiming the Archive for Rhetoric and Composition." *Rhetoric and Composition as Intellectual Work*. Ed. Gary Olson. Carbondale: Southern Illinois UP, 2002. 55–64. Print.
White, John Kenneth. *The New Politics of Old Values*. 2nd ed. Hanover: UP of New England, 1990. Print.
Wides-Munoz, Laura. "Spanish-language 'Banner' Draws Ire." *Boston Globe* 28 Apr. 2006: A5. Print.
Williams, Robert S., and Kathleen C. Riley. "Acquiring a Slice of Anglo-American Pie: A Portrait of Language Shift in a Franco-American Family." González and Melis (Vol. 2) 63–90.
Wittman, Emily O., and Katrina Windon. "Twisted Tongues, Tied Hands: Translation Studies and the English Major." *College English* 72.5 (2010): 449–69. Print.

Wolfram, Walt. "Reaction to: *For Teaching Standard English* . . ." July 1974. TS. PA70–444. Ford Foundation Archives, New York.

Woo, Elaine. "Immigrants—A Rush to Classrooms." *Los Angeles Times* 24 Sept. 1986. Web. 8 Mar. 2010.

Wright, Richard. "Reaction to *For Teaching SE* . . ." July 1974. TS. PA70–444. Ford Foundation Archives, New York.

Yazzie-Mintz, Tarajean. "From a Place Deep Inside: Culturally Appropriate Curriculum as the Embodiment of Navajo-ness in Classroom Pedagogy." *Journal of American Indian Education* 46.3 (2007): 72–93. Print.

Young, Vershawn Ashanti. "Your Average Nigga." *CCC* 55 (2004): 693–715. Print.

Zentella, Ana Celia. *Growing Up Bilingual: Puerto Rican Children in New York*. Malden: Blackwell, 1997. Print.

INDEX

AAA (American Anthropological Association), 132
AAU (Association of American Universities), 132, 134
Abbott, Martha, 126
academic writing, materialist conception of, 172
African American language, 19, 38, 51, 185n2, 187n10. *See also* Black English Vernacular (BEV)
Akaka, Daniel, 131, 193n1
Alexander, Lamar, 114
Allen, Harold, 86–87
American Anthropological Association (AAA), 132
American Council of Education, 132
American Ethnic Coalition, 80, 189n3
American identity, 73, 75–79, 114, 139
Amit, Arie, 119–20, 193n1
Arabic language, 138
Arizona, English-only movement, 10–11, 80, 115
assimilationist model of education, 35–37
Association of American Universities (AAU), 132, 134
asymmetrical warfare, 120–21
Avidon, Elaine, 56

back-to-basics educational movement, 58–59, 62–63
Ball, Arnetha, 19, 108, 177–78
Baum, Joam, 58–59
Baxter, Milton, 44–45, 59, 86–87, 186n6
Benjamin A. Gilman Scholarship Program, 131
BEV. *See* Black English Vernacular (BEV)
bilingual education, 16–17, 81–85, 102
Black English Vernacular (BEV): arguments against use of, 35–37; continuum of rhetorical styles, 50–51; contrastive analysis exercises for SE and, 38, 47–48; cultural contexts of, 51, 54; differences and similarities to SE, 37–38; LCRG course, 31–32, 55; systematic nature of, 46–47; teachers' common questions about, 52–53; use of designation, 184–85n2; valuing in the composition classroom, 49–51
Bloom, Lynn, 87–88
Bridge reading program (Simpkins, Holt, and Simpkins), 67–68
Brooklyn College, School of Education, 53–54

221

Bruch, Patrick, 11, 31, 41
Bush, George W., 117–18, 130, 140
Butler, Melvin, 39
Byrnes, Heidi, 5, 146, 156, 173

California, English-only movement, 6, 16, 80, 88, 99
Call to Action for National Foreign Language Capabilities, A (DOD), 129–30, 193n1
Canagarajah, Suresh, 155, 157
Carter, Jimmy, 74–75
CCCC. *See* Conference on College Composition and Communication (CCCC)
"CCCC's Role in the Struggle for Language Rights" (Smitherman), 30
Center for Applied Linguistics, 59, 60
Charter of the French Language (1977), 17–18
Chávez, Linda, 82–83
children's internalization of patterns of first language or dialect, 38
Chu, David S. C., 123–24, 127–29, 168, 195n10
CIE (Coalition for International Education), 132, 134
City University of New York (CUNY), 33–35, 44–45, 54–56, 59, 63–64, 186n5
civil rights movement, 33, 58
Coalition for International Education (CIE), 132, 134
Cohen, Paul, 45–46, 186n8
Colorado, English-only movement, 80
Combs, Mary Carol, 80, 168

Committee on CCCC Language Statement, 30, 39–44
Committee to Study the Advisability of a Language Statement, 86–87
Common European Framework of Reference for Languages, 17
composition scholars and scholarship: action needed to develop new language policy, 170, 179–80; debate over national security language, 145; engagement in implementing national language policy, 144; interdisciplinary efforts, 154–55; recasting the work of, 100; redesigning composition instruction, 119; research-based projects to promote public discussion, 148–49; role in increasing language diversity, 110–11, 148, 173–74; stake in language policy debate, 141
composition studies: accounting for marginalized students, teachers, and scholars, 24; bridging the gap between sociolinguistics and, 46–49; changes needed in field of, 28–29, 157; contribution to U.S. language policy, 12; fostering language diversity in, 18–21, 31–33, 107–9, 141; history of, 24–25, 62–63, 68–69, 73; language policy work within, 9–14; National Language Policy and, 72; paradigm shift in publication and teaching practices, 113; relevance in policy debates about multilingualism, 162–66; reworking departmental language policies, 157–59; valuing BEV in, 49–51

Conference on College Composition and Communication (CCCC): 1988 convention, 90; Committee on CCCC Language Statement, 30, 39–44; Committee to Study the Advisability of a Language Statement, 86–87; language policies, 1, 3–4; orientation packets for committee members, 167; Progressive Composition Caucus, 88; role in public debate on language policy issues, 88; Statement on Ebonics, 10; Statement on Second Language Writing and Writers, 10; in struggle over American values definition, 85. *See also* Language Policy Committee (LPC); National Language Policy (CCCC); Students' Right to Their Own Language resolution (CCCC)

Cotillion (Killen), 42

critical-need languages, 117–18, 131, 135

Critical-Need Language Supplements, 131

cross-dialect interference, 45, 47

Cross-Language Relations in Composition (Horner, Lu, and Matsuda), 12, 119

cross-language relations within U.S., 141

CUNY. *See* City University of New York (CUNY)

curriculum reform, 56–62, 67, 145, 152–53, 156. *See also* Language Curriculum Research Group (LCRG)

Daniels, Harvey, 2–3, 104

David L. Boren Scholarships and Fellowships, 134

Defense Language Institute (DLI), 125, 137, 193–94n2

Defense Language Transformation Roadmap (DOD), 124–26, 193n1

Diekhoff, John S., 128–29, 195n8

DOD. *See* U.S. Department of Defense (DOD)

Du Bois, W. E. B., 36–37

Edited American English (EAE), 186n9

education: assimilationist model of, 35–37; back-to-basics movement, 58–59, 62–63; bilingual, 16–17, 81–85, 102; foreign-language, 117–18, 128–29, 131, 146, 151–54, 158. *See also* language education

ELA. *See* English Language Amendment (ELA)

English First, 80

English Language Amendment (ELA): English-only movement and, 8; S. I. Hayakawa and, 71, 79–80, 87; Inhofe and, 135; isolating effect of, 112; lack of support for English-language learning in, 83; National Language Policy as alternative to, 110; voters' misunderstanding of significance, 168

English-language courses, waiting lists for, 99

English-language learning, 83, 85, 89

English Language Unity Act (2009), 114–15, 135

English-only legislation: debate over, 91–92; lack of English-language courses and, 99; LPC in debate over, 11, 72, 91–92, 192n14; National Language Policy as alternative to, 4, 71, 89–90, 105, 118; sources in support or opposition to, 15; teachers and, 104

English-only movement: in Arizona, 10–11, 115; assumptions about conditions for learning English, 98; in California, 6, 16, 88, 99; campaign for national language and culture, 79–85; focus on reducing services, 110; heritage language learning argument, 102; interests of, 189n4; linguistic minorities' participation in U.S. society and, 93; literacy myth as basis for, 111; LPC's public opposition to, 72, 91–92, 190–91n8, 192n14; public opinion on, 112–13; Reagan-era political discourse and, 73–74; rhetorical strategies of, 80–83, 85, 109; victories for, 80, 109

"English-Only Movement" panel discussion, 190–91n8

English Plus Information Clearinghouse (EPIC), 91–92, 111, 191n10

English-plus policy, 91, 190n7

Enhancing Foreign Language Proficiency in the United States: Preliminary Results of the National Security Language Initiative (U.S. Department of Education), 130

EPIC (English Plus Information Clearinghouse), 91–92, 111, 191n10

Errors and Expectations (Shaughnessy), 33–34

ESD (Standard English as a Second Dialect), 38, 47–48, 65–66

Feal, Rosemary G., 5, 126, 145–47, 163–64

Federal Communications Commission, 7

federal entitlement programs, Reagan and, 75–76

Florida, English-only movement and, 80

Ford Foundation, 45–46, 59–61

foreign-language capability, 5, 121–22, 136, 140

foreign-language education, 117–18, 128–29, 131, 146, 151–54, 158

Foreign Language Education Partnership Program Act, 131

foreign-language learning, 89, 141, 158

foreign languages, as military tools, 137–38

foreign-language scholars, 129, 143, 151

Fulbright Critical Language Enhancement Awards, 130–31

Fulbright-Hays legislation, 132

GAO (U.S. General Accounting Office), 121

Gardner, Bruce, 136

Gilman scholarships, 131

Gilyard, Keith, 19, 24, 177

global war against terrorism, 119–21

Grognet, Allene, 59

Harris, Joseph, 25, 173–74

Hayakawa, S. I., 70–71, 79–82, 87, 189–90n5

heritage languages: influence on Latino students' oral and written texts, 19; National Language Policy and, 89; national security language policy and, 137–38, 141–42; public support needed for maintenance of, 100–102, 192–93n5; revitalization programs, 16–17
Hesse, Doug, 165
higher education, and national security language policy, 131–34, 152
Higher Education Act (1965), 131–32
history of composition studies, 62–63, 68–69, 73
Holt, Grace, 67–68
Holt, Rush, 127–28, 131, 168
Horner, Bruce, 2, 11–12, 63–64, 119
Houghton Mifflin, 67–68
Huebner, Thom, 6–7
Hunger of Memory (Rodriguez), 83–85, 87–88, 105–6
hypercorrection, 187n11

immigration to the U.S., 76–77, 188n1
indigenous languages, government policies toward, 184n4
institutional critique, 159–61
"Institutional Critique" (Porter et al.), 175, 197n16
institutional culture, changes in, 161–62
instructors' manual of activities and classroom assignments (Smitherman, McPherson, and Lloyd-Jones), 68
Interagency Language Roundtable, 146

interdisciplinary collaboration, 152, 154, 156

Joint Vision 2020 (DOD), 194n5
Judd, Elliott L., 16, 109
Judy, Stephen, 1–2
just-in-time literacy, 163

Kelly, Ernece B., 38–39
Kinloch, Valerie, 64, 68–69, 177
Krashen, Stephen, 16

Labov, William, 16
Lacey, Richard A., 60–61
language acquisition, commodity approach toward, 141
Language and Area Studies Centers, 195n7
language and cultural knowledge deficiencies, effects of, 122–23
language competencies, advanced, 126, 152–53, 194n6
language crisis, 62, 121–23, 189n3
Language Curriculum Research Group (LCRG): CCCC language policies and, 4; collaborative learning sessions, 53–54; in composition histories, 62–63, 185–86n4; end-of-course evaluations, 61; funding sources, 185n3; linguistic and racial politics introduced into classroom by, 63–64; members of, 44–46; origins of, 31; sociolinguistics research and, 46–47; student research projects, 49–50; study of writing by BEV-speaking students, 47; teacher training, 52, 54–57; textbook manuscript, 47–48,

Language Curriculum Research Group (LCRG) (*continued*) 50–51, 53, 57, 59–60; translation of research into pedagogical methods, 31–33, 45–49, 64–66

language diversity: debate over, in the public sphere, 71; fostering in composition theory and pedagogy, 18–22, 31–33, 107–9, 141; processing new perspectives on, 112–13; role of composition scholars in increasing, 148, 173–74; survey on teacher attitudes toward and knowledge of, 3, 104–8. *See also* Language Curriculum Research Group (LCRG); multilingualism

Language Diversity in the Classroom (Smitherman and Villanueva), 21, 92, 107–8, 176–77

language education: contexts of, 22–24; fiscal and political support necessary for, 101, 110, 130; ideal aims of, debated, 127–28; legislation for, 134; need for expanded vision of, 157; in officer training programs, 122; shared vision for, 154; Students' Right resolution and, 44

language justice, and democratic justice, 111–12

Language Knowledge and Awareness Survey (LPC), 3, 104–8

language leadership vacuum, 72–73, 145

language learning, commodity approach toward, 140

language learning, material needs of, 98–103

"Language Learning for European Citizenship," 17

language policies: of the 1980s, 73; CCCC role in public debate over, 88; composition scholars and debate over, 141, 144–45; confusion about purposes and consequences of, 167–68; contextual nature of, 170; covert, 7; defining, 6–9; embodiment in pedagogies, 18–22, 31–33, 108–9; and expanded definition of "academic writing," 171–72; historical analysis of, 169–71; limitations as stand-alone documents, 169; long-term perspective in assessment of, 175–76; as matter of justice, 102–3; as national security concern, 5; overt, 6, 14–15; as pedagogical heuristics, 176–79; public attitudes, political values, and, 73; and realizing professional possibilities, 179–80; and redesign of professional and institutional policies, 174–75; restrictive, 16; writing into histories of composition studies, 24–25

Language Policy Committee (LPC): alignment with groups fighting for justice, 111; attempts to fill language leadership vacuum, 145; dissolution and reconstitution of, 103–4, 191–92n11; efforts to outline pedagogy that builds linguistic diversity, 108–9; English-only debate and, 72, 91–92, 192n14; focus on language education funding, 98–99, 101; formation and funding of, 88; *Language Diversity in the Classroom*, 21; *Language Knowledge and Awareness Survey*, 3, 104–8; National Language Policy and, 71–72, 89–91, 104, 112, 191n9; promotion of multilingual competence, 95–97; reading in preparation for first working session, 190n6; rhetorical strategy employed by, 110; survey of CCCC and NCTE members, 92; "The English-Only Movement" panel discussion, 190–91n8; types of activities pursued by, 88–89; "What You Can Do," 94

language policy work: CCCC's intervention through, 39–44; within rhetoric and composition studies, 9–14

language practices, influences on, 16

language readiness of the military, 122–26

language resources, existing, 126–31, 143

language rights, 30, 65–67. *See also* Students' Right to Their Own Language resolution

language skills, as war-fighting tools, 122, 135, 194n5

Lardner, Ted, 19, 177–78

LCRG. *See* Language Curriculum Research Group (LCRG)

Limited English Proficiency students, Arizona, 10

linguistically diverse communities, advocacy for, 162

linguistic minorities: changing public ideas on, 94; debate over, in the college classroom, 33–39; languages of, 20; national security language policy and, 137, 139; NDEA and marginalization of, 136; social and economic issues, 111; social and political atmosphere for, 114

literacy practices, defined, 22

Lloyd, Donald, 9–10

Lowenthal, Sylvia, 44–45, 186n6

Lu, Min-Zahn, 23, 62, 119, 138–39, 150

Marback, Richard, 11–12, 31, 41

Martin Luther King Junior Elementary School Children v. Ann Arbor School District, 10

Martus, Marjorie, 45, 59

Matsuda, Paul Kei, 12–13, 119

micro-level policy writing, 175

military. *See* U.S. Department of Defense (DOD)

Modern Language Association (MLA): action needed to develop new language policy, 170, 179–80; Ad Hoc Committee on Foreign Languages, 146, 151–52; on interdisciplinary, team-taught courses, 154; Language Map, 147–49; national security language policy and, 118; on redesigning language majors, 152–53; response to national security language policy, 5; vision for translingual and transcultural competence, 153–54

Mok, Samuel, 126–27

monolingualism, 157–58, 192–93n15

Moore, Samuel, 45–46, 52, 186n8

Morse, J. Mitchell, 35–37, 42

multiculturalism, 78–79, 188–89n2
multilingualism: in alternative to national security language policy, 141; communal responsibility for, 95, 102; composition's relevance in policy debates about, 162–66; deployment of, in name of national security, 127–28; for English language scholars, 157–59; LPC's promotion of, 95–97; and national unity, 112; as pedagogical tool, 158–59; revitalizing national core values through, 93–98; in rhetoric and composition's range of disciplinary concerns, 113; seen as threat to national identity, 78–79; as strategic military weapon, 122, 135, 194n5; theoretical and pedagogical frameworks for promotion of, 118
multilingual language arts curriculum, 145
multilingual rhetorical education design, 151–57
multilingual writers, 155–56
multilingual writing pedagogy, 152

national anthem, Spanish-language version of, 114
National Assembly of Quebec, 17–18
National Council of Teachers of English (NCTE), 2–3, 10–11, 45, 87, 92
National Foreign Language Coordination Council, 130–31
national identity, 73, 75–79, 114, 139
"National Language Conference: A Call to Action," 126–27, 193n1

national language policy: academic conversations about, 10; contribution of composition studies to, 12; examination through multidisciplinary lens, 14–18; in international context, 13; material and symbolic effects of, 11–12; student engagement through research and writing projects, 149–50. *See also* national security language policy
National Language Policy (CCCC): adopted as official policy of CCCC, 89; as alternative to English Language Amendments, 110; brochure and educational efforts, 90, 105; changing material conditions for language learning, 98–103; conversation at "National Language Conference," 126–27; as counterstatement to English-only movement, 118; criticism of, 2–3; debate over language diversity in the public sphere and, 71; efficacy of, for present-day composition studies, 109–16; English-plus policy and, 190n7; on heritage language learning and use, 101; inventing a pedagogical theory of, 103–9; learning emphasis of, 140–41; long-term perspective in assessment of, 112–13; LPC and, 71–72, 191n9; multilingualism promoted in brochure of, 97; purpose of, 8, 98; rhetorical strategy, 109; text of, 70; use of, 1, 112; vision of civic dialogue promoted by, 93–94

National Research Council of the National Academies, 132
National Security Education Program, 134
National Security Language Act, 131
National Security Language Initiative (NSLI), 5, 117–18, 130–31
national security language policy: composing an alternative to, 141–43, 164–65; debate over, as opportunity, 3–4, 119; foreign-language literacy and, 117–18, 136; formalization and implementation of, 130, 132; foundations of, 5, 134–41; heritage languages and, 137–38, 141–42; "language crisis" and, 121–23; leadership in debate over, 145–49, 165–66; linguistic minorities and, 139; multilingualism deployment in name of, 127–28; 9/11 and, 118; and production of just-in-time literacy, 163–64; purpose of, 8; theoretical foundations of, 134–41
National Security Strategy report, 122
national unity, multilingualism and, 112
nation's language needs, U.S. military and, 128
Native American Languages Acts, 184n4
NCTE (National Council of Teachers of English), 2–3, 10–11, 45, 87, 92
NDEA (U.S. National Defense Education Act), 128–29, 136
New London Group, 23
9/11 attacks, 121, 128

9/11 Commission, 121–22
NSLI (National Security Language Initiative), 5, 117–18, 130–31
"Nuestro Himno" ("Our Anthem"), 114, 193n16
Nunberg, Geoffrey, 14

Panetta, Leon, 168
points of leverage, in institutional critique, 160–61
policy writing, revising institutional values and practices through, 159–62
Porter, Clifford, 120–21
Pratt, Larry, 159–61, 192n14
Pratt, Mary Louise, 5, 137, 146, 173
Prendergast, Catherine, 13
private enterprises, language policies of, 7
Progressive Composition Caucus, 88
Psycholinguistics Project Staff, Chicago Board of Education, 67

Quebec language policy, 17–18

Reagan, Ronald, 75–78, 111
Reagan era, 73–74, 94, 96–98
Redrick, Jacqueline, 45–46, 186n8
Reed, Carol, 32, 44–46, 62, 186n6, 186n7
reflective language pedagogy, 52–56, 154
research projects: community-based, 148–50; reflective, for students, 149–51
Resolution on English as the "Official Language" (NCTE), 2–3
Rich, Adrienne, 34, 36, 42
Richardson, Elaine, 19, 107–8, 177

Rodriguez, Richard, 11, 83–85, 87–88, 105–6

Schildkraut, Deborah, 15, 139
Scholastic Aptitude Test (SAT), 58
SE. *See* Standard English (SE); Standardized English (SE)
SEEK (Search for Education, Elevation, and Knowledge) program, 33–34, 44–45, 186n5
Seward, Doug, 157–58
Shaughnessy, Mina P., 33–35, 55
Sheils, Merrill, 57–58, 70
Simone, Michael R., 137, 140
Simpkins, Charlesetta, 67–68
Simpkins, Gary, 67–68
Singapore, bilingual education policy, 17
Sledd, James, 39, 109
Smith, Allen, 2, 40
Smitherman, Geneva: on bidialectalism, 39; on CCCC's language policies, 30, 144; as chair of LPC, 88; on Committee to Study the Advisability of a Language Statement, 87; EPIC and, 91; as expert witness, 10; instructors' manuals of activities and classroom assignments, 68; *Language Diversity in the Classroom*, 21; on language policy work, 9–10; on learning Third World languages, 96; on limitations of language policies, 167–68; LPC and, 71–72, 103–4; on motivations for learning English, 99–100; on National Language Policy, 3; *Not Only English*, 11; public leadership of, 148, 173; reports on developments in English-only movement, 92; on Students' Right resolution and National Language Policy, 113; *Talkin and Testifyin*, 19
sociolinguistics, bridging the gap between composition and, 46–49
sociolinguistics research, 19, 37, 43, 46–47
Spolsky, Bernard, 7–8
Standard American English (SAE), 186n9
Standard English (SE), 37–38, 47–48, 186–87n9, 187–88n12
Standard English as a Second Dialect (ESD), 38, 47–48, 65–66
Standardized English (SE), 36–37, 48–49, 58, 183n1
Standardized-English-as-a-Second-Dialect course, 31–32
"Statement of Principles and Standards for the Post-secondary Teaching of Writing" (1989), 197–98n1
Statement on Ebonics, 10
Statement on Second Language Writing and Writers, 10
Stewart, William, 38, 186n7
Students' Right to Their Own Language resolution (CCCC): background statement and annotated bibliography for, 41–44, 198n2; CCCC entry into public conversations and, 10; Committee on CCCC Language Statement and, 39–44; disciplinary legacy of, 62–69; ethnic minorities and, 4; LCRG project

and, 61–62; learning emphasis of, 140–41; and linguistic rights of all marginalized students, 65–67; passed by general membership of CCCC, 40; pedagogies inspired by, 32; purpose of, 8; reception of, 1–3, 31, 44; on teacher training, 52; text of, 40
Sundberg, Trudy J., 2, 85, 87

Talkin and Testifyin (Smitherman), 19
teachers: in Arizona, 10; common questions about BEV, 52–53; CUNY open-admissions policy and, 34–35, 59; English-only legislation and, 104; focus on accents and pronunciations of, 10, 115; manuals of activities and classroom assignments, 68; prompting reflection by, on racial and linguistic differences, 52–56; survey on attitudes toward and knowledge of language diversity, 3, 104–8
teacher training, 21, 52, 54–56, 107–8, 177–78
terrorism, global war against, 119–21
textbook projects: LCRG writing textbook manuscript, 47–48, 50–51, 53, 57, 59–60; Students' Right-era, 68
Title VI of Higher Education act, 132
toasts, 50–51, 188n13
translingual and transnational composition, 20–21, 144
Trimbur, John, 12, 58, 95

United States (U.S.): crisis of confidence, 74–75; as "shining city on the hill," 109
University of Maryland, Center for Advanced Study of Language, 126, 194n6
U.S. Department of Defense (DOD): *Call to Action for National Foreign Language Capabilities, A*, 129–30, 193n1; Defense Language Institute (DLI), 125, 137, 193–94n2; *Defense Language Transformation Roadmap*, 124–26; existing language resources and, 126–31; higher education's relationship with, 131–34; *Joint Vision 2020*, 194n5; language education in officer training programs, 122; language needs of, defined as nation's language needs, 128–29, 138; linguistic readiness of, 122–26; National Security Language Act, 131; national security "language crisis," 121; National Security Language Initiative, 5, 117–18, 130–31; national security language policy and, 119. *See also* national security language policy
U.S. Department of Education, 81–82, 132
U.S. English, 83, 100–101, 189n4
U.S. General Accounting Office, 121
U.S. National Defense Education Act (NDEA), 128–29, 136
U.S. State Department, 131

Valdés, Guadalupe, 19
van der Heide, Marijke, 126–27
vertical curricula, 156
Villanueva, Victor: in debate over English-only legislation, 11; on effect of Rodriguez's story, 105–6; *Language Diversity in the Classroom*, 21, 92; on Rodriguez speech, 87; on Students' Right resolution, 65

"Why Johnny Can't Write" (Sheils), 57–58, 70
Williams, Jean C., 24
Williams, Robert S., 16
Wolfram, Walt, 60
Wright, Richard, 60–61

Zaeske, Lou, 189n3
Zentella, Ana Celia, 19, 101–2, 143
zero copula, 47, 187n10

Scott Wible is an associate professor of English at the University of Maryland, where he directs the Professional Writing Program and teaches courses in rhetoric and composition. His previous publications include essays in *College Composition and Communication, College English, Cultural Studies,* and *Rhetoric Society Quarterly.*